GOVERNMENT BEYOND THE CENTRE

SERIES EDITORS: GERRY STOKER AND DAVID WILSON

The world of sub-central governance and administration – including local authorities, quasi-governmental bodies and the agencies of public–private partnerships – has seen massive changes in the United Kingdom and other western democracies. The original aim of the **Government Beyond the Centre** series was to bring the study of this often-neglected world into the mainstream of social science research, applying the spotlight of critical analysis to what had traditionally been the preserve of institutional public administration approaches.

The replacement of traditional models of government by new models of governance has affected central government, too, with the contracting out of many traditional functions, the increasing importance of relationships with devolved and supranational authorities, and the emergence of new holistic models based on partnership and collaboration.

This series focuses on the agenda of change in governance both at sub-central level and in the new patterns of relationships surrounding the core executive. Its objective is to provide up-to-date and informative accounts of the new forms of management and administration and the structures of power and influence that are emerging, and of the economic, political and ideological forces that underline them.

The series will be of interest to students and practitioners in central and local government, public management and social policy, and all those interested in the reshaping of the governmental institutions which have a daily and major impact on our lives.

Government Beyond the Centre
Series Standing Order
ISBN 0–333–71696–5 hardback
ISBN 0–333–69337–X paperback
(outside North America only)

You can receive future titles in this series as they are published by placing a standing order. Please contact your bookseller or, in the case of difficulty, write to us at the address below with your name and address, the title of the series and an ISBN quoted above.

Customer Services Department, Macmillan Distribution Ltd
Houndmills, Basingstoke, Hampshire RG21 6XS, England

GOVERNMENT BEYOND THE CENTRE

SERIES EDITORS: GERRY STOKER AND DAVID WILSON

Published

Richard Batley and Gerry Stoker (eds)
Local Government in Europe

Bas Denters and Lawrence E. Rose (eds)
Comparing Local Governance

Sue Goss
Making Local Governance Work

Clive Gray
Government Beyond the Centre

John Gyford
Citizens, Consumers and Councils

Richard Kerley
Managing in Local Government

Desmond King and Gerry Stoker (eds)
Rethinking Local Democracy

Steve Leach, John Stewart and Kieron Walsh
The Changing Organisation and Management of Local Governance

Arthur Midwinter
Local Government in Scotland

Christopher Pollitt, Johnston Birchall and Keith Putman
Decentralising Public Service Management

Lawrence Pratchett and David Wilson (eds)
Local Democracy and Local Government

John Stewart
The Nature of British Local Government

Gerry Stoker
Transforming Local Governance

Gerry Stoker (ed.)
The New Management of British Local Governance

Gerry Stoker and David Wilson (eds)
British Local Government into the 21st Century

Helen Sullivan and Chris Skelcher
Working Across Boundaries

Tony Travers
The Politics of London

David Wilson ad Chris Game
Local Government in the United Kingdom (3rd edn)

Perri 6, Diana Leat, Kimberly Seltzer and Gerry Stoker
Towards Holistic Governance

Forthcoming

Steve Martin
The Transformation of Public Services

Lawrence Pratchett
Local Democracy in Britain

Rajiv Prabhakar
The Future of Public Services

Comparing Local Governance

Trends and Developments

Edited by

Bas Denters

and

Lawrence E. Rose

First published 2005 by
PALGRAVE MACMILLAN
Houndmills, Basingstoke, Hampshire RG21 6XS and
175 Fifth Avenue, New York, N.Y. 10010
Companies and representatives throughout the world.

PALGRAVE MACMILLAN is the global academic imprint of the Palgrave
Macmillan division of St. Martin's Press, LLC and of Palgrave Macmillan Ltd.
Macmillan® is a registered trademark in the United States, United Kingdom
and other countries. Palgrave is a registered trademark in the European
Union and other countries.

ISBN 0–333–99555–4 hardback
ISBN 0–333–99556–2 paperback

This book is printed on paper suitable for recycling and made from fully
managed and sustained forest sources.

A catalogue record for this book is available from the British Library.

Library of Congress Cataloging-in-Publication Data
      Comparing local governance : trends and developments / edited by
      Bas Denters and Lawrence E. Rose
         p. cm.—(Government beyond the centre)
      Includes bibliographical references and index.
         ISBN 0–333–99555–4 (cloth)—ISBN 0–333–99556–2 (pbk.)
         1. Local government—Case studies. 2. Comparative government.
I. Denters, S. A. H. II. Rose, Lawrence E., 1944– III. Series.

JS78.C63 2004
320.8—dc22   2004054824

10 9 8 7 6 5 4 3 2 1
14 13 12 11 10 09 08 07 06 05

Printed and bound in China

Contents

v

List of Exhibits, Figures and Tables

Tables

Notes on the Contributors

Chris Aulich is Senior Lecturer at the School of Business and Government, Division of Business, Law and Information Sciences, University of Canberra, Australia.

Luigi Bobbio is Associate Professor at the Department of Political Studies, University of Turin, Italy.

Olivier Borraz is Senior Research Fellow at the Centre de Sociologie des Organisations (FNSP/CNRS), Paris, France.

Graham W.A. Bush is Honorary Research Fellow at the Political Studies Department, University of Auckland, New Zealand.

Bas Denters is Professor of Urban Policy and Politics at the Department of Political Science, School for Business, Public Administration and Technology, University of Twente, The Netherlands.

Susanne Eisenmann is Chairwoman of the Christian Democratic Party in the Stuttgart Municipal Council, Stuttgart, Germany.

Oscar W. Gabriel is Professor and Head of the Comparative Politics Unit at the Department of Social Sciences, University of Stuttgart, Germany.

Mike Goldsmith is Professor of Government, University of Salford, England; Visiting Professor at Foundation Nationale de Sciences Politiques, Paris, France.

Pieter-Jan Klok is Assistant Professor at the Department of Political Science, School for Business, Public Administration and Technology, University of Twente, The Netherlands.

Andreas Ladner is Assistant Professor at the Centre of Competence in Public Management, University of Berne, Switzerland.

Patrick Le Galès is Director of Research CNRS at CEVIPOF and Professor of Politics and Sociology, Sciences politiques, Paris, France.

Yves Plees is a Fellow at the Institute of Public Management, Katholieke Universiteit Leuven, Belgium.

Lawrence E. Rose is Professor of Political Science at the Department of Political Science, University of Oslo, Norway.

Hank V. Savitch is Brown and Williamson Distinguished Research Professor at the School of Urban and Public Affairs, University of Louisville, Kentucky, USA.

Krister Ståhlberg is Director of the Foundation of Swedish Culture in Finland, Helsingfors, Finland.

Paweł Swianiewicz is Associate Professor at the Faculty of Geography and Regional Studies, Warsaw University, Poland.

Ronald K. Vogel is Professor of Political Science and Urban and Public Affairs at the School of Urban and Public Affairs, University of Louisville, Kentucky, USA.

David Wilson is Professor of Public Administration and Dean of the Faculty of Business and Law, De Montfort University, United Kingdom.

Preface

The publication of Osbourne and Gaebler's well-known book *Reinventing Government* in 1992 was something of a landmark event. It served both to register developments that had been taking place in some countries – perhaps most notably the United Kingdom and the United States – and to set the terms of debate among laymen, practitioners and academicians alike over the future direction of the public sector. In the years since the book was published the field of public administration and politics has witnessed a virtual explosion of articles and books dealing with the organization and operation of government. Much, albeit certainly not all, of this literature has tended to focus on single countries and developments at the level of national government. There has been substantially less emphasis on cross-national analyses at the sub-national – especially local – level.

The present work was in large measure undertaken in response to this situation. Our desire was to illuminate in a more systematic fashion whether or not local government across a broader spectrum of political systems had been undergoing a process of fundamental transformation during the past decade or so. Was it indeed the case that *local governance* was more than a catchword applying to developments in only a few selected settings? To answer this question we decided upon a strategy that would draw upon a number of country experts, all of which were asked to fashion a contribution around a set of predetermined questions. This book is the result of this approach.

In pursuing this project, we have been supported by our respective academic institutions. The Institute for Governance Studies research programme 'Governance in a Complex Society' at the University of Twente has been especially generous in backing this project. Among other things it provided support for the translation of preliminary versions of all of the country chapters contained in this book for publication in a series which appeared in the Dutch journal *Bestuurswetenschappen* during 2002 and 2003. We are grateful for this support. A special word of thanks is also due to Mike Goldsmith, who has added encouragement to the project as well as offering helpful comments on a number of the chapters. The editorial staff at Palgrave Macmillan and the editors of the Government Beyond the Centre series have likewise made valuable contributions at several critical junctures. Above all, however, we are deeply appreciative of the support and understanding shown by our families, without which this project would not have reached fruition.

Hengelo   BAS DENTERS
Oslo   LAWRENCE E. ROSE

1 Local Governance in the Third Millennium: a brave new world?

Bas Denters and Lawrence E. Rose

Some fifteen years ago Joachim Jens Hesse published an edited volume containing analyses of local government in 20 Western industrialized countries (Hesse 1990/91). Since then the vocabulary used in discussing local government, both among academics and practitioners, has changed considerably. Terms like 'governance', 'new public management', 'contracting out', 'community partnerships' and 'multi-level and multi-actor governance' are but a few of the neologisms that pervade current publications on local politics and government (for example John 2001; Leach and Percy-Smith 2001; Le Galès 2002).

In the early 1990s Hesse and Sharpe concluded that local governments throughout the Western industrialized world played a 'major role *in the delivery of* fundamental *collective public* and *quasi-public goods*' (Hesse and Sharpe 1990/91: 608). They considered this as a sign of local government's vitality. In the decade that now lies behind us, local government's service delivery tasks have, at least according to one student of local government in the UK, been 'squeezed by financial constraints and challenged in their management by competitive tendering, opting out and performance targets' (Stoker 1999a: 14). This, however, should not automatically be considered as evidence of the demise of local government, since local governments meanwhile 'have begun to develop a leadership role in some of the broader challenges of community governance' (*ibid*).

If these observations are correct we may have entered a new era for local government – the age of local governance. If so, this shift must inevitably be seen in light of major transformations in the contexts within which local governments operate in most contemporary democracies. Before formulating the central themes of this volume it is appropriate to identify what the nature of these changes in the world surrounding local governments may be.

Broadly speaking changes have taken place along two dimensions. On the one hand local governments have witnessed important changes in their external socio-economic and broader political environments – that is, what may be termed their macro-environment. On the other hand, local authorities have been confronted with changes in the nature of their local communities – that is, what may be termed their micro-environment (and to some degree their meso-environment as well). Citizen orientations to the public sphere appear to have changed and their patterns of association may similarly have changed. Whereas these macro- and micro-trends may be differentiated analytically, it is of course important to recognize that changes in the macro-environment are frequently interlinked with changes at the micro- and meso-levels. The principal thrust of each of these changes may be briefly outlined as follows.

Macro-trends

In characterizing changes with respect to the socio-economic and political environments within which local governments perform their functions, three major catchwords predominate – urbanization, globalization and Europeanization.

Urbanization

Urbanization, conceived of in terms of increases in the percentage of the national population living in urban places, is a phenomenon that has long historical roots. Nonetheless it is a process that has increased dramatically over the last fifty years, since the end of the Second World War, and is likely to continue in the future. Whereas in the 1970s two-thirds of the population of the more developed world was urbanized, this proportion had increased to almost three-quarters in the 1990s, and by 2030 the urban population is expected to have gone up to five-sixths (Champion 2001: 144). Manuel Castells (2002) has identified this process of urbanization as one of the key spatial processes in the early twenty-first century. In his view the process of urbanization implies the development of *metropolitan regions*. This trend, according to Castells, will imply the demise of the countryside as we have known it. Increasingly the countryside will develop into a set of urbanized villages that are part of 'urban constellations scattered throughout huge territorial expanses' (Castells 2002: 549). These metropolitan regions will presumably be characterized by a considerable degree of functional interconnectedness of people and activities. Socio-spatial interdependencies in such metropolitan regions provide a significant challenge for multiple political jurisdictions existing within these regions. Some analysts talk about a problem of fragmentation and consider it as a major force behind far reaching reforms of the local government system – both amalgamation reforms as well as the introduction of new tiers of government at the meso-level (see, for example, Sharpe 1993, especially 3–26). Others, however, conceive of the multiplicity of political jurisdictions in urbanized regions as an asset and argue that coordination problems can be solved through voluntary cooperation between local authorities (for a review of both arguments see Ostrom 1972, among others).

Globalization

Castells has not only pointed to the increasing interdependencies within metropolitan regions, but also emphasizes the embeddedness of these regions (and their centre cities) as nodes in global networks. Castells points to the multidimensionality and the partial nature of such linkages; whereas some residents and activities in these regions are more or less strongly connected to a particular global network (for example finance), most of its citizens are 'engaged in a very local life' (Castells 2002: 554). The external interdependencies of metropolitan regions, moreover, are a reflection of a wider trend towards economic globalization. According to Patrick Le Galès (2002: 152–5), three features distinguish these processes of globalization, summarized as follows:

- the strong growth of international trade and the emergence of global markets and global rules of the game;
- the globalization of finance through interconnected financial markets; and
- the attempts of firms to cope with new challenges by means of strategies of concentration and coordination through processes of horizontal and vertical integration.

In the light of these developments, Le Galès (2002: 159–60) and others (for example Mayer 2000: 231–2) have claimed that local political organizations are increasingly important in the realm of economic development:

> The economy of the city cannot be seen solely from the point of view of firm's strategies in deciding where to set up. By virtue of its materiality,

the city is also a site for the construction, management, and production of services that are an important vector for capitalist accumulation. (Le Galès 2002: 160)

Whereas globalization as well as Europeanization (see the following) have tended to render the nation states' traditional macro-economic policy instruments largely obsolete, local governments have become more prominent actors in the economic policy domain. Hence, while local governments in the USA have traditionally been active in economic development policies, many of their European counterparts are now also claiming a role in this area. These new circumstances also raise the issue of the nature of the local political agenda. What, for example, are local government's priorities with regard to economic development, social inclusion and environmental concerns?

Europeanization

In Europe the process of European integration is becoming ever more important for local governments. Since the European Economic Community (EEC) was set up by six European nation states in 1955, the scope of Europeanization has increased both territorially and functionally. In a territorial sense the scope of Europeanization has widened with successive extensions of the EC and EU membership. Now the EU has 25 members and is likely to be further enlarged in the future. But the scope of Europeanization has also been functionally extended. Initially European integration focused largely on issues of economic integration, whereas subsequently the range of functional responsibilities of the EU has been broadened considerably.

It is claimed that the rising importance of the EU has had both direct and indirect effects on European local governments (for a review of various perspectives on Europeanization, see Le Galès 2002: 5–8 or John 2001: 71–4). This is true in both member countries and in accession countries as well as in those countries remaining on the periphery. Local authorities may be directly affected by EU policies when these policies imply rules and regulations that impact upon local government activities, or when the EU provides local government with new sources of funding for local programmes. But there are also a variety of indirect effects. The rise of the EU has in many instances changed the balance of power between central and sub-national governments. Partly stimulated by EU subsides, moreover, many local authorities have also broadened their horizons and become more active in all sorts of international networks and partnerships.

Micro- and meso-trends

Recent years have also witnessed important changes within local communities, changes that have influenced their relationships with local governments. Many observers have pointed to the modernization of individual citizens for example, a phrase that encompasses both a substantive and a formal dimension (Fuchs and Klingemann 1995a: 12). In *substantive* terms it suggests that citizens' orientations towards governments have changed, increasingly being dominated by instrumental considerations concerning the performance and efficiency of governments in meeting citizen demands (Fuchs and Klingemann 1995a: 15–16). Thus, Fuchs and Klingemann (1995b: 439), on the basis of extensive longitudinal analyses in a variety of European countries, anticipate that:

> the attention of citizens will be directed more strongly than before to the performance of the state in the fields of economy and security. For this reason, the legitimation of Western democracies will depend more heavily on the performance of governments. In this case, it is a matter of output-related performance.

These changes occur at a moment in time when local governments are already facing a variety of new challenges related to the macro-trends and associated changes discussed above. An increased multi-cultural character of many Western societies, for instance, is one development that is particularly evident in urban areas.

In *formal* terms the phrase individual modernization refers to the increase in personal skills of citizens and an associated rise of new demands for participation. A secular trend observed in most Western societies is a marked rise in citizens' levels of formal education (Topf 1995a: 33–8). With increased education more people have acquired politically relevant skills and a sense of political competence, characteristics which in many instances result in demands for more extensive opportunities for political participation going beyond that of voting (Fuchs and Klingemann 1995a: 17–18). Studies indicate that in various European countries citizens are becoming ever more critical of governments and have extended their political action repertoire beyond the traditional modes of institutionalized forms of political participation (Topf 1995a, 1995b).

In addition to its impact on new substantive and participatory demands, the emancipation of citizens may also have had other consequences. There have been fears that individual modernization, rising mobility and a breakdown of people's traditional social ties would weaken people's integration within social networks, and increasing urbanization may very well have strengthened this trend. Robert Putnam, for instance, has argued that a variety of factors, urbanization among them, have contributed to a decline in people's participation in voluntary associations and decreasing interpersonal trust. Such a decline in 'social capital' may further contribute to reducing a government's institutional performance (Putnam 1993: 163–85). A decline in organizational participation, moreover, may also lead to a deterioration of the linkages between local communities and their governments. Such linkages are crucial for the articulation of social and political cleavages and, by consequence, for a healthy democracy (see Aarts 1995: 227–8).

In his book *Bowling Alone*, Putnam (2000) has collected evidence for the empirical validity of such a decline in social capital for the USA. Whether there is a similar downward trend in other Western countries is less clear. Aarts (1995: 255), for example, has concluded that 'there is generally little evidence' for a trend that membership of traditional social and political organizations is declining. In another respect, however, there is evidence that, even in Europe, traditional linkages between society and government may be in a period of transition. Political parties have generally been conceived of as cornerstones of modern representative democracy: 'It was essentially the political parties which articulated citizens' interests on their behalf, and it was the parties which introduced citizen interests into the decision making process' (Fuchs and Klingemann 1995b: 435–6). Yet the key role played by parties is under pressure. Increased education, and an extension of the political action repertoire of individual citizens that has accompanied this, have contributed to the erosion of the articulation function of parties. This function is also eroded by a decline in people's overall attachment to political parties (*ibid.*: 425).

These changes imply a dual challenge for local governments. On the one hand, the rise of more output-oriented, more demanding, more critical and more action-prone citizens forces local governments to improve their capacity for effective and efficient governance. In many respects this has made them receptive for the adoption of many innovative management techniques and may also have led to attempts to increase the system's problem-solving capacity by engaging various actors from within the local community in partnerships. On the other hand, new participatory demands and the partial decline of traditional political party linkages between local government and the local community require municipalities to reconsider channels of communication with the local community, and to consider new forms of local democracy.

How does local government respond to its 'brave new world'?

Up to this point we have identified some major changes in the world of local government and some of the main challenges for local authorities that arise as a consequence of these trends. In this volume we seek to elaborate how local governments in a variety of countries have reacted to these challenges, and to do so we have invited authoritative specialists to analyse recent developments in their own country. In order to secure a degree of comparability among the various national contributions, we have suggested that our authors deal with a number of questions identified in Exhibit 1.1, each prompted by one or more of the previously identified trends and challenges.

It should be emphasized that the challenges noted in Exhibit 1.1 are not solely associated with or generated by one specific trend alone. Urbanization, for example, may be a significant factor that creates a need for coordination of activities among various sub-national governments, but other trends such as globalization and Europeanization may be just as important. Moreover, not all of the trends and themes are equally relevant in all countries. This is blatantly obvious, for example, with regard to the impact of Europeanization, which is mainly relevant for actual and aspiring EU member states; but this is probably also the case for some of the other trends, challenges and themes highlighted in Exhibit 1.1. The country experts have therefore been given fairly wide discretion in how they wish to address the central issues, allowing them to emphasize some of these themes and to de-emphasize others as may be deemed appropriate. In addressing the questions, however, we have suggested that the authors concentrate their attention on *local government*, by which we loosely refer to the level of government in a political system that is closest to the citizen and that bears or shares responsibility for a relatively wide range of services and policies, rather than *regional* or other levels of international government.

In dealing with these themes and questions, the combination of the contributions will provide an answer to the central question underlying this volume: *What have been the major changes and continuities in various systems of local governments in selected Western countries?* In many recent analyses of changes in contemporary political systems, analysts have observed a shift from government to governance. The recent stream of publications on the rise of governance initially had a rather heavy British accent (see, for example, Rhodes 1997; Stoker 1999b, 2000, 2003). Generally this literature concludes that for a satisfactory understanding of contemporary political processes the concept of 'government' should be replaced by the

Exhibit 1.1	Comparing local governance: major trends, challenges and questions	
Trend	**Challenge**	**Questions**
Urbanization	Coordination of activities of various sub-national governments	*1 Have there been any changes in the relations between sub-national governments or at the local and meso-level of the local government system?*
Globalization	Development of new divisions of labour in the territorial state to meet the socio-economic consequences of globalization	*2 Have there been any changes in relations between local governments and higher tiers of government?*
Europeanization	Secure or even increase the role of local government in the newly emerging European polity	*3 What are the major implications (direct and indirect) of the rise of the EU for local governments and systems of local government?*
New substantive demands	Increase local capacity for effectively and efficiently solving community problems	*4 What are the major changes in systems of local government management and community partnerships?*
New participatory demands	Respond to new participatory demands and secure the responsiveness of local government	*5 What are the major changes in the system of local democracy?*

notion of governance. Thus, in a recent monograph about the British case Leach and Percy-Smith (2001: 1) conclude that the traditional notion in which 'local government is "what the council does" ' has to be replaced by a conception in which it is conceded that public decision-making concerning local issues 'increasingly involves multi-agency working, partnerships and policy networks which cut across organisational boundaries' (that is governance).

Some critics have argued that such a shift might be a British peculiarity. Le Galès (2002: 262), for example, has argued that 'announcements of the demise of local government and the triumph of public private partnerships probably reveal slightly too much of a British tropism'. There are indications, however, that a shift from local government to local governance is not a phenomenon that is typical for the UK only. On the basis of an ambitious comparative approach, John (2001: 174) concludes that: 'the charge of [UK] exceptionalism should be rejected, since the Netherlands, Germany and Spain are as reforming as the UK on certain dimensions [of governance]'. John's analysis is based on an effort to combine the author's expert knowledge about the UK and France with an impressive body of secondary literature on other countries. Yet the author is well aware that limitations in expertise and language skills might have resulted in biases (John 2001: xii). In this volume we have sought to overcome the limitations of a single-author volume by drawing on the collective expertise of a group of national experts, each of whom have access to a much wider range of research and source material in other languages. Chapters 2 to 13 of this book contain the country reports by these authors. These are followed by two chapters aimed at a broader cross-national comparison relating to two central issues. In Chapter 14 Goldsmith provides an overview of changes in intergovernmental relations – both horizontal and vertical – focusing on the first three trends, challenges and questions identified in Exhibit 1.1. Chapter 15 provides a similar overview of the evidence that pertains to the fourth and fifth trends and the associated challenges and changes.

The selection of countries

This volume contains 12 'country' chapters: Australia, Belgium, France, Germany, Italy, the Netherlands, New Zealand, the Nordic countries (Denmark, Finland, Norway and Sweden), Poland, Switzerland, the United Kingdom and the United States of America. The main consideration in selecting these countries for inclusion has been a desire to provide a balanced account of the developments in local government over a wide geographic area. Our main objective has been to select countries that would 'represent' various traditions of local government found among advanced industrial democracies. In the contemporary literature on local government, several typologies of local government systems have been proposed. On the basis of a comparison of six European unitary states, for example, Page and Goldsmith (1987a: 156–63; see also John 2001) distinguish between Northern and Southern European systems, based on three criteria – functional responsibilities, discretion and access. The most obvious difference between the Northern and the Southern systems lies in the range of local government functions: in Northern European countries local governments tend to have a relatively wide range of functions, whereas in Southern Europe these functions have traditionally been narrower. On the basis of 22 Western industrialized countries, Hesse and Sharpe (1990/91: 605–8) have proposed a related but somewhat more refined distinction. They refer to the Southern European systems as the Franco or Napoleonic group, but within the Northern European group they distinguish between an Anglo-variant and the Middle European variant. The major difference between the latter two groups is that in the Middle European variant local governments typically possess and exercise a general functional competence, whereas in the Anglo variant local governments are restricted to those functions that central government explicitly grants to local government (the *ultra vires* principle).

In addition to this threefold distinction, which is essentially based on the nature of local government functions, it also makes sense to employ a second dimension in selecting cases for closer inspection. This second dimension pertains to the distinction between federal and unitary systems. One major difference between unitary and federal systems is that in federal systems the role of national government *vis-à-vis* local government tends to be more limited. Moreover, there may be a considerable degree of within-system variation in the systems of local government found in a federation, whereas in a unitary state there is generally only one system of local government throughout the country.

If both of these dimensions are combined, we get a matrix with six cells (see Exhibit 1.2). In selecting our cases we have aimed at a balanced coverage of all these different systems of local government. With regard to the Southern European or Napoleonic models, it is important to recognize that this model is historically based on a unitary system. In recent years, however, it is possible to observe a trend in which some traditionally Napoleonic countries, such as Italy and Belgium, have been moving towards a (quasi-)federal type of system. In the United Kingdom recent devolution policies might indicate that there, too, traditional unitarism may be undergoing fundamental change. In selecting countries we have also tried to achieve a mix of small- and medium-sized countries (such as Belgium, Italy, the Netherlands, the Nordic countries, Switzerland and New Zealand) and large countries (such as France, Poland, Germany, the UK, the USA and Australia). Considered together the mix of countries covered in this volume should therefore serve to provide a broad basis for understanding important trends and developments relating to local government and local governance at the beginning of a new millennium.

Exhibit 1.2   A typology of local government systems illustrated by countries in this book

	Unitary systems	Federal systems
Southern European	France Italy Belgium →	
Middle European	Netherlands Nordic countries Poland	Germany Switzerland
Anglo	United Kingdom New Zealand	Australia United States

2 France: the intermunicipal revolution

Olivier Borraz and Patrick Le Galès

Local government in France is on the move. After three decades of increasing local autonomy, a trend highlighted by the much-celebrated Decentralization Acts of 1982 and 1983, France is no longer the Jacobin centralist state it used to be. Local government nevertheless faces a paradoxical situation. On the one hand, legitimized by decentralization reforms, it has so far avoided strict financial controls by the state and its representatives are colonizing national politics. Local and regional politicians now control an expanding share of public resources and their power has increased within the main political parties and central government. Political leaders on both the left and the right are building powerful urban and regional bases, and the new generation of national political leaders is firmly rooted in local and regional governments. Even what was regarded as the main weakness of the system – its division into more than 36,000 municipalities – is now moving towards integration within new structures of cooperation. Only in the area of local democracy has there been little progress so far, as more participatory forms of government remain limited.

On the other hand, local government is enshrined within a world of conflicting norms, competitive politics, mosaics of local and regional governments and a restructuring state which, while less present in day-to-day politics and policies, also distances itself from the immediate demands and needs – including financial – of local government. Local government autonomy, therefore, is a very mixed picture (Balme *et al.* 1999). It is clearly an illusion for small communes without resources, expertise or strong mayors, but a great opportunity for powerful municipalities or intermunicipal governments able to mobilize different types of resources to support their own strategy.

This chapter aims at analysing the main dynamics and current characteristics of French local government. This is not a simple story, and at the outset it is necessary to stress the changing but decisive role of the state

(Cassese and Wright 1995; Jessop 2000; Le Galès 1999). Although French national government, as elsewhere, may have lost some of its power due to the impetus of the European Union, internationalized economies, and the 'crisis' of the welfare state, it still retains capacities in shaping political and administrative institutions. Yet local factors determine the content given to these institutions. We provide evidence of strengthened local government – in particular in terms of innovating and implementing public policies, but also with respect to its increasing political capacity for collective action – in a context of more diverse and fragmented patterns of local governments.

In what follows, we first consider recent changes in French local government and then move on to a more precise analysis of the revolution taking place in intermunicipal cooperation. After this the impact of new procedures for local democracy is considered, and finally the role of large utilities firms and of other procedures in integrating public policies at the local level are assessed. In keeping with the general focus of this volume, our emphasis is on local government. The meso tier – that is, regions and departments – are not treated in any detail in this chapter. One must never-theless be aware of the far-reaching financial and political interdependence between the different levels of government.

French local government: a brief overview

France currently has 36,565 municipalities (see Table 2.1), almost 98 per cent of which have a population of less than 10,000. Yet little more than half the total population lives in these municipalities while almost a third lives

Table 2.1 *Distribution of municipalities and population in France by size of municipality, 2002*

Population size	Municipalities		Inhabitants	
	Number	*Per cent*	*Number*	*Per cent*
Less than 1,000	27,794	76.0	9,393,701	15.7
1,000 to 5,000	6,922	18.9	14,298,005	23.9
5,000 to 10,000	975	2.7	6,729,792	11.2
10,000 to 30,000	633	1.7	10,647,377	17.8
30,000 to 100,000	205	0.6	9,844,714	16.4
100,000 to 300,000	31	0.1	4,885,416	8.2
Over 300,000	5	0.01	4,152,430	6.9
Total	36,565	100.0	59,951,435	100.0

Source: Data from Direction Générale des Collectivités Locales (2002: 7).

in cities with a population over 30,000. To these municipalities must be added a little over 20,000 *ad hoc* associations of municipalities or more formalized intermunicipal organizations managing utilities and services. Last but not least, sub-national government encompasses a meso tier with 100 departments and 22 regions plus four overseas regions.

The world of local government also comprises a myriad of other organizations. Some of these have a nongovernmental status, such as associations acting as quasi service-producers for local government. Others such as *sociétés d'économie mixte* (private agencies with majority public ownership) have a mixed status, often acting as subsidiaries or managing services for local government (cf. Caillosse *et al.* 1997). While some organizations such as those running social housing are public, others involved in, for example, town planning are quasi-public or public–private agencies running services operated by private firms. Finally, a number of organizations are clearly private, engaging in activities relating to the environment, transport and housing management. What has been termed the 'municipal public sector' (Lorrain 1991) thus comprises a diversity of organizations, many of which do not have genuine public status (even though they may well operate on public funding) and whose integration is highly problematic, if only because they do not always operate on the same geographic scale.

The functions of local government

Ever since the Revolution suppressed municipal corporations, France has been a Jacobin state, built on mistrust of local institutions. The Napoleonic organizational model provided for uniform municipal institutions, but it was not until the Third Republic – notably in 1884 – that major laws granted municipal freedoms. Yet the commune, preserved by the Revolution, long remained a largely mythologized foundation of French democracy (Joana 2001). Local elected political representatives, often powerful, have held legitimacy through their access to the centre achieved through either the practice of multiple office-holding or through political party ties. Local government, however, had few resources and little expertise, most of which remained monopolized by the state administration, either in Paris or in field offices operating at the departmental level.

The first step towards genuine change occurred with the decentralization reforms of 1982–83, which gave wider resources, powers and legitimacy to all levels of sub-national government, from the municipalities to the departments and newly created regions. The foremost impact of the decentralization acts was to strengthen local autonomy. Mayors gained greater authority, both in financial and legal terms, and the position of urban governments was strengthened. Symbolic of the new legal autonomy of local government was the retreat of the deconcentrated branches of the state bureaucracy and the suppression of prior administrative control. The Ministry of Social Affairs' departmental services were largely dismantled, for example, as these became a new power of the *départements*. Important transfers also took place from the powerful Ministry of Infrastructure and Housing's departmental services. These and other changes served to under-cut the executive power of the prefect and created a situation in which the prefect has had to look for an alternative role, particularly with respect to the coordination of state services (cf. Reignier 2001).

A more complex picture of local government has emerged, a more mosaic-like pattern resembling the situation found in many other countries throughout Europe and very different from the previous well-organized system controlled by civil servants and enshrined within financial and legal constraints set by the state. The reforms of 1983 gave more or less specific competences to each level of government. Thus, municipalities were awarded powers in the fields of town planning, culture and primary educa-tion. In addition to these formal provisions, local councils took on tasks in other areas where they felt they had political legitimacy to act, much as they always had, although the prefect had previously limited their initiatives. Economic development, for example, was primarily assigned to the regions, but both departments and municipalities developed policies in this domain. Similarly, while social services were assigned to the departments, large municipalities have maintained extensive services in this area. The same is true in other fields such as culture, the environment and social infrastructure.

All in all, a complicated picture has emerged, and one finds a confusing pattern of intergovernmental policy networks and complex financial arrange-ments. These overlapping policy networks and the resulting 'crossed financing patterns' (Gilbert and Thoenig 1999) have proven to be major obstacles to efficiency and accountability. But this complex system has also resulted in considerable innovation and new forms of coordination.

Financial autonomy

Despite its centralist reputation, 'the financial autonomy of French local authorities seems to be extensive, effective, strongly supported by decen-tralization, and guaranteed by the political influence that local politicians have within national elected representative bodies' (Gilbert 1999: 159). Several facts underline such a conclusion. First, local and regional government or agencies now undertake about 70 per cent of all public investment in France. Second, between 1985 and 1996 local taxes increased from 3.8 to 4.7 per cent of GDP. In cities with a population above 10,000, taxes now account for 45 per cent of resources, the rest coming in through state grants (31 per cent), bank loans and local user fees and charges. Third, even though local government expenditure as a percentage of GDP is not very high (just under 10 per cent in France by contrast to around 30 per cent in Scandinavia), the discretionary authority accorded French local government in spending is very high. Hence, according to Gilbert (1999), comparatively France ranks second in terms of local government's overall spending autonomy. In this respect it is in the same league as the Scandinavian countries, and far ahead of Italy and the UK.

These figures not only differentiate the well-known stereotype of French centralism but also help provide a better basis for interpretation than do the laments heard from spokesmen of local government, who characteristically start by asserting that there is a general financial crisis of local government. Actually French cities and conurbations were by no means in a state of financial crisis in the 1980s; their financial situation only became strained in the 1990s.

Recent changes in the shape and functions of local government

After two decades of decentralization, differentiation among local government has become the norm. The long-standing doctrine of a uniform legal status among 36,500 plus communes has become ever more fictitious. The changing role of the state within the European polity and economic restructuring have gradually signalled the decline of the old communal France of the Third Republic dominated by rural interests. Regions and regional capital cities, which have obtained more resources and political support than rural communes and small towns, dominate the 'new urban system'. Unless they join a large urban region, small communes are becoming more and more marginalized. Although institutions such as the Senate, the departments or the *Association des Maires de France* (the national organization of all communes) retain sufficient resources to resist and celebrate a slightly conservative view of the Republic, urban interests – represented for instance by the *Association des Maires de Grandes Villes de France* (association of large city mayors) – have gained a decisive advantage.

Recent changes can be considered under three general headings: legislation aimed at improving local political capacities, the growing influence of the European Union on local policy-making, and the management of utilities.

New institutions and instruments for local policy-making

Decentralization over the last 20 years has gone hand in hand with increasing local expertise and resources. Within a context in which political legitimacy seems more related to public policy outcomes and the capacity to implement programmes (Duran 1998) and in which classic vertical, state-led policies have collapsed (Muller 1992), local government plays an increasingly important role in terms of public policy. During the 1980s and the 1990s, several 'new' public policies (urban, social, environmental and health) were initiated by the state which gave sub-national governments, along with social and political groups from the local communities, responsibility for integrating different policy programmes. The aim was to provide a territorial logic and a degree of coherence to a whole range of programmes and policies, and to compensate for the decline of the old vertical integration through national interest groups and state administrative elites. The territorial integration and coherence achieved was in fact more often a myth (a mobilizing myth) than a reality, inasmuch as fragmentation and the multiplication of intergovernmental/private–public networks continued to prevail (Gaudin 1999; Le Galès 2001). Urban elites, however, were busy building new alliances, networks and partnerships, and seemed to be at the forefront of new forms of governance (Cole and John 2001; Jouve and Lefèvre 1999).

In particular, the use of contracts – both with other levels of government and with private actors – became a central policy instrument for cooperation (Marcou *et al.* 1997). Contracts take different forms. Frequently they are inspired directly by corporate law and have helped to introduce market mechanisms into public management. At the same time, the use of contracts flies in the face of efforts to achieve intergovernmental coordination of policies and programmes by the use of public rather than private means (Le Galès and Mawson 1995). Similar tensions arise with partnership approaches. Because of the rules governing public accounts in particular, partnerships require the development of complex bureaucratic structures. These structures, however, represent an additional barrier to engaging local residents and small associations in such partnerships. Local governments, moreover, are only keen on developing such partnerships when they do not conflict with the political interests and legitimacy of local political elites (Loncle 2000).

At the end of the 1990s, several additional laws were passed to organize local development and planning through compulsory urban strategies, projects and contracts. These laws mainly aimed at fostering cooperation between local governments in both urban and rural areas. These cooperative efforts were designed to secure the development of economic development strategies, planning strategies and the management of services and utilities.

Additionally, new policy tools were also introduced, most notably in the fight against poverty and social exclusion. Such tools usually called for the allocation of resources through contracts negotiated and signed between local authorities and state officials, an approach applied in different contexts. Initially they were focused on the neighbourhood, then were extended to the city level, and more recently to the larger urban area. Their application was also extended to other policy domains – from urban renewal to development and physical planning, then to social and health policies, and more recently to area-wide strategies for transport or housing. The multiplication of such schemes, however, brought a new incoherence into the system. Each policy instrument is supposed to be inclusive, to embrace a transversal global approach and to promote some kind of partnership, but political rivalries between local governments and ministries produce different frontiers for each contract and each development strategy. While stronger municipalities may be able to achieve some coherence and develop a mode of integrated governance for the whole area, extensive confusion is the norm.

The Europeanization of local government

There has also been a marked shift in the context of French local government. The political playing field has seen changes of scale and a proliferation of new players: no player now possesses a monopoly on rule-production or coercion. The European Union represents a particularly significant political opening in this regard, offering a wide range of new options for local governments. They may appeal state decisions through the European Court of Justice, organize lobbies in Brussels to influence policies, obtain resources, develop horizontal transnational relationships with other local authorities, become deeply involved in various policy networks, claim to represent the interests of their citizens, and question the state's formulation of the common interest. But the EU represents something of a double-edged sword. While EU programmes and funds provide new political horizons, local governments have also learned that EU institution-alization is accompanied by a new set of constraints. Thus, although still important, the old antagonism between the state and local government has been reduced to merely one dimension among others. This factor has almost automatically transformed hierarchical central–local relations into overlapping policy networks (Smith 1995).

A key indicator of the emergence of more Europeanized local government is the increased density of transnational relations and networks among social and political actors. Together with their European counterparts, French local governments have joined hundreds of horizontal networks across the EU, nearly always related in one way or another to EU programmes and incentives. If the initial focus of twinning agreements was very much on cultural exchanges, day-to-day life and peace related issues, the EU has provided a new impetus and a new focus for transnational networks of local government. Typical now are policy-domain networks, especially networks oriented towards economic development (Vion 2002) or specific networks of local and regional governments organized to represent their own collective interests. These transnational networks are privileged sites for obtaining information, exchanging experiences, ideas and knowledge of various kinds, and challenging European programmes or national policies – in short, places for learning new policy norms and styles. French local governments were not pioneers in this trend, but they have gradually taken these networks seriously and learned the rules of the new game (Balme and Le Galès 1997; Goldsmith and Klausen 1997).

This is a significant development but not a crucial one. So far, the restructuring impact of these transnational networks is often limited, since they reflect existing power structures and hierarchies. Although they bring some fluidity into these, they do not replace them. It is in this context that the growing role of large urban areas must be emphasized, inasmuch as these tend to consolidate powerful local governance patterns.

The management of utilities

Another factor that has strongly affected local politics is the changing management of public utilities. The privatization of services and utilities in the 1980s, which gave prominence and power to large utility firms, was in many respects a silent revolution for local government. These firms became major actors, offering technical and financial solutions to cities, whether to solve their technical problems or to carry out major projects. They ran various public utilities (from water to new metro and tramway lines), but also entered into new urban markets, built new neighbourhoods and were involved in flagship projects. They also became the providers of funds for political parties and political leaders (Lorrain 1993, 1996).

Firms still play an important role in running urban utilities, but recently they have somewhat distanced themselves for various reasons. Large utility firms became world leaders with less interest for running local utilities

(Lorrain and Stoker 1996). They have restructured their activities at a regional level, thus accompanying the move towards more integrated forms of local governance. Political corruption scandals have also encouraged firms to keep some distance from local politics – and in this respect, the relationships they build at the intermunicipal level are more 'technical'. But increasing distance was also induced by changes in the attitudes of local politicians and citizens. As a reaction against privatization, state officials, green movements and local governments have demanded stricter controls over contracts with utility firms. After a few years of rapid growth, moreover, major infrastructure projects (office space, shopping centres, parking lots) proved to be a financial black hole and thus less attractive to the firms.

It must be noted, however, that leading utility firms have supported the intermunicipal revolution inasmuch as the rise of this development offers them an opportunity to rationalize their organization and to concentrate on markets of a reasonable size. Yet this does not imply that local councils are without resources in dealing with these firms. The firms need public space, access to refuse collection and coordination for carrying out their work: in short, if there were open conflict with a city council, network operators might find themselves in a difficult position. Local government therefore remains a major player in running urban utilities and faces more and more political pressure from citizen groups to make sure fair prices and environmental and sanitary norms are respected.

The intermunicipal revolution

Municipal amalgamation has always been a politically sensitive subject in France, and the central government has systematically failed in attempts to reduce the number of municipalities. To manage this municipal fragmentation, therefore, different forms of intermunicipal cooperation have been pursued over the years, in particular in the provision and production of goods and services (water, waste, public transportation and so forth). In 1980, for example, over 10,500 syndicates (the minimal form of cooperation between towns) existed. By 1992 this figure had risen to 17,000, a reflection of the decentralization acts and the new competences and responsibilities given to local government. Alongside these syndicates, more integrated bodies with specific taxes and compulsory activities also existed. One voluntary form of inter-communal cooperation was the district, the number of which increased from 147 in 1980 to 214 in 1992, along with urban communities and 'new-city' syndicates of which there are nine of each.

Confronted with these multiple and overlapping structures, the central government attempted to simplify forms of municipal cooperation in 1992.

Three forms were introduced, each supported by generous financial incentives, but only one – *communautés de communes* (medium-sized towns) – achieved rapid success. The number of these authorities rose from 193 in 1993 to 1,349 in 1999. Significantly, during the same period the number of single or multipurpose bodies (the syndicates mentioned above) continued to rise. Even more noteworthy, however, is the rise in the number of districts during the first years after the law's introduction, since the new structures were supposed to replace districts, not encourage them. Overall, in other words, rather than introducing greater simplicity and increasing transparency, the new legislation made the situation even more complex and difficult to control. In 1999, different intermunicipal bodies employed more than 110,000 civil servants.

The 1999 Chevènement Act was a response to this situation. It was intended to reduce the variety in the different forms of cooperation once and for all. To do so, the government adopted an approach that combines *direct constraints* with strong financial incentives. Three modes of cooperation were made available with a stipulation that preexisting intermunicipal bodies would have to adopt one of the three new modes of cooperation by 2002. To ensure this, the prefect was granted the authority to force a commune into cooperation, even against its will. Furthermore, over time the new cooperative bodies must achieve a uniform business tax (instead of permitting taxes to vary between neighbouring towns). Finally, each entity finds itself with a set of compulsory competencies and the obligation to choose other optional competencies.

As a result, 14 urban communities (in general the largest urban areas), 120 *communautés d'agglomération* (large-sized communities) and 2,033 *communautés de communes* had been established by 1 January 2002. Together with the remaining eight new city syndicates, this amounted to a total of 2,175 intermunicipal bodies, each having a specific and distinct tax base. These institutions encompassed 26,748 municipalities with a total population of over 45 million (75 per cent of the French population). Simplification, in short, is finally at hand and a large majority of municipalities are today integrated in some form of cooperation. In the years ahead, it is expected that all municipalities will have joined some intermunicipal body and that the old syndicates will slowly disappear, their competencies being transferred to the new institutions.

The success of the 1999 law has been interpreted as a 'return of the state', and indubitably the 1999 law implied strong state intervention in the process of building metropolitan governments. Yet this intervention is of a particular type: it rests more on a constitutional focus rather than on substantive policies. The state, in other words, defines rules and procedures, roles and settings, but it does not go into details as to how exactly these will contribute to a particular purpose. The latter is left to local officials. In this respect, the 1999 law is perfectly congruent with a whole series of other laws that see central government as defining priorities and procedures to achieve particular goals while allowing local actors to choose the requisite means (Duran and Thoenig 1996). Hence, the state still has significant capacities to act, but the nature of its interventions has changed in such a way as to imply a weakening of its control over exactly what goes on inside the new intermunicipal arenas it has established.

To understand this radical change, political factors need to be considered, since this revolution has much to do with municipal patterns of leadership, stabilized forms of political exchange and organizational learning through preexisting forms of cooperation between different levels (Gaxie 1997; Le Saout 2000a; Baraize and Négrier 2001). Major policy domains are now under the responsibility of the new inter-communal authorities: economic development, planning, social housing and environmental protection (including water and waste) respectively. These domains share some common characteristics: they can be costly, call for professional expertise, and entail political risks (in case of an accident or crisis, or simply because they are unpopular). More precisely, they require political and administrative officials to show some capacity for building consensus on issues that can be highly controversial and which are, at the same time, characterized by interdependencies between a wide variety of stakeholders in a given territory. Regulating these interdependencies calls for modes of coordination and decision-making that are well-beyond the technical, political and financial capacity of municipal governments. This is further aggravated by increasing demands emanating from the EU (in terms of regulation and financing), along with numerous political requirements and technical and professional standards. The new intermunicipal governments are therefore not only subjected to central government rules and procedures, but for a whole range of activities also have to work under supranational norms – something that municipal governments, due to lack of expertise and scope of action, found difficult to achieve. New expertise is required both at the political and the administrative level – expertise in mastering European funds and regulation, managing networks of cities, putting together coalitions in favour of large projects, and so forth.

These new forms of cooperation between local governments will have important effects on the institutional framework and on issues of coordination, and the future of these new units will largely depend on their legitimacy. For the time being, these structures are still indirectly elected by the municipal councils of the member towns, which could hamper their capacity for authoritative action. Were these structures to achieve political autonomy through direct election (a point on which both right- and leftwing parties have agreed in their party platforms), this capacity will get a considerable boost. In turn, this could result in styles of decision-making that differ radically from the rather authoritarian style prevalent at the municipal level. Intermunicipal governments will also offer new opportunities for local leaders willing to establish strongholds on a larger territorial basis (Baraize and Négrier 2001). A large majority of the *communautés* are already now chaired by mayors, often the mayor of the central city around which the *communauté* was built (Le Saout 2000b). But if intermunicipal councils are directly elected, and if as some national politicians suggest there is independent democratic legitimation for the chairman of the intermunicipal authority, this could give birth to a system of more collective forms of leadership unknown in French local government up to now.

The issue of coordination *between* these structures will also arise. Tensions are already visible between existing *communautés* and the towns that have chosen to remain outside or that have formed their own 'defensive' *communauté*. Will the coordination of these units be a new task for the prefects or for officials of regional or departmental governments? Or will *communautés*, through conflictual or cooperative interactions, develop their own capacities for coordination? Up to now the consequences of this 'intermunicipal revolution' have hardly been considered.

New procedures for local democracy

Although the major local government acts did not contain measures to revitalize local democracy, there has recently been a move towards more participatory forms of decision-making.

Representative versus participatory democracy

French municipal government is based on a complex system of representation often overlooked by observers who have been all too eager to focus on the position of the mayor (Mény 1992; Mabileau 1995). Municipal council elections are based on a majority system with a touch of proportional representation. Elections are contested between party lists, and the list that obtains the most votes receives half of the council seats. The remaining half is then distributed on a basis of proportionality among all of the lists, including the winning list. Thus, the party that gets the most votes is certain to obtain a large majority on the council. The municipal council then elects its mayor, usually the head of the winning list, and appoints a number of deputy mayors to whom the mayor then delegates some of his powers. Frequently deputy mayors are selected on the basis of their capacity either to represent or to work with different local groups.

This system rests on the personal relationships which the mayor is able to develop with his municipal councillors and deputy mayors. In particular, deputy mayors act as spokespersons or mediators between the mayor and different groups and interests in the municipality, thereby building legitimacy for the mayor and municipal government. They also have specific responsibilities within local government; they act on behalf of the mayor to promote policies and answer requests and in so doing work with a variety of professionals and local groups. In this way the deputy mayors are at the centre of a largely informal system of functional representation that reflects local policy networks. This informal system of functional representation complements the electoral system of representation which provides the basis for the mayor's authority (Borraz 1998, 2000).

The present system is currently under pressure in terms of both electoral representation (due to a decline in voter turnout) and functional representation (due to multiple and fragmented local interests). Despite some variation, municipal elections in France have generally long been characterized by high voter turnout. From 1983 to 2001, however, turnout levels have steadily dropped, declining from 78 per cent to 61 per cent on the aggregate level. Electoral participation among some groups (in terms of social class, ethnic origin or area) is particularly low. This implies a potential problem of representation: the needs and demands of such groups, individuals and areas may receive less attention and understanding from political officials. Low electoral turnout, of course, does not preclude alternative modes of mobilization and political activity, but in a political system based on representation, low levels of turnout may provide an argument for questioning the legitimacy of elected officials. This is particularly true in the French system where the mayor's authority heavily rests on his capacity to represent different interest and social groups in their diversity and heterogeneity.

Another difficulty faced by local officials arises from an increasing variety of political parties competing during elections (Chiche *et al.* 2002). From an average of two to three parties in the 1970s, the average number has recently risen to nearly four, and even five in major cities. This increasing fragmentation of the party system goes hand in hand with increasing electoral volatility (Hoffmann-Martinot 1999). Electoral fragmentation, however, tells only part of the story. New forms of non-electoral participation are emerging, including various types of consultations, referendums and procedures designed to promote dialogue. There is, in short, a shift from representative democracy towards a more participatory type of democracy. Some of these new participatory forms (such as consultative committees, referendums and popular initiatives on planning issues) are based on national laws and regulations. Others stem from local government initiatives, and still others from citizen-initiated collective action. On issues such as environmental protection, planning, transportation infrastructures, social housing, work promotion, health, industrial pollution and risks, a wide variety of forms and actions exist through which demands are formulated, priorities set, resources distributed, information produced and decisions made. Such channels are used to engage a wide array of stakeholders, professionals and other participants in collective decision-making.

A further channel for citizen involvement in France is through voluntary associations. It is relatively easy to form an association which can then take part in local issues and the promotion of interests. It is estimated that there are currently about 700,000 such associations and groups, the vast majority of them being active at the local level (Barthélémy 2000).

These 'new' types and forms of participation are at present almost inevitable – if only from a policy-implementation point of view. But clearly many of these forms of activity exert strong pressures on local elected officials, both in terms of generating conflicting legitimacies (between representative and participatory modes) and as a test of the officials' capacity to take demands into consideration, provide answers and arbitrate between contradictory pressures. From this perspective, the new participatory channels appear to offer advantages both in terms of effectiveness and efficiency, but also constitute a challenge in a quest for greater legitimacy.

This tension, along with the growing importance of intermunicipal governments and declining participation in local elections, prompted the government to pass a new law on 'democracy and proximity' in February 2002. Among other things, the Act makes the creation of neighbourhood councils compulsory in cities with over 80,000 inhabitants, as well as consultative committees for local utilities in cities with over 10,000 residents and intermunicipal structures over 50,000. The law also makes it easier for citizens to participate in the decision-making process on major infrastructure projects – for example through public enquiries and consultations. Finally, the minority in the local assembly has seen its powers enlarged. All in all, the aim has been to promote new forms of participation and to stimulate political debate in what formally remains a representative system of government.

Parties and elites

In general, political parties have played a limited role in setting the local political agenda. They have, however, often established close links to the local community (Sawicki 1997). Since the 1990s parties have changed, most notably under the influence of legislation on party funding, the imposition of limits on multiple office-holding, and an obligation for parties to present lists of candidates for elective office with an equal number of women and men. Rather than their traditional function in developing party platforms, parties have gradually evolved into a vehicle for the recruitment and selection of candidates for elective office at different levels. The creation of a regional level and the success of *communautés* have multiplied the number of seats to be distributed and given even more weight to political parties.

In this regard, the role of local political elites has also been subject to change. Paradoxically, legislation passed in 1985 to reduce opportunities for multiple office-holding instead promoted this practice. After passage of the legislation no single individual held five or six offices, as had occasionally occurred previously, but almost all the members of parliament (both national assembly and senate) subsequently held at least two, and likewise many mayors also held at least one other mandate. Under constraints imposed by recent legislation, the transformation of political parties, and a change in public opinion, however, this practice has been progressively restricted. The 2001 municipal elections saw new profiles emerge, and at least initially mayors appear less concerned about starting a national career. Rather, they seem keen to establish strong ties with their constituency and to promote integrated forms of cooperation with neighbouring towns.

Another important group of actors in French local government are local civil servants, and more precisely top officials (CEOs and the like – see Klausen and Magnier 1998). Highly qualified and highly mobile, they constitute a new class of experts that play a critical role in decision-making – a role that up to the 1970s used to be played by state personnel or agents working for major public firms and corporations. But more recently, local officials have taken on a more prominent role, contributing to the rapid spread of ideas and professional models through national and international networks, professional associations and academic training courses (Faure 1994). With the development of *communautés*, their role will be even more decisive in building up these new institutions, giving them expertise in their various domains of action and in managing relations with the other levels of local, national and European government.

Clearly the intermunicipal revolution offers new opportunities for collective action at the local level. It provides opportunities for the *communautés'* political and administrative personnel to establish their institution's legitimacy and political capacity. New opportunities also exist for local organized interests to push forward their demands and obtain recognition by public officials. But new forms of participation, local initiatives, patterns of mobilization and the capacity for elites to build coalitions outside urban government also contribute to a shift towards more complex forms and processes of governance. Urban government, in other words, is not the locus of transformation in local policy-making; the impetus comes either from the intermunicipal level or from mobilization around issues outside the realm of city politics.

At the supra-local level of urban regions, local political elites – often but not always urban – work hard to create stabilized forms of governance, regimes or coalitions to develop collective action and long-term political goals for the urban area (Pinson 2002). In cooperation with other local elites (business, unions, university, and so on), they try in particular to organize cities as collective actors within a system of governance emerging in Europe (Le Galès 2002).

Conclusion

Reorganized French local government is enjoying more autonomy in terms of resources, legitimacy and expertise, but it evolves within a system of constraints now defined by the EU, a restructured state and regions which may not be easier to accommodate. This calls for the invention of new styles of leadership, new processes of policy-making (notably through citizen participation) and new institutionalized procedures for collective action. French local government remains dynamic, launching and developing a variety of procedures and experiments to develop political participation and debates ranging from the inter-communal to the neighbourhood scale. The same applies to the policy process where forms of consultation and inhabitant participation are rising, sometimes backed by national law. Policy instruments are used to aggregate demands, but interestingly the rise of urban strategies, projects or strategic planning reveals the sense of unity and the attempt to define some forms of common good or general local interest collectively. At the same time, fragile political elites also use these new forums and procedures to manipulate the process, to eliminate political rivals and to strengthen their political control of the territory without too much interest for policy effectiveness and democracy. This tension lies at the heart of French local government and leads to serious differentiation within it.

The intermunicipal revolution is gradually reorganizing French local government into a system wherein a few thousand intermunicipal governments play an increasingly important part within a more diverse and differentiated system. The almighty commune remains, but is now gradually associated with other communes, and the long-term anti-urban bias of state elites is fading away. The development of new public policy networks and the extension of existing ones has kept pace with the fragmentation and the overlapping responsibilities among different levels of government. Yet despite these changes, local political leaders and their officers, together with satellite organizations, have remained clearly dominant within the networks that matter most at the local level. The political legitimacy of the French mayor remains very strong, and even private-sector representatives do not often challenge his leadership. Politics and government, in short, are still central in the new forms of municipal and intermunicipal governance.

3 Italy: after the storm

Luigi Bobbio

In international comparisons, the Italian system of local government is usually traced back to the Franco-Napoleonic family: it originated in the nineteenth century based on the French model, and during the twentieth century typical features of that model continued to dominate – centralization, prefects who exercise control over local government, uniformity of territorial subdivisions and organizational form. Local governments played a marginal role (though a growing one) in the management of public policies. Still today, the local share of revenue, expenditure and employees is much lower than in Northern European countries (Bobbio 2002). However, the original framework, still visible in some formal aspects, was increasingly eroded after the Second World War, literally crumbling during the 1990s. If continuity could still be said to prevail at the beginning of the 1990s (Vandelli 1990), by the end of the decade the dominant element was undeniably discontinuity.

The 1990s was the decade that saw the most intense change in the age-long history of Italian local governments. The decade opened with the law reforming local authorities (1990), awaited for 50 years; it continued with the introduction of direct election for mayors (1993), numerous measures to modernize the administration and a vast process of decentralization (1997); it concluded with two constitutional reforms (1999 and 2001) tending to transform Italy into a quasi-federal state. The reforms from above were accompanied by initiatives from below that had the effect of strengthening the process of change. The trend running through these transformations is not very different from that begun, in many cases earlier, by other European countries, but the engine driving the changes lies in the political crisis that struck Italy during those years, and this may explain why the change has been more intense (and perhaps also more confused) than elsewhere.

Characteristics of Italian local government at the end of the 1980s

The local government system and intergovernmental relations

At the end of the 1980s, Italian local government consisted of three sub-national tiers, encompassing 20 regional governments (*regioni*), 95 provincial governments (*province*) and approximately 8,000 municipal governments (*comuni*) respectively. The autonomy of each level of government is guaranteed by the Constitution. The introduction of regional governments in 1970 marked a complete break with the old system, but only marginally changed the position of local governments, which still chiefly revolve around the nation state. Municipal and provincial governments are regulated under national law and are thus uniform throughout the country. The Ministry for Internal Affairs supervises them through representatives in each province – the prefects – and the Minister has the power to dissolve municipal councils that are unable to function and to call new elections. All decisions made by the municipal governments (including the most trivial) are subjected to legal review. At one time this review was the prefect's responsibility, but in 1970 it passed to the regional governments. The municipal administration, furthermore, was under the direction of a municipal secretary who was appointed by and served under the direct authority of the Ministry for Internal Affairs. The municipal secretary was the guardian of legality: he did not interfere with the political choices of the mayor, but was a sort of legal consultant of the mayor, and the secretary's interpretation of the rules normally had a great influence on the decisions of local government.

Italy is among those European countries (above all the Southern European countries) in which local government has never been reorganized from the territorial standpoint. Indeed, the number of local governments has slightly increased over the years. The 8,000-plus Italian municipalities (*comuni*) have on average just over 7,000 inhabitants, which is much higher than, for example, France, but lower than in some Northern European countries, and 74 per cent have fewer than 5,000 inhabitants (see Table 3.1). For historical reasons, moreover, the size of municipalities differs widely from one region to another. Piedmont, with four million inhabitants, for instance, has 1,200 municipalities, whereas Sicily, with five million inhabitants, has only 390.

During the 1960s and 1970s, following the Northern European example, a debate on the amalgamation of municipalities also developed in Italy, but remained fruitless. National policy-makers preferred not to challenge the force of municipal identity or the civic pride of micro-municipalities. Nor

Table 3.1 *Distribution of Italian municipalities and local government characteristics by size of municipality, 2001*

Population size	Number of municipalities	Number of seats in the council	Number of assessori in the cabinet
Less than 3,000	4,630	12	2
3,000 to 10,000	2,359	16	4
10,000 to 30,000	820	20	6
30,000 to 100,000	250	30	6
100,000 to 250,000	29	40	10
250,000 to 500,000	7	46	12
500,000 to 1,000,000	3	50	14
Over 1,000,000	3	60	16
Total	8,101		
Average population size	7,036		

Source: Data from Istat, *14° Censimento Generale della Popolazione e delle Abitazioni 2001*, www.istat.it for column 1, national law on local government ('Testo unico delle autonomie locali', d.lgs. 267/2000) for columns 2 and 3.

was the long-running debate on the government of metropolitan areas resolved. Supporters of a 'hard solution' – that is, a new local government at the metropolitan level built over the preexisting municipalities – were not able to defeat the partisans of a 'soft solution' – that is, metropolitan problems tackled by special agencies or by *ad hoc* agreements among metropolitan municipalities (Rotelli 1999).

The continuation of this highly fragmented picture pushed the country into intermunicipal cooperation. The traditional and most widespread form consists of intermunicipal associations (*consorzi*), to which member municipalities devolve the management of specific services (waste collection and disposal, transport, administrative functions, social and welfare services, and so on). The majority of Italian municipalities belongs to at least one such consortium. Furthermore, since 1971 all municipalities in mountainous areas (half of all Italian municipalities) have been obliged to belong to a specific association (*comunità montana*) of which there are approximately 350, whose boundaries are drawn up by the regional governments and whose councillors are elected from among members of the councils of the municipalities involved. They replace the member municipalities in several functions (transport, infrastructure and economic development) defined by the regional government or delegated by the municipalities themselves.

Functions and finance

Italian municipal governments have general jurisdiction – that is they may undertake any initiative that is not prohibited by law – but this does not prevent them from being subject to numerous obligations. The municipal governments are obliged to exercise some state functions (register of births, deaths and marriages, electoral rolls, and so forth) and in this case the mayor acts as a 'government official' under the direct authority of the Ministry for Internal Affairs. They must also perform numerous functions entrusted to them by national laws or, increasingly often, by regional laws. However, the general jurisdiction they possess has historically enabled Italian municipal governments to develop innovative policies in numerous fields, starting from the experiences of 'municipal socialism' in the early years of the twentieth century. Above all, the municipal governments of central and northern Italy have compensated for gaps or failures in national policies, setting up their own services in many different fields: day nurseries, kindergartens, welfare, production and distribution of energy, school services, professional training, promotion of cultural activities, museums, and so on. In many different circumstances the more dynamic municipal governments have anticipated the formulation of policies that were later introduced at the national level.

   The principal functions of Italian municipal governments may be divided into three areas: environment and territory (the fundamental function being that of drawing up development plans, which is the direct responsibility of the municipal government, subject to subsequent approval by the regional government), social services, and economic development. The biggest difference compared to Northern European countries lies in the fact that, with the development of the welfare state, Italian municipal governments have not become the chief managers of welfare policies: numerous functions have remained the exclusive jurisdiction of the state, especially in the areas of education, health and labour policies. In the field of education, local governments are responsible for school-building and maintenance, whereas teachers are state employees and school programmes are national, drawn up by the state. Health services are provided by specialized authorities, which were initially under the control of individual or associated municipalities, after which they became fully autonomous. The labour market is managed directly by the state (through a network of employment offices) and welfare and social security services (pensions, unemployment benefit, etc.) are also dispensed throughout Italy by a single state agency. Naturally, with the development of the welfare state, municipal governments, too, have enormously extended their functions, but not to the same extent as their British or Scandinavian counterparts. Suffice it to say that in 1990 municipal employees were still only 12 per cent of all public employees.

This subdivision of functions between the state and local governments has one important consequence: the nation state continues to act in peripheral areas through its own decentralized units in numerous sectors – school, work, national heritage protection, vehicle licensing, social security, and so on. In theory, the prefect coordinates the state field agencies, chiefly operating at the provincial level; however, unlike France, prefects have a weaker role in Italy. Thus, policies carried out at the local level are the result of complex intergovernmental relations between local governments and national ministries operating through their peripheral agencies.

At the financial level, local governments were completely dependent on the state until the beginning of the 1990s. The fiscal reform of 1973 suppressed all the most important local taxes and provided for finance to municipalities exclusively through the transfer of state funds. This complete lack of fiscal autonomy was not entirely unpopular with local administrators, who were able to expand public spending without shouldering the burden of increasing local taxes. But in the 1970s, municipal deficits reached alarming dimensions and forced the national government to take restrictive measures to limit local spending. This gave an advantage to municipalities that had been more generous, since the reductions were in proportion to the preexisting spending levels of each local government.

Internal organization

Until 1993 the internal organization of Italian local governments was largely fashioned on the national model, which is a system of the parliamentary type. Thus, citizens elected an assembly or council (*consiglio*), which in turn elected the mayor (*sindaco*) and his cabinet (*giunta*), where only parties comprising the majority of the council were represented. The council was elected every five years from party lists using a system of proportional representation. Except in the smaller municipalities, the principal contestants of municipal elections were the national political parties, and indeed municipal elections, most of which take place at the same time throughout Italy, were seen as an electoral test of national importance.

Between the council and the mayor (and his cabinet) there was a relationship of confidence. If confidence was withdrawn, the cabinet had to resign and the council selected another mayor and cabinet by the same method: a new mayor would be elected and a new coalition could replace the old one if it could obtain the confidence of the council. If no solution could be found, the national government had the power to dissolve the council and call for new elections.

Given the fragmentation of Italian political parties, municipal cabinets were normally coalitions of a number of parties, and were exposed to marked instability depending on the varying equilibrium among them. The average life of municipal cabinets in the 95 provincial capitals between 1972 and 1989 was 22 months: much shorter than the council's mandate which is five years (60 months) (Cazzola 1991). Although the law gave the mayor clear supremacy within the cabinet, his or her powers were in fact limited by the need to mediate between the divergent thrusts of the parties in the coalition and by continual threats of crisis. Throughout the history of the Italian Republic, some 'historic' mayors have governed for long periods with great personal prestige, but these are exceptions made possible by the dominance of a single party (the Christian Democrats or the Communist Party) in some cities. With the progressive weakening of the two mass parties, unstable cabinets and frequent replacement of mayors became the norm.

Despite this situation, turnout for local elections has traditionally remained high (between 80 and 90 per cent) compared to that for national elections. In part this has been due to the widespread belief that voting is compulsory (the constitution defines the vote as a 'civic duty' but does not provide any sanction for failing to vote). Even more so, however, it has depended on the highly politicized nature of Italian society, characterized by hard competition between the Christian Democrats and Communists.

Two political shocks of the 1990s

During the 1980s, Italy did not espouse the neo-liberal trend that was gaining ground in Western democracies with the collapse of the Keynesian–Fordist model. Pressure to introduce a leaner state, privatize public corporations and manage the public sector with corporate methods following the dictates of New Public Management was only weak in Italy. But at the beginning of the 1990s, the situation changed drastically under the effect of two interconnected political crises.

The first political shock was the rapid and unexpected success of independence or separatist movements in northern Italy. In 1990 the Northern League (*Lega Nord*) achieved a spectacular result in municipal elections in Lombardy and Veneto, and in the general election of 1992 it became the second largest party in northern Italy, with 17 per cent of the vote. In 1993 it won numerous mayorships in northern Italian municipalities, including Milan. For the first time in the history of the Republic, a new entrant succeeded in denting the monopoly of the historic parties. The success of the Northern League has its roots in the protest by small-scale entrepreneurs and workers in the richest areas of the country against the historic inefficiency of the central state and against forced solidarity, imposed from above, with the poorer southern areas. The main effect was to put the federalist option, which had fallen into total oblivion on its defeat immediately after national unification (1861), solidly back onto the political agenda.

The second political shock came from the judicial investigations into bribery that, within two years (1992–93), swept away an entire political class. Numerous politicians were arrested or prosecuted, and none of the historic parties succeeded in surviving the storm. The general election of 1994 was fought by political forces that were either completely new on the scene or had been renamed (and in many cases remade). At the outbreak of the judicial crisis, a movement for reform loudly demanded that the government system and the electoral rules be reformed, against the 'partitocracy', in the name of honesty, efficiency and 'clean hands' (an analogy may be drawn with the Progressive Reform Movement in early twentieth-century America). And its first success concerned local governments, which incidentally were found to be permeated by widespread practices of favouritism and bribery. In order to avoid a referendum on municipal electoral law promoted by this movement, Parliament adopted a law in 1993 that, out of the blue, introduced a majoritarian electoral system combined with direct election of the mayor in all Italian municipal governments.

These two political shocks brought to light the deep crisis in which the overextended and inefficient Italian government was wallowing, and brought the theme of administrative reform crashing onto the political agenda. As shall be seen, this was a reform that would above all profoundly affect local government. This step was facilitated by the rise of new political leaders with only weak links to the traditional parties, now in disarray, who were determined to modernize the institutions. The vacuum left by politics was filled by new 'technical' figures, frequently recruited from among university professors. Two examples of this are Ministers for the Civil Service, Sabino Cassese (1993–94) and Franco Bassanini (1996–2001), who launched the most extensive administrative innovation programme ever attempted by the Italian state.

Processes that occurred after signing the Maastricht Treaty tended to accentuate this process. The impressive public deficit accumulated by Italy during the 1970s and 1980s required a particularly intense commitment to respect the Maastricht parameters, yet the heavy sacrifices imposed by budget cuts did not cause any reaction or protest. Rather, Europe was generally seen as the force that would enable the country to leave behind the

traditional vices of the Italian state and move towards a rapid modernization process. In a word, there was a widespread awareness that Italy was
being 'saved by Europe' (Ferrera and Gulamini 1999).

All of these developments had a very strong impact on the organization
of local governments, which in the end were quicker to innovate and
showed greater conviction than the national state structure.

The new position of local governments in intergovernmental relations

Relations between the centre and the periphery is an issue that has dominated public debate since the beginning of the 1990s. The key words were
decentralization, federalism and subsidiarity, taken on board by all of the
political parties, including those traditionally adopting a more centralist,
nationalist and statist position. Pressure towards decentralization appeared
inexorable.

Decentralization

Proposals to reform the constitution in a federal sense were put forward
throughout the decade, and in 2001, though in a highly polemic climate, a
constitutional reform was finally approved. While erasing the word 'federalism', it completely redrew relations between state and regional governments, giving the latter a very wide range of legislative functions (some
competing and others exclusive). Meanwhile, the 'Bassanini Law' of 1997
started a process whereby administrative functions concerning all the most
important public policies (transport, work, social services, the environment,
and so on) were transferred from the state to regional and local governments, the process still being underway. The autonomy of the municipal
governments has been greatly extended in several respects: since 1990 they
have been allowed to write their own municipal charters that are not subject
to any form of approval from higher authorities; since 1997 checks on the
legitimacy of individual acts have been almost completely abolished; and
the municipal secretary is no longer under the authority of the central government and may be freely chosen by the mayor. Furthermore, with the
introduction of a municipal property tax, municipal governments have
regained fiscal capability, though within a range of rates that is fixed centrally. While in 1990 only 19 per cent of municipal revenue was provided
by their own taxes, this share rose to 40 per cent in 1998 (see Table 3.2).

Table 3.2 *Sources of Italian municipal government revenue, 1990 and 1998 (thousands of euros)*

Source of revenue	1990		1998	
	Amount	*Per cent*	*Amount*	*Per cent*
Local taxes	5,816	19	17,454	40
Tariffs and other incomes	4,737	16	9,113	21
Transfers from state	19,845	65	17,331	39
Total	30,398	100	43,898	100

Source: Data from Brosio *et al*. (2001: 78).

If the tariffs that municipalities get for their services are also considered, we can observe that their dependence on state transfers decreased from 65 per cent in 1990 to 39 per cent in 1998 (Brosio *et al*. 2001: 79).

Decentralization has been accompanied by a covert conflict between regional and local governments. In the main (following American and German models) the federalists sought to give the regional governments a dominant role, and aimed to bring local government within an exclusively regional orbit. But this perspective has met with solid opposition from the municipal and provincial governments, who have shown themselves to be more afraid of regional centralism than of state centralism and have loudly demanded that they maintain a dual link (with the state and with regional governments), the idea being that it is better to be the periphery dealing with two centres than dealing with a single centre (and what's more one which is closer). Thanks to the strength of municipal traditions and to the rather murkier characteristics of regional governments, local governments have obtained some undoubted successes in this regard.

Intergovernmental cooperation

Ever since the 1970s, a national body coordinating state and regional governments has existed – the 'state–region conference' – which in recent years had become the most important occasion for negotiation between the two tiers of government. In the 1990s, at the request of local governments, a second central coordination body was instituted, the 'state-city conference', formed by representatives of the municipal and provincial governments and the state. Since 1997, the two conferences also meet jointly. Although the 2001 constitutional reform sought to strengthen the institutional position of regional government, it left the state with the power to establish electoral and organizational rules for local governments, which have thus avoided falling completely under regional influence. And it is significant that when the Committee of the Regions of the European Union was constituted, Italy chose to share its 24 seats equally among regional and local governments, whereas in other European federal states (Germany, Belgium and Spain) the regional governments took the lion's share.

It would thus appear that Italian federalism (if we may speak of federalism) is not so much seeking to introduce a bipolar model characteristic of classic federal states such as the USA and Germany founded on two pillars consisting of the federation and the confederate states, but is rather aiming towards a completely new three-pole model in which the state, regional governments and local governments constitute three pillars and interact on a substantially equal basis. It is not clear how this three-pole model will be institutionally consolidated, but it is difficult to imagine that Italian local governments could be brought completely under the influence of regional governments, as occurs in federal states.

Public debate on decentralization now revolves around the regional governments' demands (especially in northern Italy) for increasingly wide powers that are clearly separated from those of the state, almost as though the goal were the dual federalism imagined by the American founding fathers. In reality, the functions of the different tiers of government have long become so inextricably interwoven that the idea of a dual federalism appears seriously naive, although it is probably effective from a propaganda standpoint. There is not a single public policy that is not under the contemporary management of all levels of government, and that does not require some form of explicit cooperation to deal with the inevitable overlap of functions. Over time, the state, the regional governments and local governments have, in various policy areas, built up innumerable meeting places for coordination, so that from the factual standpoint the cooperative model appears to be the dominant one.

The drive towards intergovernmental cooperation has been accentuated by the continuing fragmentation of local governments. The measures finally introduced in 1990 to induce the amalgamation of local authorities have had derisory results: the number of municipalities has not decreased and the number of provinces has even increased (from 95 to 103). In this framework, pressure towards intermunicipal cooperation is increasing and the support offered by provincial governments to the smaller municipalities has strengthened. Regional and state laws have provided for obligatory cooperation among municipalities to manage certain services (for example waterworks, sewage, waste disposal) on a supra-municipal basis.

The metropolitan question fared little better. In 1990 supporters of a hard solution won the battle in parliament with passage of a national law providing for the institution of metropolitan government in nine Italian metropolitan areas. Metropolitan governments were to have been elected directly and should have replaced provincial governments whereas the territory of the central municipalities would have been subdivided into smaller municipalities. But their success turned out to be a Pyrrhic victory. Ten years after the law was enacted, none of the nine metropolitan governments provided for in the law has been instituted. The law had entrusted the regional governments with the responsibility to define the boundaries of the metropolitan areas, but even this first step generated so much conflict that it was impossible to proceed further. Hence, the Italian metropolis, frequently consisting of a large number of municipalities, is still governed by means of agreements or specialized agencies.

One of the most characteristic features of the decade was the birth and development of contracts between public administrations (local governments, regional governments, ministries and other agencies) to put in place projects of joint interest. The introduction of contract regulated relations between governments was particularly disruptive in a country like Italy, based as they are on administrative law and thus on a clear distinction between acts of public law (unilateral) and acts of private law (bilateral) (Bobbio 2000; Cassese 2002). During the decade different types of 'contracts between governments' were gradually defined. State–regional government contracts (*Intese istituzionali di programma*, started in 1999) determine policies of common interest to be put in place during the subsequent five-year period and ways to share the costs entailed. Through 'programme agreements' (*accordi di programma*), introduced in 1990, different authorities, including those belonging to different tiers of government, may reach an agreement to put in place works, measures and programmes that require integrated action and establish reciprocal commitments in terms of the duties each of them must accomplish and the resources each must contribute to the project. In the first decade of their application, the regional governments of Lombardy and Tuscany stipulated 210 and 110 agreements respectively with municipal or provincial governments or other public authorities, above all in the field of infrastructure.

Another tool that has spread rapidly is that of 'territorial pacts' (*patti territoriali*), that is a form of agreement between municipalities, public authorities and private interests aimed at revitalizing the economy on a local scale. They originated in southern Italy in 1994–95 to stimulate development 'from below' after the failure of development policies managed 'from above' (through 'special interventions for southern Italy'), and then spread rapidly throughout the country. At present more than 200 territorial pacts involving approximately 25 per cent of Italian municipalities have been approved or are in the process of being drawn up (Cersosimo and Wolleb 2001). The territorial pacts cover a much smaller area than the provinces, and therefore tend to redraw Italian administrative geography on a voluntary basis since it is the municipal governments that decide the extent of the territory involved in the pact. The most successful experiences have given rise to stable aggregations that tend to strengthen the position of a supra-municipal area in competing for development (Barbera 2001).

New structures of local government

Directly elected mayors

The 1993 reform introduced the direct election of mayors and a modified system of proportional representation for the municipal council, with a premium for the parties associated with the winning mayoral candidate. The two elections (both mayor and council) take place simultaneously every five years. In municipalities with more than 15,000 inhabitants the mayor is elected under a two-ballot system, similar to the French presidential system, whereas in municipalities with less than 15,000 inhabitants a single-ballot system is used, according to the 'first-past-the-post' rule. The council is elected from party lists on a proportional basis, but the parties linked to the winning candidate for mayor automatically obtain 60 per cent of the seats (two-thirds in the smaller municipalities). The mayor is thus guaranteed a majority within the council.

The mayor has the power to appoint and revoke members of the cabinet (*assessori*) without council approval. In larger municipalities cabinet members cannot belong to the council; if a councillor is appointed as member of the cabinet, he or she must resign. This provision aims at introducing a clear separation between the executive and legislative bodies. Following the reform, the council may still pass a vote of no confidence, but in this case the council is also dissolved and new elections are held for both bodies. The reform has greatly reduced the powers of the council in favour of the cabinet. Before the reform, all decisions had to be approved by the council, while the cabinet was limited to drawing up proposals. Today the council is only involved in decisions of a strategic nature (for example approval of the budget), with all other decisions being reserved to the cabinet.

The most important effect of the reform, however, 'was that of placing the mayor in the central position once held by the parties' (Baldini and Legnante 2000: 69). Indeed, new mayoral figures have emerged from the ashes of the old Italian political system. These figures have come from outside the party machinery and may have great personal prestige, as for instance Valentino Castellani in Turin, Riccardo Illy in Trieste or Massimo Cacciari in Venice. The 'new mayors' have not only greatly increased stability for the governments of their cities, but have also taken on a role of increasing importance in national political debate, as had never previously occurred. Some mayors of large cities, such as Antonio Bassolino (Naples) and Enzo Bianco (Catania), have been called into the national government, and it is significant that in the 2001 general election the centre–left coalition chose the mayor of Rome, Francesco Rutelli, as its candidate premier.

Bettin and Magnier (1995) have shown that the increasingly frequent recruitment of mayors from among professionals and entrepreneurs has brought with it the 'bourgeoisification' of the local political class, to the detriment of politicians of popular extraction, which the old party channels were better able to promote. This phenomenon is fairly similar to what occurred in the United States previously. Yet it must be added that over recent years, due to the effect of the 'reshuffle' of the political system, party politicians' control over the designation of candidate mayor has been restored, and the number of outsiders has dropped sharply. But it is undeniable that the reform has helped to give stability to municipal executives, offering new drive and new autonomy to municipal governments and bringing new actors into the field in connection with the decentralization process.

Reform of local administration

The reform of government was accompanied by numerous less visible but equally important reforms of the local government administration. The decisive step was the introduction (established in 1990 and reinforced by subsequent laws) of a clear separation between political and administrative functions. In the past, due to the principle of 'ministerial responsibility', the mayor and members of the cabinet were responsible for everything the administration did, while the administrative managers worked behind the scenes. This system enabled politicians to meddle even in the most trivial administrative practices, giving them the opportunity to force decisions for reasons of particularism or favouritism. It also obliged the council or the cabinet to approve hundreds of resolutions at each sitting, without being able to discuss or even to read them.

Much in keeping with a precept of New Public Management philosophy, the reforms of the 1990s have now established that the mayor and councillors must limit themselves to setting goals, whereas the choice of means and use of resources is the exclusive province of the executives, who take full responsibility for this and who, for this purpose, have their own budget. This innovation met with some resistance both from the politicians (who did not want to give up their traditional powers of petty intervention) and from the executives (who were reluctant to come out into the open and take on clear responsibilities). But, step by step, it has been introduced quite effectively in almost all Italian municipalities, thanks to the general crisis of the party system and to civil servants' increased professional awareness.

To provide a link between the political and administrative spheres, Italy has chosen to import from the USA the figure of City Manager (though in a diluted form). Since 1997, the mayor has the option of recruiting a professional manager who takes the title of general manager (*direttore generale*). This appointment does not require approval from the council: it is entirely the mayor's prerogative. The City Manager has responsibility for managing the municipal administration as a whole, remaining in office for as long as the mayor's mandate lasts. All of the larger municipalities have taken advantage of this possibility and have a City Manager at present.

In addition to the idea of management by objectives, other principles of New Public Management (NPM) have, at least on the surface, also enjoyed wide diffusion in municipal government. English expressions such as 'customer satisfaction', 'strategic planning', 'benchmarking', 'outsourcing', and 'contracting out' are on the lips of any executive who wants to appear up to date. It is difficult to say whether this is only a facade, having become obligatory lip-service to fashion, or whether there has actually been a change in behaviour. Indications in both senses may be found. It is in any case certain that NPM has brought about a sudden overturning of Italy's dominant administrative culture, which was both formalistic and legalistic, and has obliged public executives to look at real processes instead of simply paper shuffling, to measure performance and output instead of hiding behind conformity to regulations.

Two factors can explain the diffusion of NPM in Italian local government. First, the rise of a new political class, at both the national and local levels, strongly committed to modernizing Italian administration. Second, the growing contacts of Italian local governments with their European counterparts and with the European Union: applying for structural funds under EU programme, for instance, obliged Italian local governments to learn new tools and techniques (setting objectives, monitoring, evaluating results), which were completely foreign to the domestic administrative culture.

A national law of 1993, moreover, made it obligatory for all local governments to adopt performance reviews, with the aim of replacing the old and formalistic preventive checks of legality with a more substantial control over processes and management. These new provisions include recording indicators of efficiency and effectiveness, project management, control over budget process and spending, evaluation of managers' performance and distributing incentives to the managers who reach best results. The actual implementation of these tools has been slow and uneven (stronger in the central and northern municipalities, much weaker in the south), and the practices already adopted have differed widely (Lippi 2001). The mere development is nonetheless interesting given that municipalities in Italy have traditionally been accustomed to following uniform rules established centrally. It is also of interest that local governments have been much more ready than national ministries to take up the challenge of organizational innovation.

Processes of privatization and outsourcing, by comparison, have enjoyed steady development during the 1990s. Municipal governments in the larger cities had direct control over a series of municipal corporations, many of which dated back many years and which managed various services (transport, energy, waste collection, waterworks, and so on). Most of these have now been transformed into joint-stock companies, and some of them (especially in the energy sector) have been completely or partially privatized, operating beyond 'their' old municipal boundaries.

The phenomenon of outsourcing has been particularly marked in the field of social services. Here the prescriptions of NPM have been extended by pressure applied by voluntary groups and service associations (above all Roman Catholic in inspiration) that wanted to take over the management of certain services, offering lower costs, more personalized services and less bureaucracy. Curiously, a union has come about between the personalistic anti-statism of the Catholic movements and the corporate individualism of NPM. This massive process of delegation to organizations in the 'private social sector' has not failed to produce alarm and concern, since it risks fragmenting social policies, weakening their egalitarian and universalistic scope and moving towards the triumph of 'privatism' (de Leonardis 1998).

Citizen involvement

The direct involvement of citizens in local decisions has also made some progress. The most important field is that of projects for urban renewal, of which the last decade has seen many, a number of which have been at European urging. Numerous experiences now exist in Italy of shared town planning, of citizens' involvement in drawing up Agenda 21 plans, or in infrastructure policies (Balducci 2001; Sclavi 2002). In a number of circumstances diffusion of the NIMBY syndrome with respect to the question of locating facilities for waste disposal, high-speed railways, power lines and dams, and so on, has obliged local governments to negotiate with neighbourhood committees in order to find agreeable solutions (Bobbio and Zeppetella 1999). Italian local governments also have the possibility of holding local referenda in response to citizen demands. Such referenda only have an advisory status, but in practice end up being quite compelling. Hence, in the last decade referenda led to the banning of cars from the city core in several Italian cities (Milan, Bologna, Florence, Turin).

Citizens' involvement and referenda may be seen as the way in which local governments attempt to reach consensus on a single issue (for example traffic policy, urban renewal, waste policy, and so on), since the general consensus coming from party organizations and from polls seems to be weaker than in the past. It is interesting to note in this connection that from the early 1990s onwards, turnout has started to decline more rapidly for local elections than for general elections. The difference is not large (approximately 5–10 per cent), but it is generally interpreted as an indicator of disaffection that is growing more quickly with respect to local politics, and which contrasts with the high turnout Italians have traditionally shown both nationally and locally.

Between government and governance

The renaissance of Italian cities during the 1990s is due not only to political and administrative reforms (although these have helped); it is also the offspring of a more general trend towards city activism which has characterized all European countries due to globalization and the weakening of nation states. The urban and social cohesion policies promoted by the European Union have had a determinant effect. Although not all Italian cities have been able to take advantage of the opportunities offered by Brussels (Ercole 1997), many have opened offices for international relations, developed their own 'foreign policies', entered European networks and successfully competed for European Community funds. The cities that have shown greatest dynamism are those that have had to tackle serious crises, whether due to de-industrialization processes (Turin) or to endemic factors (Naples). But it is interesting to note that even medium-sized or small towns (above all in central and northern Italy) have shown marked activism in international competition.

These tendencies have brought development policies sharply into focus, and everywhere these have become the top priority for local governments.

Other policies (transport, the environment, culture, museums, parks, and so on), which used to be seen as services for 'their' citizens, today tend to be reformulated with an eye to their potential external users, so as to increase the city's attractiveness (commercial, industrial, tourism). The accent placed on development policies has made it necessary to create coalitions among local elites and to strengthen internal cohesion. Local governments have thus had to open their doors to economic, industrial and social partners, giving life to complex processes of local governance. In some cities, this process has been structured in an open, public form, breaking with the traditional practice of concealed committees by drawing up strategic plans. The first case is that of Turin, whose strategic plan was drawn up in the year 2000, after two years' work involving all the city's most important public bodies, associations and private firms. Today, realization of the plan is stimulated and monitored by an association of over a hundred member organizations, of which the municipal government is only one among many partners. Similar experiences are underway in other cities (for example Rome and Florence), and it should not be forgotten that for smaller municipalities a similar role is played by the territorial pacts, which have already been mentioned.

Lights and shadows

It is not easy to assess the changes that have taken place during the last decade. Many of them are still underway and it is not always clear what final direction they will take. What is least in doubt is that the situation is evolving, but this does not mean that the old problems have been solved. To a great extent municipal governments still depend on the central government, both financially and through the dense network of legislation to which they are subjected. The financial restrictions that European requirements have obliged the central government to impose have pushed local governments to 'count on their own forces' and to modernize their organizational structure, but they have also set insuperable limits on the development of local policies. Equally unresolved is the historic split between central and northern municipalities and those in the south. The latter are behind in the modernization process across the board, as well as in the quantity and quality of services offered.

There are other factors of uncertainty as well. It is still not clear whether the process that has developed during the 1990s will be supported or contrasted by the Berlusconi government, which indeed expresses contradictory tendencies. The rightwing coalition that won the 2001 election, and which is probably destined to govern Italy for a long period, includes the Northern League as a full member: their historical leader has filled the post of 'Minister for Devolution'. Thus the government cannot ignore pressure towards decentralization, which the Northern League cannot give up; indeed, it is working to reform the 2001 constitutional reform with the goal of giving regional governments full responsibility for health, education and local public order. And since the trend within the Northern League is towards devolution to regional governments, local governments might see the new decentralization process as an attack on their autonomy.

On the other hand, the Berlusconi government, due to its corporate, decision-oriented and vaguely Thatcherite vocation, instinctively tends towards centralism and appears intolerant of the tortuous processes of inter-governmental negotiation. On one hand it solemnly proclaims devolution, while at the same time it daily gives the lie to this process through a series of measures showing little respect for regional and local autonomy, when not actually slighting it (although many regional and local governments are in rightwing hands). A recent analysis by the secretariat of the Conference of Regions reported that 85 state measures already approved or being drawn up are in contrast with the constitutional provisions for devolution estab-lished in 2001. For the same reasons, the cooperative intergovernmental relations that have grown up over previous decades might suffer a setback. After the storm of the early 1990s, changes in local government have with-out doubt been very important, but some confusion still dominates the scene and brings with it more than a few uncertainties about future developments.

4 Belgium: the changing world of Belgian municipalities

Yves Plees

A Sunday morning in Belgium is not normally the most exciting moment of the week. Once every six years, however, on the first Sunday in October, things are totally different. On that day the political fate of tens of thousands of Belgian councillors and of 589 mayors is decided. Weeks before the event, brochures and election pamphlets bulge out of people's letterboxes, and no festivity can be held without a local dignitary paying his respects. In these weeks the number of free rounds of beer bought in numerous bars by office-seeking politicians is also at its peak.

In this chapter the role of various actors in Belgian local government – the mayor, the aldermen and councillors – are considered more closely. But as a frame of reference, major changes that Belgian local government has undergone in recent decades are also discussed.

General characteristics of the system of local government

Historically, the area that was later to become Belgium was characterized by strong cities. As such, it is not surprising that the position of these entities would be safeguarded when the new independent Kingdom of Belgium was created in the 1830s. Indeed, while the Constitution of 1831 only indirectly acknowledged the position of the municipalities, already in 1836, just five years after the creation of the kingdom, adoption of the local government act formally recognized municipalities as important actors in the organization of the state and determined their organization.

Up to 1928, rising population figures led to the creation of new municipalities, bringing the total to 2,675, the highest number ever to exist. New demands upon local governments caused by rising industrialization and

47

changes in the social structure, however, made it clear that there was a need for a thorough restructuring of the municipal landscape. Plans in this direction had been made at the end of the 1930s, but during the Second World War German occupation authorities altered the municipal scene by an Act that was considered illegal and that was revoked after the war. As a result, a large restructuring of local government was for many years taboo. Yet the perceived need for a large-scale amalgamation of small municipalities, and a supra-communal structure for big urban agglomerations, remained. This view, which was held by central government, received support in 1958 when the Central Council for Industry, a central government advisory board, concluded that an amalgamation of local authorities with less then 2,500 inhabitants was desirable. Legislation allowing for a more flexible approach to amalgamation of municipalities was introduced in the wake of this report and was ultimately passed. Yet the initial impact of this legislation was rather limited; the number of local authorities declined only moderately, to 2,359 entities.

It was first in 1977 that the number of local authorities was drastically reduced – to a mere 595 – in an operation strongly contested by the population, but to no avail. Six years later, the suburbs around the city of Antwerp were merged with the core city, thereby creating the largest local authority of the country and further reducing the number of local authorities to 589. Since 1983 the number of local authorities has remained unchanged, though their average size has increased slightly, and the number of municipalities with fewer then 10,000 inhabitants has declined further (see Table 4.1).

Despite a drastic reduction in the number of units and an increase in the size of local authorities, the basic system of organizing local governments has

Table 4.1 *Distribution of Belgian municipalities by size of municipality, 1977 and 2003*

Population size	1977	2003
Less than 5,000	108	87
5,000 to 10,000	183	166
10,000 to 20,000	180	200
20,000 to 50,000	91	109
50,000 to 100,000	19	19
Over 100,000	8	8
Total	589	589
Average population size	16,678	17,582

Source: Data from official statistics.

remained remarkably stable. This does not mean, however, that municipal size is no longer an issue. It is generally accepted that local authorities must be effective and responsive to the needs of their citizens, and on these grounds some observers insist that the issue of a minimum size – in terms of scale, staff and financial possibilities – cannot be ignored (De Leemans 2001).

Municipalities during the transition of Belgium to a federal state

Despite such views, the issue of local government reform has not figured prominently on the political agenda of central government. Most attention in postwar Belgium politics has rather been devoted to managing ethnic tensions between the Dutch-speaking Flemish population in the north of the country and the French-speaking population in the south. From the 1960s up to this day, Belgium has been gradually transformed from a unitary to a federal state, with an ongoing transfer of competencies to the sub-national units (*regions* and *language communities*). In this process, the bilingual central government first created new, geographically defined political institutions – the so-called *language communities* – and then shifted more and more competencies in which language has played an important role (such as education or health care) to the institutions of these communities. Three such language communities were created: (1) the Dutch-speaking '*Vlaamse Gemeenschap*' in the north, (2) a Francophone '*Communauté Française*' in the south and (3) the German-speaking '*Deutschsprachige Gemeinschaft*' in the east. All three language communities are unilingual. This implies that even if there are French-speaking residents in the Flemish town of Ghent, these Francophones fall under the jurisdiction of the Flemish language community. The Brussels area is the exception to this rule. Here both the French-speaking and Dutch-speaking language communities have competencies and citizens decide on their own whether they want to be under the jurisdiction of the Flemish or the Walloon language community.

Whereas language-related matters have been decentralized to the language communities, spatial issues concerning such matters as roads, land-use planning and economic development have been transferred to regional authorities. For this purpose three *regions* were created: (1) the Dutch-speaking region '*Vlaanderen*', (2) the Francophone region '*Wallonie*' and (3) the bilingual region '*Bruxelles-Capitale/Brussels Hoofdstedelijk Gewest*'. In this case the German-speaking area falls under the jurisdiction of the Walloon region. As of 2000, 58 per cent of the Belgian population lived in Flanders, 33 per cent in Wallonia and 9 per cent in Brussels.

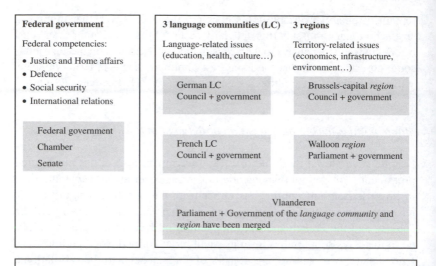

Federal government	3 language communities (LC)	3 regions
Federal competencies: • Justice and Home affairs • Defence • Social security • International relations	Language-related issues (education, health, culture…) German LC Council + government	Territory-related issues (economics, infrastructure, environment…) Brussels-capital *region* Council + government
Federal government Chamber Senate	French LC Council + government	Walloon *region* Parliament + government
	Vlaanderen Parliament + Government of the *language community* and *region* have been merged	

10 provinces: 5 in the Flemish *region* and 5 in the Walloon *region*
(the Brussels *region* has no subdivision in provinces)

589 municipalities: 308 in Flanders, 262 in Wallonia, 19 in Brussels

Figure 4.1   *The institutional infrastructure of Belgian government*

Both the regions and the language communities have a separate legislative assembly (council or parliament) and executive (government). The exception is Flanders, where the political institutions for the region and language community have been merged (see Figure 4.1). It is important to recognize that in their areas of competency, the regions and language communities constitute a form of central government; in their sphere of competence, they cannot be overruled by federal government. On the contrary, in the areas where they have acquired competencies, the legislative acts of the regions and language communities replace former 'national' legislation. The Brussels region, where the federal government has retained a right to interfere for very specific reasons, is an exception in this respect.

This process of transferring competencies to the regions and language communities dominated the political agenda for most of the 1980s and early 1990s, without having much impact on local authorities. It was first in the mid-1990s, during formation of the second Dehaene (federal) coalition government, that the main political parties agreed that competencies regarding the organization of local authorities should also be decentralized to the regions. But inasmuch as it was generally accepted that this would require a change in the constitution, the cabinet could do no more than prepare the decision, since in the Belgian constitution a revision of the constitution is only possible after the outgoing parliament designates the articles of the constitution to be revised. Subsequent disagreement between French and Dutch-speaking representatives in Parliament, however, appeared to signal the end of this reform, and the constitutional amendments were shelved. Despite the reluctance of French representatives, the decentralization issue was nonetheless resuscitated and ultimately included in a package deal reached after the accession of the new cabinet. The parties agreed, moreover, that this reform did not require a constitutional reform after all; a special law would suffice. This Act was subsequently approved on 28 June 2001, and under the provisions of this legislation, competencies to organize local authorities (provinces and municipalities) were transferred to the regions on 1 January 2002. Given the different characteristics of local government in the three regions, it can therefore be expected that local government Acts will gradually start to diverge.

The fact that municipalities have not been subject to major reforms during the postwar years, it should be emphasized, does not mean that nothing has changed. For one thing, what from local government's perspective is 'central government' has changed profoundly. In the Belgian federalist model, the federal government has to be considered as the central authority for some issues (for example for issuing passports or the organization of security forces), whereas for other issues (for example regulation of land use) the regions figure as such, and for still others (for example education) the language communities serve as central government. Each of these bodies can supervise particular local decisions and provide local government with instructions on specific topics. This will not change with the new round of state reform; the only difference the latest reform makes is that it is no longer the federal level, but the regions that decide on the organization of local government.

Internal organization of municipalities

The highest political body at the local level is the municipal council. Under existing legislation, municipal councils are elected once every six years. All citizens living in Belgium who are at least 18 years of age are entitled *and obliged* by law to vote. EU citizens can also opt to be registered as eligible voters. More and more voices also support granting voting rights to non-EU inhabitants in local elections, on the condition that these foreigners have spent a minimum number of years in the municipality, but this has not yet been enacted. The council, which may be considered as the 'legislative' body of the municipality, meets at least ten times a year or whenever one-third of the representatives asks for a meeting. The number of councillors is fixed by law, varying from 7 to 55 according to the number of inhabitants of the municipality. Decisions are made by simple majority, and in principle council meetings are open to the public.

Since 1999, municipalities with more than 100,000 inhabitants have had the option of intramunicipal decentralization by means of creating so-called districts, to which a number of competencies can be transferred. Just as is the case for municipal councils, each district has a directly elected district council, out of which a bureau and president are elected. Elections for the district councils coincide with municipal council elections, and legal stipulations prevent individuals from being members of both municipal and district councils.

The districts originate from a desire to create easier access to the political level in the larger cities. Indeed, given the fact that the number of councillors is set by law, the ratio of inhabitants per councillor in bigger centres could be well above 8,000, while a smaller municipality of only 8,000 inhabitants would have 19 councillors – a ratio of roughly 1 to 420! It is therefore no surprise that it was especially Antwerp, the largest Belgian city, which rapidly introduced districts. In Brussels, by comparison, the problem of representation was not acute, since it consists of a constellation of 19 different municipalities, the largest of which is Brussels city with 133,000 inhabitants.

Council meetings are presided over by the mayor. Formally, the mayor is appointed by the King, but in reality members of the political majority in the council propose one of their colleagues, and the Minister of the Interior ratifies this nomination. In many municipalities the council nominates the individual who has obtained the highest number of personal votes. The importance of personal votes is in this respect one explanation for the intensive canvassing which occurs in local election campaigns. As already noted, the mayor has a dual loyalty: besides occupying a local political role, the mayor is also the representative of the central (regional and federal) government. In the first role the mayor functions as the political leader of the municipality and its administration, and in this role chairs council meetings. In the second role the mayor is responsible for such tasks as keeping public order and maintaining respect for the law.

The political majority of the council also selects members of the *College van Burgemeester en Schepenen* (the Court of Mayor and Aldermen, CMA) from among themselves. The mayor, who is also a member of the CMA, chairs the meetings of this body. The number of aldermen varies from two in the smallest villages to ten in the major cities. Together with the mayor, the aldermen are responsible for execution of council decisions. Theoretically, aldermen have no individual executive powers, but can only act on the basis of collegial responsibility. In practice, however, there is a functional division of labour among the members of the CMA for purposes of preparing and implementing particular decisions. The mayor, moreover, can delegate certain of his powers to one or more aldermen. Despite the fact that the CMA has to act as a collegial body, and theoretically aldermen have no direct power over the local administration, it is not exceptional that an individual alderman will directly instruct the local administration to perform certain tasks. Occasionally this causes problems, as is clear from the words of one Chief Executive Officer (CEO):

> I try to coordinate services, when this alderman walks in and instructs some of the workers to repair a small window in the sports hall. The fact that they were ordered to repair the heating in the nursery school did not seem to be his concern. After all, he lived close to the area of the sports hall.

Although this example might suggest otherwise, Belgian local administration in general is not directly managed by the political level, but rather by the CEO, who is responsible for coordinating the work of the local administration 'under the authority' of the political level. In reality, the CEO, who is referred to as the 'municipal secretary' in the Local Government Act, is the second most powerful individual actor in the local authority, after the mayor. The CEO acts as secretary of the local council, and has to sign all outgoing mail from the municipality. By law the CEO should refuse to sign if he discovers any illegalities, thereby insuring the legality of actions of the authority. To ensure that this role be fulfilled adequately, the Local Government Act explicitly specifies the educational qualifications required of the CEO and clearly defines his duties. Moreover, it is very difficult to dismiss the CEO, giving him additional leverage to play the role of 'neutral technician'.

In addition to the CEO, the municipal administration has a treasurer who is responsible for the payments and accounts of the local authority. In smaller municipalities it is possible to confer this task to a 'regional treasurer', but authorities above 10,000 inhabitants must have their own treasurer. The role of the treasurer can hardly be overestimated; his role in financial management of the local authority can be safely compared to the role of the CEO in general management. He is personally responsible for local finances, and has to deposit a financial guarantee to ensure that he does his work correctly.

Changes in intergovernmental relations in the 1990s

Two main issues have dominated the Belgian political scene for most of the
1990s: first, the traditional tensions between the linguistic groups; and second, the race against time to fulfil the criteria of the Maastricht Treaty. The
first led to a further refinement of constitutional arrangements, with a new
step being taken in reforming Belgium from a unitary to a federal state. The
second issue implied the introduction of stringent budgetary discipline and
high taxation. As a result, much needed improvements in the functioning of
the administration and police forces were not acknowledged, or could not be
funded. The political elite therefore woke up in shock when the dramatic mismanagement of a series of murders led to the so-called 'White March', the
largest public demonstration ever to occur in the country, in which more than
200,000 people marched in silence through Brussels. The result was that all
political attention turned away from constitutional reform and shifted instead
to refining the administrative machinery of government, a move that was
reinforced by the food scare during the summer of 1999 in which dioxins
were found to have contaminated chicken feed. The government rediscov-
ered its citizens, and learned that they wanted better and cheaper services.

These changes occurred in a setting in which the newly established
regional governments tried to assert their position *vis-à-vis* local government. This sparked off a fierce reaction on the part of municipalities. The
main complaint was that the regions conferred new tasks upon the municipalities (for example in the case of land-use planning) without transferring
corresponding financial resources. In the Flemish region municipal reactions inspired a pact between the regional authorities and local governments
(Decoster 2000). The pact established principles for intergovernmental
relations, such as clarity of rules regarding funding by the region, and on
the way the region would supervise the municipalities.

Problems nevertheless continued to exist. Indeed, renewed attention paid
by different levels of governments to citizen concerns imposed new financial burdens on municipalities. The merger of national and local police
forces provides a good example. Municipalities have rightfully claimed that
the costs of this reform, imposed by the federal level, were not adequately
covered by the additional funds provided to local government.

These additional financial burdens were imposed in a general climate of
discontent about fiscal relations between central and local government.
Local authorities were in particular incensed at central government decisions on the income tax that had a direct negative effect on local revenues.
The reason for this is that municipalities have two main sources of revenue:
one is a grant from central government based on the number of residents; the

other is based on personal income taxes. The amount of the latter is a function of a tax rate determined by the municipal council as a percentage of the overall amount of personal income paid by citizens to federal authorities. Hence, when federal authorities lower the national tax rate, local government income is *de facto* lowered as well, unless the municipal council counters this decrease by raising the local tax rate. This latter option, however, is politically difficult since it means that what the federal government has announced as a *decrease* in personal income taxation is turned into an unpopular *increase* in taxes by local authorities.

Further complicating the picture is the fact that another major source of local revenue has also been under threat. Traditionally local governments have taken part in the distribution of electricity, an arrangement that has provided a much-welcomed addition to the local coffers. Liberalization of the energy market and changes in legislation on intermunicipal cooperation (in which private-sector involvement is to be phased out), however, have made this source of income uncertain.

Another facet of central–local relations which has become ever more noticeable is that local politicians have become increasingly prone to the NIMBY ('not in my back yard') syndrome. Thus, in a number of cases where national government has undertaken projects such as construction of high-speed rail links, building of waste incinerators or opening reception centres for refugees, local politicians have joined citizens in their protests. It was expected that a fundamental debate on key responsibilities of public authorities and the proper division of these responsibilities among various tiers of government would provide a possible solution for such tensions in intergovernmental relations. On the basis of such a debate an agreement was in fact reached between various levels of Flemish government in April 2003. But this agreement did not imply a major reallocation of tasks and the consequences for intergovernmental relations remain to be seen.

From local service provision to community governance?

> All citizens of the municipality are responsible for the attacks committed on their territory, be it against persons, or against properties.

This statement, found in a decree regarding police services written in 1795, still provides an apt summary of the role of the local community in providing security for its citizens. Of course much has changed in the 200 years since this statement was written. At present local authorities provide a lot more to citizens than physical security. And with changing tasks, new forms of service delivery are often needed. But the 'vogue' of New Public Management, so readily observed in several other countries, arrived in Belgian municipalities with some delay, since they have long been bound by strict legal provisions. From the mid-1990s onwards, however, signs of movement in this direction have been noticeable. One can, for example, point to the creation of autonomous municipal companies as well as other developments that allow for more flexible service provision. Changes in executive leadership in local government are also noteworthy. In addition citizens have expressed a desire for more participation than that provided by merely casting a vote every six years. Before considering these developments in greater detail, however, it will first be useful to sketch out the tasks fulfilled by local authorities.

Traditionally three different types of tasks of local authorities have been distinguished. In decreasing order of local discretion, these are autonomous tasks, bounded tasks and co-government tasks respectively. *Autonomous tasks* are based on the right of local governments to organize everything that is considered to be of 'local importance'. Since what is considered to be of local importance is nowhere legally defined, it is generally accepted that local authorities have a general competence to undertake any activity that is not strictly assigned to another level of government. *Bounded tasks*, by comparison, are those tasks for which central government sets out the framework within which local governments have to execute certain responsibilities. An example of such a task is a system of local employment offices. Here local authorities organize schemes to reintegrate long-term unemployed. In other areas local authorities only have to respect central norms if they want to receive subsidies. In such cases municipalities are directed by so-called 'golden ropes'. Finally, *co-government tasks* are those in which local government acts as an agent of central government; both the tasks and the procedures to fulfil the tasks are determined by the central government. An example of this is the issuing of passports.

As this would suggest, local authorities engage in a wide range of activities. In total local authorities spent €12.5 billion during 2000, or 5.5 per cent of Belgian GDP, and the local sector accounted for 60.7 per cent of all investments made by the public sector. In providing for service delivery, municipalities have a number of options. One alternative is direct provision by municipal employees, and at the end of 1998 Belgian municipalities employed more then 142,000 people with responsibilities for everything from registering births to issuing building permits and clearing snow from roads.

Although local authorities can opt for in-house service production, many municipalities have chosen forms of intermunicipal cooperation for the provision of services. Examples are found in the distribution of electricity and waste incineration. From a legal perspective intermunicipal cooperation (or 'intercommunales') can take the form of a limited company, an association or a cooperative. Under terms of existing laws, 'intercommunales' may be created for a period of not more then 30 years, after which partners have the possibility of a prolongation of their collaboration. Participation in such intercommunales is not limited to municipalities however; involvement is also open to other public and private organizations. Regardless of their share in the capital of the organization, local authorities must nevertheless hold the majority of the votes in the different bodies of the intercommunale at all times. The distribution of votes among the different cooperating municipalities is determined by their share of the capital and the respective municipal councils elect their representatives to the governing bodies of the intercommunale.

A number of intercommunales have developed into very powerful organizations, being active in a wide range of activities – everything from electricity provision and waste disposal to regional development. From this perspective, it is striking how little attention local politicians devote to the operation of these intercommunales. In a questionnaire of the Flemish authorities, one mayor even replied that 'the general council of the intercommunales is not a place to create tensions, but a cosy meeting of local politicians of the same region, where surely there is no room to discuss problems!' (Van Overheyden and Verhulst 2000). The importance of these so-called 'auxiliary structures' makes it quite understandable that a number of concerns have been voiced regarding their power, and that efforts have been made to strengthen the position of the municipal council *vis-à-vis* the intercommunales throughout the country.

In 1993 the power to pass legislation on intermunicipal cooperation was transferred to the regions. In Wallonia this led to the passage of new legislation in 1996; the new Act ruled that a decision of the intercommunale would not only require a majority of votes in the intercommunal council, but also a majority of the municipalities represented. Another striking feature of the new Act is that the Walloon region has the right to participate in intercommunales. Given the limited size of a number of Walloon municipalities, this is necessary for reasons of capital provision.

The Flemish region, by comparison, decided not to change the old 'Belgian' legislation immediately, waiting rather for the moment when the region would not only have power regarding intermunicipal cooperation and supervision of local governments, but full competency in matters of the organization of local governments as well. At the end of 2000, when the transfer of these powers to the regions was finally accepted, the Flemish

regional government also drafted a new decree on intermunicipal cooperation. This decree was approved by the Flemish parliament in 2001. The
decree introduces alternative structures for intermunicipal cooperation,
ranging from a loose form of cooperation without any legal personality, via
a project organization which exists for a maximum of six years, to a service
delivery or task-oriented organization with delegated responsibilities for
service provision existing for 18 years. Similar to the Walloon case, the role
of the local authorities has been strengthened. Another remarkable implication of the decree is the gradually diminishing role of the private sector in
the decision-making bodies of the intermunicipal organizations. This aims
to strengthen the role of local authorities, which until now have sometimes
found themselves confronted with a private partner who was *de facto* far
more important than themselves. However, it remains possible for an intermunicipal organization to cooperate or have contracts with the private
sector. But unlike the Walloon case, regional participation in intercommunales is not possible.

Besides in-house production and intermunicipal provision, a host of
possibilities exist for local service delivery outside the traditional administration. One of these is *regie* or a 'municipal company', a possibility
existing since 1939. In this case, the 'company' has its own financial management and accounting system, yet has no independent legal status. Any
profit has to be transferred to the local authority, and losses are to be paid
by the municipality. Originally this approach was limited to a number of
well-defined industrial or commercial tasks, such as the exploitation of sea-
ports, markets or the distribution of electricity. But since 1995 the approach
is also open for use in non-commercial activities such as museums or sports
centres.

For the management of industrial infrastructure, a new structure has also
been made possible – the autonomous municipal company. This option is only
open for a number of well-defined duties in the commercial or industrial
sphere, and this type of company has independent legal status. A management
council and a board of directors are responsible for managing the company,
but the majority in the management council must be members of the local
council. Moreover, all political factions in the council must be represented, but
this representation need not necessarily be fully proportional (Dujardin 1997).

An autonomous company also has the possibility of taking part in other
public or private companies, organizations and institutions, whose aims
correspond with that of the autonomous company. Yet regardless of the
importance of the investment of the different parties, the autonomous company must have a majority of the votes and the presidency of the council of
the organizations in which it participates. Needless to say, these regulations

are not very conducive for the participation of autonomous local companies in other entities (Van Hooydonk 1997).

It should also be mentioned that all citizens have the right to create non-profit associations having legal status – the so-called VZWs (*vereniging zonder winstgevend doel*). Inevitably, some of these associations have purposes that can be considered to be of local interest, and this sparked a discussion as to whether local authorities could also participate in such associations. It is now generally accepted that legally they can do so, as long as they do not transfer decision rights to this association, and the rights of individuals are guaranteed. In practice, especially in the management of sports- and cultural infrastructure, local authorities have relied heavily on this approach. After passage of legislation regarding autonomous municipal companies, municipalities have been under substantial pressure to use the company approach rather than the VZW structure. Because of its flexibility, however, the VZW structure remains a very attractive option.

Strengthening executive leadership?

In considering the role of executive leadership, it is necessary to take into account both the (dual) role of the mayor, and the role of the chief executive officer. As previously noted, the mayor, as representative of the central government, has a number of executive duties in making sure central legislation is enforced. On the local level, however, when it comes to implementing decisions made by the council and the CMA, the formal head of the administrative staff is not the mayor, but the chief executive officer.

The position of the CEO is actually characterized by a high degree of professionalization (cf. Plees and Laurent 1998). In part this is due to the educational requirements to qualify for this office and the extreme stability of the job. As such the CEO is a strong player in local government. Mayors tend to consider CEOs as the person they rely on most in doing their job (Ackaert 1997). Until recently this relationship was further enhanced by the fact that the level of compensation provided to mayors was so low that most had to combine their position with other gainful activity. This situation implied that the CEO was quite often 'master of the town hall'.

While the formal role of the mayor has not changed noticeably, a great deal of effort has been put into making the position more attractive for well-qualified people. Indeed, since the beginning of 2001 levels of compensation for mayors and aldermen have been dramatically raised. Depending on the size of the municipality, they now earn between 75 and 120 per cent of the maximum salary of the CEO.

Table 4.2   *Role expectations among Belgian mayors, 1997*

Role expectations	Average ranking of role expectations*	Per cent spontaneously mentioning these expectations
A person of trust for the population	2.57	47.7
Directing the council and the CMA	2.93	43.6
Policy-making	3.84	55.2
Making sure the administration functions correctly	4.95	36.0
Functioning as head of the police	5.05	10.5
Lobbying on behalf of the municipality	5.06	12.8
Promoting participation	5.58	4.7
Bridging differences in the population	6.27	6.4
Promoting the situation of his political party	8.10	0.0
N	138	172

* Figures are based on a survey of 172 Flemish mayors. During the interview mayors were asked what they considered as the most important mayoral task. They were also asked to order the role expectations of the mayor according to importance, the most important first, then the second most important and so on. The item which thus on average scores the lowest, is the most important.

Source: Ackaert (1997: 33). Reproduced with the permission of the author and *Res Publica*.

This professionalization contrasts somewhat with the self-perception of the function of the mayor. Research published by Ackaert (1997) shows that mayors do not primarily consider themselves as managers. Rather they see themselves first and foremost as trustees acting on behalf of citizens or as a kind of 'father' of the citizens (see Table 4.2). Being a political leader in making public policy ranks only third, whereas promoting participation and bridging differences in the community are ranked much lower. This latter finding is very surprising given the increasing possibilities for citizen participation at the local level (see below).

Linked to efforts to make the function of mayor more attractive financially, there are also a number of proposals to strengthen the mayor's executive position. In the Flemish region, for example, it was proposed that the mayor should be directly elected. In a study undertaken prior to preparing a draft local government act for Flanders, however, the possibility for a direct election of the mayor was rejected in order to preserve the position of the local council as the highest body in the municipality (Gekiere 2001). It was instead proposed to separate the role of mayor as head of the executive branch of the local authority more clearly from the legislative position of the council, by separating the executive function of the mayor from that of being president of the council. Linked to this, the study proposed the introduction of a 'motion of no-confidence' allowing the council to replace the mayor and/or aldermen if they should fail to execute the council's policies.

These more moderate reform proposals appear to be in agreement with the dominant opinions among local party leaders. A study among these shows that there is a broad support for the idea of a motion of no-confidence, whereas only the liberal parties are in favour of the direct election of the mayor (Rihoux 2001). Nevertheless, the issue of a direct election of the mayor remains high on the political agenda and no formal decision has yet been taken.

Increasing citizen involvement?

There are clear indications that many citizens are no longer satisfied with a political role that is limited to participation in periodic general elections. Indeed, a general decline in confidence in government, fired by a number of scandals, a decline in party loyalty and the rapid depillarization of Belgian society suggest that the expectations of citizens at the beginning of the twenty-first century are substantially different from those of their mid-twentieth-century predecessors. Recent democratic innovations have attempted to respond to this shift, clearly recognizing residents' roles as active political participants and as consumers of public goods and services in addition to their roles as 'subjects' of law and decision-makers (Maes 1997). Among the most noteworthy innovations are (1) citizen consultations, (2) citizen surveys, (3) advisory councils, (4) *ad hoc* initiatives and (5) individual contacts with citizens.

Citizen consultations
After the negative experiences of the 1950s with the only national referendum ever held (a referendum on whether the King should be permitted to return from exile following the Second World War), the idea of using referenda as a tool of political decision-making has long been taboo. Because of this unhappy experience, there is still no legal possibility for organizing a referendum at the national or regional level, and possibilities for citizen consultation at the local level have only existed since the mid-1990s. In introducing this option, moreover, the term 'referendum' was carefully avoided in order to make clear that a decisive referendum was out of the question. Following passage of the law in 1995 it has instead become possible to organize local non-binding consultations. These are held at the

initiative of the council or when at least 10 per cent of the voters ask the council to put the organization of a citizen consultation on its agenda. In the latter case there is no guarantee that the council will organize the consultation, or will respect the outcome if the consultation is held.

While voting in elections is compulsory, this is not the case for consultations. Since a minimum turnout level is required to validate the consultation's result, abstaining can in a number of cases also become a significant means of expressing an opinion. Initially the turnout threshold was set at 40 per cent of all voters, but recently this threshold (and the threshold for the organization of the referendum) was lowered to a figure between 10 and 20 per cent of the inhabitants, depending on the size of the municipality. The impact of this revised legislation has not as yet been tested.

Citizen surveys

A second means of consulting citizens is through citizen surveys. In the second half of the 1990s a number of local authorities started to organize surveys, hoping that this would bring the local authority closer to local residents and improve services. These surveys differ considerably in their methodology (interviews or mail surveys), the selection of 'customers' (from a sample of voters to all inhabitants), and the issues under investigation. There are, furthermore, a number of conditions linked to the use of this instrument. For example municipalities are not allowed to ask questions about issues which are not in their sphere of competencies, and they have to make sure that citizens do not confuse surveys with consultations (Van Speybrouk 2000). Besides, it remains to be seen whether such surveys are really an appropriate device for stimulating citizens' local political involvement (Bouckaert *et al.* 2001).

Advisory councils

The use of advisory councils is another way of increasing citizen participation, with two principal alternatives:

● *Local advisory councils that have been created by specific legislation.* In this case, a law or decree of a *region* or *language community* defines the existence, composition and competencies of the body in question. This type of advisory council has a long history and a solid legal basis. Examples are the municipal commissions on land-use planning, and councils that are responsible for the management of cultural infrastructure.
● *Purely local advisory councils.* In this case, the local council determines the composition and duties of the advisory council. Formal

competencies of the municipal council cannot be transferred to such advisory boards, but they may be used to solicit citizens' views on a variety of issues.

The latter type of advisory council is widespread. For instance a culture council advising the local authority on which cultural activities to subsidize is found within virtually every municipality. The same is true of sports councils, migrant councils, youth councils and senior citizen's councils.

Ad hoc initiatives
Local governments can also decide to consult with citizens in a variety of other ways. Organizing *ad hoc* meetings in neighbourhoods where individuals can ask questions and formulate remarks on the intentions of the council is one such approach, and sometimes such meetings are institutionalized. An example of this is the city of Leuven, where an information house was opened at the start of a major construction project. Anyone interested in the project could come and ask questions at this house. Following completion of the project, it was determined that the house should continue to play a role by channelling remarks and questions regarding a discussion paper the city launched on land use in the city.

Individual contacts with citizens
Last but not least in importance are individual contacts between councillors, aldermen and mayors with the general public. At present almost all mayors and aldermen organize weekly consultations in their town halls, allowing individuals the opportunity to directly address the politician who is supposed to serve him or her.

Conclusion

While Belgian municipalities have remained outside state reforms and their formal position has remained extremely stable, beneath the surface a number of important changes have taken place in recent years. From the perspective of local authorities, complexity has increased by the creation of regions and language communities. This complexity has been further increased by the fact that municipalities increasingly rely on new forms of providing services at some distance from the municipal administration as an alternative to traditional in-house production. In addition, there is a slow move towards professionalization of political personnel and local service provision. Gradually, structures for more flexible management are coming into place. Moreover, there is a slight increase in citizens' participation and involvement, which quite often leads to a situation in which local actors and citizens jointly protest against central government decisions. Towards creating ways of promoting citizen involvement, however, there is nonetheless still a long road ahead, both in terms of the mentality of local politicians and in terms of legal work.

This gradual transformation and modernization has been needed to guarantee the position of local authorities at the beginning of a new century. Given changing expectations of citizens, Belgian local authorities cannot escape the logic of modernization and professionalization and retain their legitimacy.

5 The Netherlands: in search of responsiveness

Bas Denters and Pieter-Jan Klok

The grapes must have been sour. For years Tilburg was widely recognized as a paragon of a modern well-governed municipality. Not only in the Netherlands but also in neighbouring Germany the 'Tilburg model' was widely copied. Hence, when the prestigious Carl Bertelsmann Foundation in Germany organized an international contest to select the world's best-governed municipality in 1993, many Tilburgers were confident that this competition would further boost the international reputation of their city. The jury, however, decided otherwise. They felt that Tilburg was too concerned with matters of efficiency and did not focus enough on being responsive to citizen demands. It took Tilburg some time to come to terms with this setback, but in 1997 the municipality went through a major reorganization to increase its openness to citizen demands.

The Tilburg case is exemplary of developments in Dutch municipalities in the past decade or so. In the early 1990s Dutch local government was preoccupied with a concern for effectiveness and efficiency. This concern was a reflection of the prevalent trend in the previous decade, in which the reduction of the size of the public sector, a stronger reliance on markets and private initiatives were dominant concerns. During the 1990s, however, the emphasis shifted to the issue of public responsiveness.

The main question in this chapter is *what were the major changes in the organization and political-administrative processes of Dutch municipalities during the 1990s?* But before this question is answered, a short description of the traditional Dutch system of local government is provided. Both the description of the traditional system and the account of recent changes focus on three broad themes:

1 Relations between municipalities and other governments.
2 Internal organization and management of municipalities.
3 Relations of municipalities to citizens and local organizations.

The traditional system of local government

The Dutch State consists of three tiers of government. Besides national government in The Hague and 12 provinces, there are currently 496 municipalities. The constitutional basis for this system of Dutch local government is stipulated in the Dutch constitution of 1848 and in the Municipal Law (1851). Although subsequently amended on numerous occasions, until 2002 these two laws set down the basic conditions for local self-government in the Netherlands.

Relations between municipalities and other governments

The constitution states that local communities have 'autonomous' powers to regulate and administer their internal affairs (Dölle and Elzinga 1993: 179–81). In theory, in short, municipalities are free to define tasks and to use all their powers, as long as these do not conflict with national or provincial statutes. This principle of general competence, of course, is very different from the English '*ultra vires*' principle. The constitution also stipulates that municipalities should, whenever possible, be involved in the implementation of national legislation at the local level (co-governance), and with the expansion of the welfare state most activities of municipal governments have been based on such co-governance arrangements. The result has been a highly complex system of shared responsibilities in which hardly any policy sector is the exclusive domain of one tier of government ('*Politikverflechtung*'; Scharpf 1976).

It is sometimes claimed that Dutch local government is little more than a front-office of national government (see, for example, Hennekens 2000), but this is a rather unbalanced picture of the reality of intergovernmental relations. Municipalities often enjoy considerable discretion in the execution of national programmes. It should also be emphasized that co-governance has served to preserve a meaningful local tier of government through which citizens can exercise at least some degree of local control over a broad range of policies and services (Toonen 1987a).

The active role of municipalities and the broad range of municipal activities is reflected in patterns of public expenditures and public employment (see Exhibit 5.1). The degree to which municipalities cover their expenses from locally raised revenues, however, is low by international standards. The major *local* source of revenue is a property tax; municipalities have some room for setting the rates for this tax and for other sources of local revenue and thereby have some discretion in determining municipal revenues.

Exhibit 5.1   Local public expenditures, public employment and sources of revenue in the Netherlands

- Total spending by Dutch municipalities (1999) amounts to 38.1 per cent of national government spending (local and national capital expenditures excluded).

- In 2000 the estimated municipal current expenditure by Dutch municipalities was €35,761 million distributed as follows:
    o   29.8 per cent for social expenditures (mainly for social security payments)
    o   16.7 per cent for physical planning and housing
    o   11.1 per cent for education
    o   10.1 per cent for roads and traffic
    o   9.3 per cent for public health
    o   8.8 per cent for culture and recreation.

- In 1999 Dutch municipalities employed 175,000 people, whereas total employment in national government was 114,000 (education sector and armed forces excluded).

- In 2000 Dutch municipalities revenues were derived from:
    o   local taxes and levies: 16.4 per cent
    o   general grants by central government: 36.7 per cent
    o   specific grants by central government: 46.8 per cent

Although there have been variations over the years, figures in this exhibit reflect the general contours of the Dutch system of intergovernmental relations over the last decades.

Sources: Expenditure data (Centraal Bureau voor de Statistiek 2001); Employment data (Ministerie van Binnenlandse Zaken en Koninkrijksrelaties 2000); Revenue data (Ministerie van Financiën 2001).

Yet in large measure Dutch municipalities rely on grants from national government for their income – a *general grant* and a variety of *earmarked grants*. Overall the largest source of municipal revenue is via earmarked grants. Such grants – currently there are more than a hundred of them – are provided by central government ministries for specific purposes. Some of these categorical grants are very rigid, while others allow for considerable local discretion. In addition to these earmarked grants, each municipality receives a general grant provided through the Municipal Fund. On the basis of an agreement between central government and the union of municipalities, the annual change in the budget for this fund is proportional to the change in national government expenditures, and the size of this grant to each municipality is determined by objective criteria. In general terms these criteria try to equalize obvious intermunicipal differences in ability-to-pay and the costs of service provision.

Local dependence on centrally provided revenues is often considered as further evidence of the subordination of Dutch municipalities to central government. Here again, however, the picture is much more differentiated. Once distributed, every municipality is free to spend the general grant according to local priorities. A good number of the earmarked grants also allow for considerable local autonomy in spending decisions.

But in terms of public debate, the territorial organization of local government has been a matter of far greater importance than matters of local finance, and two issues have dominated the debate. First, for many years central government has pursued an active policy of municipal amalgamation, resulting in a sharp reduction of the number of municipalities (see Table 5.1). By 2002 the average population size of a Dutch municipality had risen to almost 32,500. Research suggests that the empirical validity of the rationale for these amalgamations, based on the assumption that size is a condition for effective and efficient local government, is questionable (see, for example, Derksen *et al*. 1987; Denters *et al*. 1990; Berghuis *et al*. 1995; and, for a dissenting view, Toonen *et al*. 1998). Some studies, moreover, have shown that the increasing size of municipalities may have had negative effects on the quality of relations between citizens and local government (Denters *et al*. 1990; Denters and Geurts 1998).

A second issue that has regularly been on the agenda for the past half century concerns the organization of local government in matters that require *regional cooperation or coordination*. Since the Netherlands is a small densely populated country, where municipal boundaries typically cut across urban agglomerations, the salience of this issue is not surprising.

Table 5.1   *Distribution of Dutch municipalities by size of municipality, 1950–2002*

| | Number of municipalities | | | |
Population size	1950	1980	1990	2002
Less than 5,000	624	246	105	13
5,000 to 20,000	314	407	384	247
20,000 to 50,000	53	114	130	175
50,000 to 100,000	13	27	36	36
Over 100,000	11	17	17	25
Total	1,015	811	672	496
Average population size	9,879	17,375	22,162	32,466

Source: Data from official statistics.

What is surprising is the fact that, despite an enormous amount of 'verbal action' (Toonen 1993: 123), the institutions for regional governance remained essentially unchanged. Again and again, proposals for structural reform were defeated by ever-changing *ad hoc* coalitions of affected interests – provinces, municipalities, central government departments and political parties (see Toonen 1993: 123–6; Hendriks 1997).

Because of this, the Joint Provisions Act of 1950 and its successor of 1985, which provided a legal basis for voluntary intermunicipal cooperation, remained the main tool for regional cooperation and coordination. These acts allow for the establishment of 'intercommunales', the governing bodies of which are bound hand and foot to the municipalities because they operate on a consensual basis (Traag 1993: 123–248). This is a provision which implies that all municipalities have a veto-position, and this tends to reduce the capacity for effective joint action. The lack of decisiveness is particularly likely where the competitiveness of the economy is at stake, or where a joint effort is unpopular with the electorate at the 'home front' (Scharpf 1996: 19–20). For some types of cooperation such problems may be only minor. This is true, for example, in the case of joint provisions aimed at exploiting economies of scale in the case of capital-intensive production processes (refuse collection and similar activities). But the structure of decision-making in the intercommunales is less appropriate to make binding decisions in the case of key issues such as joint economic planning, acquisition of business firms, coordination of tax policies and planning decisions in metropolitan areas (Denters 1987; Van Dam 1992).

The internal organization and management of municipalities

Since the Municipal Law was enacted in 1851, the basic decision-making structure in all Dutch municipalities has been identical. In formal terms a directly elected municipal council is at the head of municipal government. There are, however, two additional offices in municipal government with independent powers – the Mayor and the Court of Mayor and Aldermen (CMA). Councillors elect the aldermen on the CMA from their own ranks, and the council may also dismiss them. After their election, aldermen continue their membership in the council and their party group in the council. The mayor – who is appointed by central government on the basis of a shortlist drawn up by a committee from the council – has several powers granted by national law in the fields of public order and public safety. The CMA, in addition to its general responsibility for the preparation and implementation of council decisions, similarly has specific powers in executing many national policies in co-governance arrangements. Both the mayor and the CMA are responsible to the council for their use of these powers. In a formal sense, in other words, the primacy in local decision-making rests with the council, but in practice the centre of power resides with the CMA. Because of their political weight, their information advantage and the professional support of their staff, relations between aldermen and ordinary councillors are normally heavily tilted in favour of the former.

The organization of the municipal administrative staff and executive agencies is a matter of local discretion, and during the 1980s municipalities experimented with a wide variety of models to restructure the administrative apparatus. The basic aim of these administrative reforms was to integrate policy formulation and policy implementation.

Relations of municipalities to citizens and local organizations

In the heydays of the Dutch segmented system of the 1950s and 1960s, relations between State organizations and citizens and local organizations were characterized by a remarkable mix of mass passivity and involvement of segregated middle-level elites (Lijphart 1977; Berkhout 1996: 90). The cornerstone of the organization of the Dutch social and political system was segmentation in five 'pillars', one for each of the major religious and economic strata (Lijphart 1977). The role of ordinary citizens was to vote in compulsory elections for the party representing one's pillar and to be a loyal member of a relevant organization in this pillar.

The role of mid-level elites in the traditional segmented Dutch system was twofold: on the one hand they were to communicate the concerns of their 'part of the nation' to the political elite; on the other hand they were to be responsible for providing an important range of goods and services to their segmented clienteles (Berkhout 1996: 90). In this manner the national and local governments delegated and subsidized the execution of many welfare state programmes to a highly segmented system of 'private governments'. With increased individual emancipation, growing prosperity and secularization, however, traditional cleavages of Dutch society lost their salience and the segmented system of governance became increasingly problematic. The role of third-sector organizations waned as the role of state organizations, at both the central and local level, increased. Municipal powers over these organizations were increased and mergers were stimulated in order to enhance efficiency (Berkhout 1996: 92; Veldheer 1996; Burger 2000: 94). Because of these developments the traditional strong

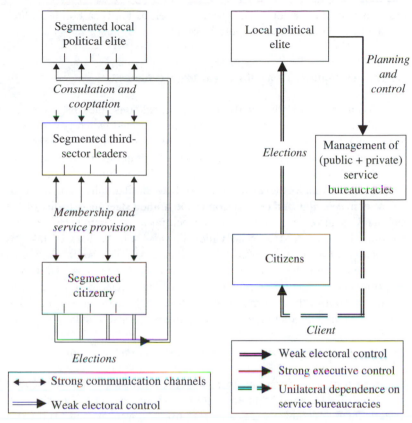

Figure 5.1 *The traditional ideal-typical Dutch segmented system*

Figure 5.2 *The ideal-typical Dutch welfare-state model of the 1970s and 1980s*

links between most third-sector organizations and their 'natural' constituencies became ever looser.

Depillarization radically changed the relations between local politicians and their electorates, gradually broke up previously close relations between pillar parties and 'their' organizational networks. As a consequence party membership declined (Van Deth and Vis 1995: 136–7) and party identification (Aarts 2002: 64–5, 71). Combined with the abolition of compulsory voting, these factor led to a gradual decline in turnout for municipal elections. Ultimately these socio-political trends resulted in a situation where the traditional institutionalized linkages between political elites and the leadership of third-sector organizations as well as between political elites and the local citizenry were largely broken.

Recent developments – a shift towards governance?

The economic crisis of the 1980s and its political consequences in the second half of the 1980s and the early 1990s transformed Dutch government. Public spending was reduced, and national government endorsed 'a rhetoric which was pro-privatization and in favour of slimming the central state' (Pollitt and Bouckaert 2000: 245). The case of Tilburg illustrates that some agents at the municipal level were moved by a similar spirit. The need for cutbacks in spending and recognition of the limited steering capacity of the national state gave impetus to changes in central-local relations, and the rising importance of the European Union likewise left its marks. Linkages between government and society also changed. All of these developments contributed in their own way to what by many is referred to as a shift from government to governance – that is a set of changes evident in intergovernmental relations, the internal organization and management of local government, and the relations of municipalities to local society.

Changes in relations between municipalities and other governments

Relations between central and local government in the 1980s and 1990s have been characterized by three major developments: (1) decentralization towards local government, (2) increasing use of covenants and (3) the rise of the EU.

The desire to slim the central state provided a strong stimulus for *decentralization*, and one of the 'beneficiaries' of this trend has been Dutch local government. In these two decades municipalities received extended powers in such areas as public housing, urban renewal, education, social security, social work, child care and youth work, among others (Denters and Veldheer 1998). The transfer of central responsibilities to the local level, however, was a mixed blessing: municipalities were permitted to take over certain tasks only if they were prepared to accept less than 100 per cent funding. The 'savings' realized (justified as 'efficiency gains' from decentralization) were gratefully collected by central government departments, who were looking for ways to minimize the pains of recurrent spending cuts (Derksen 1998: 196–7).

Expansion of municipal tasks has also taken place in the economic sphere. Whereas economic policy was long regarded as the primary responsibility of national government, municipalities – especially the major cities – have increasingly accepted responsibility for local economic development. Thus, municipalities, sometimes in close consultation with regional employment offices, central government ministries and private partners (like the Chamber of Commerce and large local employers), have developed strategic plans for local economic development – a trend that is not merely a Dutch phenomenon (Mayer 2000: 230).

A related trend in current Dutch central–local relations is increased use of *covenants* (Van Muijen 2001). In 1987 the national government and the Association of Dutch Municipalities (VNG) signed their first covenant with agreements on the principles and procedures ruling relations between central and local government. In a legal sense these covenants are not binding; their major importance stems from creating moral obligations, and as such their primary significance is in terms of reducing opportunistic behaviour in defiance of mutual agreements (Axelrod 1990). A practical problem in this regard is the fact that the VNG negotiates on behalf of its now nearly 500 members. Yet as is the case for most umbrella organizations, the VNG does not have the proper authority to make binding agreements on behalf of its members.

The most important provisions in the 1987 covenant related to the principle of proportionality in the implementation of cutbacks in public spending at national and local levels, and central government's decentralization policies. The covenant for the period 1999–2002 was also innovative in several respects (Van Muijen 2001). In particular, two major innovations are worth highlighting. First, the covenant was supposed to be result-oriented; provisions imply measurable targets and provide for periodic *monitoring of performance*. Second, the covenant provided for bi-annual consultations between the prime minister, senior cabinet ministers and the top representatives of associations of municipalities and provinces.

The overall effects of these covenants on the distribution of power in central–local relations are difficult to assess. On the one hand the new conventions open up additional channels through which central ministries are able to influence municipalities and control their performance through newly introduced performance monitors (Lako and Daaleman 1999). On the other hand, the covenants grant more local discretion and additional funding, and the consultation procedures provide previously unknown channels to access agents in central government.

In terms of its effects on the distribution of power in central–local relations, the increasing importance of the European Union provides similar ambiguities. On the one hand there is little doubt that the EU, through its regulations and directives, places additional constraints on the discretion of local governments. But also, more indirectly, the rise of the EU as a fourth level of government has had a centralizing effect by hollowing out some of the basic principles underlying the constitutional regime for municipal self-government. This is because under EU law, the national government is responsible for all incursions on EU regulations, whether these be actions by local authorities that contradict EU regulations or failure to take actions in compliance with EU regulations. Hence, there has been a tendency to concentrate all matters regarding the implementation of EU regulations at the national level (Raad voor het Openbaar Bestuur 1998: 49–50).

On the other hand the rise of the EU also provides new windows of opportunity for municipalities. New channels for access and influence have emerged which can be used to mobilize additional resources to solve local problems (Toonen and Hesse 1991: 79). The EU, for example, supports urban municipalities (under Objective 2 and through the URBAN programme) to set up innovative projects in deprived urban neighbourhoods. Moreover, EU funds (INTERREG) have also facilitated the development of cross-border cooperation between municipalities in the so-called Euregions. It is therefore not surprising that Dutch municipalities, both individually and collectively (through their union, the VNG, for instance), have invested in extending their politico-administrative networks to the European level. These efforts take two forms – formal and informal (Bekkers and Hendriks 1998: 176–7). Regarding *informal* patterns of influence, two approaches are evident:

- *Individual efforts*: municipalities may make individual efforts to lobby. Rotterdam, for example, has set up a special unit for External Funds and EU-coordination, and Amsterdam has posted a representative in Brussels (SCP 200: 107).
- *Cooperative efforts*: characteristic of such efforts is the fact that the Association of Dutch Municipalities (VNG) has set up a European Information Centre and has employed a representative in Brussels to further the interests of its members. There are also cross-national efforts such as the Eurocities-network. This network now comprises over a hundred European cities.

In terms of *formal* patterns of influence, the Committee of the Regions is the most important channel. It is an official advisory council on matters regarding sub-national governments in the EU. The Netherlands provides 12 of the committee's 222 representatives; six of them represent the Dutch provinces and the other six are municipal representatives.

No matter how important such channels for informal and formal access at the EU level may be, it is equally if not more important for municipalities to have effective access to and influence over *national decisions* that have implications for their position in the context of the EU (Raad voor het Openbaar Bestuur 1998: 53–5). This is important for both the preparation of new EU legislation and for matters regarding the implementation of such rules. The most recent intergovernmental covenant contains agreements on this topic that are in line with more general constitutional provisions on procedures that should govern intergovernmental relations.

Also noteworthy is the fact that the national government energetically continued its active *amalgamation policy* during the 1980s and 1990s. The number of municipalities was further decreased, and the average size of municipalities increased accordingly (see Table 5.1 above). Partly as a reply to critics of amalgamations, an amendment to the Municipal Law in 1993 provided a solid legal foundation for intra-municipal decentralization, but so far this option has not been widely used. Amsterdam and Rotterdam are among the few Dutch municipalities that have set up democratically elected decentralized city district authorities.

In terms of the territorial organization of local government, the 1990s also witnessed several new rounds in the continuing debate about institutional arrangements to cope with the need for supra-local (regional) coordination and cooperation. The immediate cause was the publication of a series of reports on the future of the country's major urban agglomerations in light of the increasing need to retain or possibly improve their competitiveness in a single European market and the global economy. Against the background of these developments, several commentators raised the question as to whether the traditional system of Dutch sub-national government was still adequate (Hendriks 1997: 371). The debate resulted in a series of government initiatives to provide metropolitan regions with a form of regional government. In 1994, for example, this led to the introduction of temporary special Regional Public Authorities in seven of the country's major urban agglomerations. The idea was that after a period of transition these temporary authorities would be transformed into fully-fledged, directly elected regional governments. The main responsibilities of these Regional Authorities are in the fields of economic development, infrastructure, physical planning, housing, and the environment. An executive board (with an independent chairman) and a council govern these authorities. The local councils elect the members of these bodies from the ranks of municipal councillors, mayors and aldermen. In this respect the new authorities are not very different from the intercommunales found in the

rest of the country. Even so, a major difference between the intercommunales and the new units is that the new law contained provisions to make
regional authorities more decisive.

In subsequent years, however, it became evident that the initial idea that
these seven regions should acquire the status of fully-fledged, directly
elected regional governments was unrealistic. In the second half of the
1990s and the beginning of the present decade the parliamentary majority
for such changes waned. This mirrored the widespread unpopularity of
these new bodies. Thus, in 2003 the national government introduced a new
law in which the Regional Authorities would be transformed into new
regional bodies that would have to operate under a new legal regime codi-
fied in a revised Joint Provision Act. This new legislation should be enacted
before the beginning of 2005.

Effective policy-making in supra-local matters, especially in urban
regions, is complicated by the increasing salience of regional quasi-
governmental organizations. The transfer of responsibilities of public responsibilities to independent public boards during the 1980s and 1990s provided
a widely used alternative to territorial decentralization (Van Thiel and Van
Buuren 2001). Many of these new bodies operate at the regional level. The
same also applies for field agencies of national government departments. In
coping with urban socio-economic problems, municipalities are therefore not
only obliged to cooperate with other municipalities in intercommunales or on
an *ad hoc* basis, they also have to consult, cooperate and coordinate with
important independent public boards such as police authorities, resettlement
organizations, guardianship boards and employment offices and regional
branches of national departments (for example, the Ministry of Planning,
Housing and the Environment 2000). This complex multi-actor system is further convoluted by a variety of jurisdictional boundaries existing for different
independent regional boards and ministerial field agencies.

It is therefore appropriate to argue that 'the Netherlands could still be
typified as a decentralized unitary state, in which municipalities, provinces
and national departments typically share[d] responsibility for issues of
regional concern' (Hendriks 1997: 374). Rather than a marked shift towards
governance, the increased dependence on negotiations and consultations in
intergovernmental multi-actor networks represent an element of historic
continuity.

Changes in the internal organization and management of municipalities

Whereas intergovernmental relations in the 1990s present some remarkable
continuities amidst changes, internal organization and management

practices in Dutch municipalities showed considerable and genuine change. Both relations between the council, the mayor and the CMA, and the internal management practices of municipalities were radically reformed.

The adoption of a new model

After a final attempt to save the old regime through a major revision of the Municipal Law in 1994, it was decided in 1998 that the previous system should be abandoned in favour of a more divided system of government. A Royal Commission was formed to offer advice on the new system, and in 2001 this commission published its report, that included many proposals. Some of the most important of these were:

- Concentration of administrative powers in the executive board.
- Increasing the council's powers of executive control.
- Increasing local control over the appointment of mayors, for example through direct election by the citizens, through an indirect election by the municipal council, or via a binding recommendation by the municipal council.

Most of the proposals were not controversial and made it into the draft for a new municipal law that was enacted on 7 March 2002. The most divisive issue relating to the appointment of mayors, however, was 'solved' separately. The Minister of Home Affairs retains the right to appoint mayors, but the influence of the council – and possibly that of the citizens, through an advisory referendum – on the composition of the list of nominees to be submitted to the Minister for appointment is increased. This compromise is considered to be highly unsatisfactory, so it remains to be seen whether this 'solution' will be long-lived.

Proponents of the new system have high hopes regarding its benign effects. First, they hope that the system will provide a solution for the problems of accountability that existed due to the absence of effective checks on executive powers under the old legal regime. The new law should change the role orientations and role behaviour of councillors in such a way that they will actually concentrate on scrutinizing the executive board. Second, protagonists of the reforms also hope that the reforms will allow councillors to invest more time and energy in their representative role *vis-à-vis* citizens. If so, this should contribute to more responsive municipalities. Finally, reformers hope that such changes in the role orientations and behaviour of councillors will enliven municipal politics. The hope is that this in turn will stimulate public interest in local politics and enhance electoral turnout and other forms of active citizen involvement in local politics.

Whether any of these effects will materialize remains to be seen. Results of an evaluation of experiments with the new system in 18 Dutch municipalities indicate that there is considerable aversion to changing such role orientations and behaviours among councillors (Klok *et al.* 2002a, 2002b). Without such changes, the institutional reforms are likely to fail.

The adoption of New Public Management doctrines
Doctrines of New Public Management (NPM) have been quite influential in shaping both the structures and processes in Dutch municipal administration. One of the main maxims of NPM has been that governments should engage in 'steering rather than rowing' (Osborne and Gaebler 1992: 25–48). Governments should be primarily concerned with trying to determine which goods and services should be provided to respond to citizen demands, and in evaluating the actual service production and delivery. Thus, whereas the 1980s was a period of experiments with organizational forms, the 1990s was characterized by a convergence towards a concern-model. In order to facilitate 'rowing', the municipal organization was consolidated and slimmed down. Part of this was the result of privatizing and contracting-out of municipal tasks.

At least three alternative models of production and delivery of municipal services are now widely used. First, municipalities have handed over production and delivery of services to third-sector organizations. This is a model that was typical for the segregated Dutch welfare state. A modern variant of this model is one in which the municipality sets up a new third-sector organization at arm's length from municipal government. This variant is often found in such areas as cultural policies, sports facilities and education (Van Thiel 2002: 11). Where this first model is adopted, subsidies typically provide the main steering instrument used by the municipality. Second, many local goods and services have been contracted-out to private firms or to a production unit set up with other municipalities (Joint Provision Act). This is a strategy that has been especially popular for production of goods and services that could just as well have been produced by private firms. Examples are refuse collection, maintenance of streets, parks and so on. In the case of public utilities or housing agencies, municipalities have also set up new private firms in which they command part of the shares or are represented on the board of commissioners. Third, municipalities have put service production at arm's length by introducing contract management for local administrative agencies.

Van Thiel (2002) suggests that at least the first and the second alternatives have been rather widely used. She concludes, moreover, that over the last two decades Dutch municipalities have increasingly made use of various forms of placing service production and delivery at arm's length. In many instances the transfer of powers to private-sector, third-sector or public-sector organizations is complemented by 'contracts' specifying performance criteria and a system of performance measures to scrutinize contract implementation. The use of performance-based management is therefore not only a feature of new relations between central and local government, it is also characteristic of the relations between local politicians and administrative agencies and between local government and subsidized third-sector organizations. Many municipalities have also tried to use focus groups and consumer surveys to learn more about customer preferences for services, and some municipalities are currently experimenting with citizen's charters in order to strengthen the position of the customers of local service providers.

Changes in the municipal relations to citizens and local organizations

Alongside the changes within municipal government and local service delivery, the 1990s also witnessed a reorientation in relations between municipalities and local organizations and the general public. As previously noted, the depillarization of Dutch society dissolved the close links which traditionally existed between local political elites, the leadership of local third-sector organizations and the mass public. In the 1970s and early 1980s, the ideal-typical role of the citizen was essentially that of a voter. But the 1990s have also witnessed other changes in the role of citizens in local governance (see Figure 5.3). In addition to traditional electoral controls, some municipalities have experimented with local referenda. A firm legal basis for such direct democratic experiments was lacking, however, and the status of the results of local referenda was therefore unclear. In response to this a bill has recently been enacted that allows municipalities to organize consultative referenda. Whether this law will be long-lived remains to be seen.

The introduction of 'interactive governance' in many municipalities has the potential for more fundamental changes in municipal democracy. The term interactive governance refers to modes of public decision-making in which governments to varying degrees allow for *direct participation* of interested citizens and other stakeholders (social organizations, business firms and public independent boards) in decision-making processes. In many municipalities these interactive schemes are combined with a neighbourhood approach, which in some cases also implies the delegation of

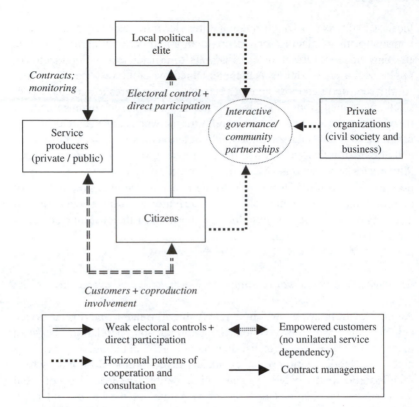

Figure 5.3   *The ideal-typical Dutch model of governance of the 1990s and 2000s*

power to decide over some neighbourhood facilities and a small budget to an association of neighbourhood residents. The more radical experiments also allow for a substantial degree of citizen involvement in making decisions that have important implications for the neighbourhood.

The nature of direct public participation in interactive governance varies on at least two dimensions. First, the scope of popular participation differs; in some cases the result of public participation is merely informal non-binding advice to the CMA or the council, in other cases municipal politicians have been willing to allow public participation to have more far-reaching influence on municipal decisions. Second, there are also differences in the openness of the interactive arenas for different types of participants. In some cases participation is essentially by professionals of third-sector organizations that are involved in the delivery of municipal ser-

vices or the civil servants of other governments or independent public
boards. In other cases municipalities primarily aim at mobilizing interested
citizens. Of course there are also examples in which a mix of organizational
and citizen participation is envisioned.

Although a systematic survey of all municipal initiatives is not available,
scattered evidence suggests that the role of ordinary citizens in most
instances is modest at best. Oftentimes the networks of interactive governance are dominated by professional third-sector organizations, public officials of other (quasi-)governments and the business community. Citizens
are either not included or their structural position in the networks is relatively weak (Denters *et al.* 1999; Denters 2002: 14–16). If we compare
these results with those of analyses of regimes in US cities (for example
Stone 1989, 1993), there are striking differences (the strong position for
professionals and civil servants) as well as similarities (the non-participa-
tion or modest role for citizens). Moreover, insofar as mobilization of citizens is successful, there are indications that the citizen participants may not
be representative for their community (Fiorina 1999; Van de Peppel and
Prummel 2000; Wille 2001: 113–14). On the other hand, there is also some
evidence that it is possible to skirt such difficulties by adopting attractive
and easily accessible modes of participation (Denters *et al.* 2002).

Conclusion

In the last decade many things in Dutch local government have changed.
But is it justified to characterize these developments in terms of a shift from
government to governance? As is so often the case, an answer to this type
of question depends on one's perspective. From a historical perspective one
is likely to emphasize continuities rather than changes. Whereas governance may be conceived as 'a *new* process of governing' (Rhodes 1997: 15)
in the context of the traditional British Westminster type of democracy,
this notion is not nearly as new in the Dutch political system. In intergovernmental relations, the Dutch polity has a long tradition of cooperative
relations and consultation. Moreover, in the conduct of local affairs, power-
sharing arrangements and the cooperation of public and 'private governments' is by no means a new phenomenon (Denters 2000). Despite these
obvious historical continuities, however, we should not be blind to some of
the marked changes that have nevertheless taken place, probably the most
remarkable of which is the emancipation of the individual citizen. This
development has been one of the important factors contributing to the dis-
integration of the traditional segmented system of linkages between the

(local) political system and citizens and civic society (compare Figures 5.1, 5.2 and 5.3).

In the 1990s, municipalities have tried to adapt to these changes. The successes of the Tilburg model suggest that some of these governance innovations may (have) contribute(d) to more efficient and effective municipalities. Yet whether innovations in public management (strengthening consumerism), in representative democracy (new roles for councillors) and in new forms of direct citizen involvement (interactive governance) have also been successful in providing for more citizen responsive municipalities remains to be seen.

6   The Nordic Countries: still the 'promised land'?

Lawrence E. Rose and Krister Ståhlberg

In many international comparisons, the Nordic countries – Denmark, Finland, Iceland, Norway and Sweden – are treated as belonging to a single model of local government. Quite often, moreover, these countries are depicted as representing the 'Promised Land' of local government. The sources of such images are numerous. Foremost among them are four considerations: (1) the countries have an interwoven historical and cultural legacy; (2) they are all unitary states, but within the respective political systems local governments enjoy, at least in theory, broad discretionary authority due to constitutional or legislative provisions permitting them to engage in all activities that are not specifically prohibited or otherwise allocated to other bodies – a situation diametrically opposed to the principle of *ultra vires* known from local government in the UK; (3) all of the countries have systems of fiscal redistribution which, to a substantial degree, assure that local governments have the resources necessary to deal with responsibilities assigned to them; and (4) local authorities, especially in recent decades, have stood for the lion's share of public employment and expenditure in these countries – a situation providing the basis for speaking of the *local* welfare state.

Whereas all of these points contain elements of truth, closer inspection reveals a much more nuanced, some might even say less idyllic, picture of the conditions that actually pertain. In what follows some important differences as well as similarities that exist among the countries are presented in order to permit a more differentiated understanding of local government in the Nordic area. First, general characteristics of the Nordic systems of local government at the beginning of the 1990s are described. Then some of the principal pressures for change that have influenced developments during the past decade are identified and changes which have occurred are discussed. The chapter concludes with an assessment of the current status of local government in the Nordic countries and some reflections on what may be expected for the future. In this review Iceland is excluded from the discussion; attention is rather concentrated on the other four countries.

Characteristics of local government in the Nordic countries

The roots of local government in Denmark, Finland, Norway and Sweden are deeply planted in the soil of history. As it is known and functions today, however, local government in these countries is of more recent vintage, stemming largely from developments following the Second World War. This has been a period of expansion of the Nordic social welfare states, an expansion in which local government was given a major role. Without exaggeration it can be stated that this expansion led to the *municipalization* of the public sector, which is particularly evident in statistics concerning public consumption and employment. At the beginning of the 1990s local government accounted on the average for roughly two-thirds or more of both public consumption and public employment in the four countries. It is important to note in this connection that local governments have not merely been passive recipients and implementers of national plans; historically they have also been active initiators in developing many social welfare practices. But the major source of growth in municipal expenditure and employment in recent decades has been a push by central authorities to realize greater equality regarding nationally set standards. Local government has been an important tool in this regard.

The political-administrative system in each of the four countries consists of three levels of government – national, regional (county) and local. A distinction can nonetheless be made between a 'Scandinavian model' on the one hand, and a 'Finnish model' on the other. This is because the Finnish system does not have regional authorities comparable to the elected county-level governments found in Denmark, Norway and Sweden (called *amtskommuner, fylkeskommuner* and *landsting* respectively). Finland, however, does have a system of intermunicipal cooperation that in many respects is the functional equivalent of regional governments found in the other three countries. The core of this Finnish alternative is the creation of joint municipal boards which exercise responsibility for specialized tasks such as healthcare, economic development and specialized education. In 1993, for example, there were roughly 300 such joint municipal boards devoted to a variety of different tasks (cf. Ståhlberg 1996: 95), and even though the total number has declined somewhat in recent years, there were still well over 200 at the beginning of the new millennium.

The difference between the two models is also evident from the perspective of public finance. Whereas municipalities in the three Scandinavian countries account for roughly 60 to 70 per cent of all local government expenditures (with the remaining 30 to 40 per cent being spent by county governments), municipalities in Finland account for roughly 85 per cent of all local government expenditures, the remaining 15 per cent being spent by joint municipal boards (Ståhlberg 1998: 53).

A further distinction that can be drawn concerns the number of municipalities found in each country and the distribution of these municipalities in terms of their population size. In this case the line of division runs between Finland and Norway on the one side, and Denmark and Sweden on the other. At the turn of the millennium both Finland and Norway had closer to 450 municipalities, whereas for Denmark and Sweden the number was less than 300 (see Table 6.1). Not only are there more municipalities in Finland and Norway, but they also tend to be substantially smaller than their counterparts in Denmark and Sweden. Over 50 per cent of the municipalities in the former two countries have fewer than 5,000 inhabitants. These conditions reflect the results of somewhat different processes and strategies relating to municipal amalgamation carried out within each of the countries during the postwar period (for details, see Albæk *et al.* 1996).

With respect to the formal institutions of local self-government, however, the four countries are quite similar. In each country the highest political body

Table 6.1 *The infrastructure of local government in four Nordic countries, 2001*

Population size	Number of municipalities			
	Denmark	*Finland*	*Norway*	*Sweden*
Less than 2,000 inhabitants	–	76	95	–
2,000 to 5,000 inhabitants	17	141	150	12
5,000 to 10,000 inhabitants	117	112	90	60
10,000 to 25,000 inhabitants	97	68	68	120
25,000 to 50,000 inhabitants	27	21	22	55
50,000 to 100,000 inhabitants	13	8	5	31
Over 100,000 inhabitants	4	6	5	11
Total	275	432[a]	435	289
Average population size	19 451	11 965	10 353	30 827
Median population size	10 239	4 977	4 392	15 264
Counties	14[b]	–[c]	19	24

Notes: [a] The 16 municipalities of Åland are not included in this total; [b] Copenhagen and Fredriksberg are not included here; [c] no formal counties exist, only regional municipalities.

Source: Data from official statistics.

at the local level is a popularly elected municipal council. Elections are held at regular intervals (currently every four years in all countries) according to principles of proportional representation, and the number of council members elected is related to the size of the municipality. Denmark distinguishes itself in this regard inasmuch as the councils tend to be smaller. As a result the ratio between citizens and council members is substantially greater in Denmark than is the case in the other three countries (Lidström 2003: 207). Finland also distinguishes itself, albeit in another respect, insofar as there is a stronger element of personalized voting in local elections. In the other three countries voting is primarily based on party lists.

Within certain limitations, the municipal councils determine the internal organization and operation of local government. Some national variations are to be found, but the major tendencies and features were quite similar in all four countries at the beginning of the 1990s. Thus, the municipal council commonly appointed a variety of committees and boards, one having overarching executive responsibility for coordination and preparation of matters for the municipal council, the others having responsibility for functionally defined areas of municipal activity. It is particularly with respect to the character of these latter bodies that variations among the countries are most evident. In Denmark and Norway board members are appointed by and from among elected council members, while in Finland and Sweden members are appointed by the council but often include non-elected representatives. The number of such boards is in all countries decided by the council, with the trend being towards a reduction in their number.

The manner in which political-administrative leadership is organized is also a point of significant differentiation among the four countries (cf. Albæk *et al.* 1996; Baldersheim and Øgård 1998; Ejersbo *et al.* 1998; Haglund 1998; Sandberg 1998). In Denmark the mayor (*borgmester*), who is elected by and among the council members, has a much stronger administrative role than his or her elected counterparts in the other countries. The Danish mayor is formally above the municipal chief executive officer and has primary executive responsibility, whereas in Finland and Norway political and administrative leadership is clearly separated. In the latter two countries CEOs are appointed by the council and serve either for a fixed period or indefinitely. Sweden, by comparison, falls somewhat in between these two models since some of the council members are employed on a full-time basis in connection with their responsibilities as heads of municipal committees or boards, and the relative importance of political leaders *vis-à-vis* CEOs varies somewhat from one municipality to another.

The formal competencies of local governments in the Nordic countries are, as already noted, broadly defined. In reality, however, municipal discretion is a bit more limited than legal stipulations would suggest. In part this is due to restrictions which arise from national legislation, in part this is due to constraints on municipal finance and stipulations requiring local authorities to maintain balanced budgets. Long before postwar welfare-state developments, local governments had been involved in providing basic infra-structural services (water and sewage, electrical production, and local road maintenance for example) as well as holding responsibilities within the educational, health, social service and cultural sectors. But these responsibilities and the attendant activities expanded considerably in the period from the 1950s through 1980s. Physical planning, environmental protection and other responsibilities were also added during this period.

Financing of these activities has been dependent on two primary sources: income taxation and intergovernmental transfers. In addition, local governments have had the right to impose various user fees and charges. Traditionally user fees and charges comprised only a small segment of local government income (cf. Albæk *et al.* 1996) and continue to do so despite increases in recent years (see Table 6.2). A noteworthy distinction regarding local government finance is the fact that in Norway local authorities have no real ability to set the rate of local income taxation. Central authorities impose an extremely limited range for these rates, and under these constraints all local governments have chosen the highest rate. Central authorities in Norway also exercise a stronger degree of macroeconomic control over local authorities. This is primarily done by means of reviewing and approving local government budgets and borrowing activities. In Denmark, Finland and Sweden, on the other hand, local governments have enjoyed a greater degree of fiscal discretion, particularly in terms of setting local income tax rates.

Table 6.2 *Sources of local government revenue in four Nordic countries, 1999 (%)*

Source of revenue	Denmark	Finland	Norway	Sweden
Taxes				
personal income and wealth	52	42	40	60
business and property taxes	8	12	1	–
Intergovernmental transfers				
block grants	10	17	23	16
earmarked grants	8	2	17	5
User fees and charges	21	25	14	18
Other sources	1	3	5	1
Total	100	100	100	100

Source: Data from table 2.3 in Mønnesland (2001: 25).

With respect to intergovernmental transfers, efforts have been made in all four countries to shift from a high degree of earmarked funding to a system of block grants. But the nature and success of these efforts have varied. Finland made the most dramatic break with prior practices in 1993 and has subsequently been the country in which block grants have accounted for the largest proportion of intergovernmental transfers, whereas shifts in Denmark and especially Sweden have been much less noteworthy. Transfers from central government in Denmark and Sweden, however, have tended to account for less of total local government income than is the case in Finland and Norway (cf. Oulasvirta 1991: 115; Mønnesland 2001: 25).

Within the constraints imposed by available income, local government authorities have considerable autonomy in deciding how they may wish to allocate funds. But an elaborate set of national regulations, particularly with respect to fundamental social welfare programmes, serves in practice to limit this discretion. A complaint commonly voiced by local authorities is not only that there has been a mismatch between the expectations placed on local government and the resources available, but that national prescriptions have been poorly suited to local conditions, often inhibiting more effective responses to local needs and problems. Criticism of excessively detailed central government control of local authorities was in fact one of the motivating forces underlying initiation of what was termed the 'free commune experiments' in all four countries during the 1980s (cf. Baldersheim and Stava 1993; Baldersheim and Ståhlberg 1994; Rose 1990). The essence of these experimental programmes was to free a selected set of local authorities from prevailing norms and regulations and to allow them to experiment with alternative solutions to local tasks and responsibilities. These programmes were an important backdrop to many of the reforms and changes relating to local government which emerged in all four Nordic countries during the 1990s.

The 1990s – dramatic changes in the context of local government

Developments in local government in the Nordic countries during the 1990s have been influenced by more than the criticisms of local officials. Equally if not more important was a set of changes in the broader context of local government. Fundamental in this regard was an economic downturn that affected all of the countries. Worst hit was Finland where, following the collapse of the Soviet Union, which had been a major trading partner, unemployment soared to nearly 20 per cent in the early 1990s. To varying degrees, however, the other three countries experienced economic decline and rising unemployment as well. For Denmark, which had encountered problems even before the beginning of the decade, the change was less dramatic, whereas for both Norway and Sweden the turn of events produced an entirely new situation, with unemployment hitting levels not previously experienced in the postwar period. As the decade drew to a close, unemployment levels had declined in all of the countries, but nonetheless remained a problem, especially in Finland and Sweden.

In coming to grips with this new reality, the Nordic countries also had to face marked changes in the international environment. As a result of ever stronger economic internationalization, the countries experienced increased competition in their export markets. International trade has long been a prominent feature of the Nordic economies, and competition from countries with lower production costs became ever more apparent as the countries attempted to cope with increased unemployment. In seeking solutions to these problems, membership in the European Union offered an especially enticing possibility for Finland, Norway and Sweden, the three countries that were not yet members. Following negotiations, all three countries submitted the question of membership to approval in popular referenda during the fall of 1994. The issue obtained a clear majority in favour of membership in Finland and a narrow majority in Sweden, but even the pull of these favourable decisions among their Nordic neighbours was not sufficient to sway Norwegian opinion, where the result was a narrow majority against membership (cf. Jenssen *et al.* 1998). Norway's fallback option was continued membership in the European Free Trade Area (EFTA), and the European Economic Space (EES) agreement on economic cooperation between EU and EFTA countries that had been signed previously.

Whether members or not, all four Nordic countries have experienced the effects of the four freedoms upon which the EU is built – freedom in movement of individuals, capital, services and products. Being countries with relatively small population bases and hence domestic markets, this situation has had a noticeable impact, contributing in varying degrees to a significant restructuring of social as well as economic life in all four countries. Most noteworthy in this respect has been increased demographic mobility, not least because of increased economic competition and the concentration of production facilities that has accompanied this. Migratory tendencies have largely followed classic patterns of movement from more peripheral areas towards urban or regional centres, particularly those where new production facilities based on high technology have been located. This development has been most evident in Finland and Sweden, somewhat less so in Norway, and least pronounced in Denmark where distances are smaller and the transportation infrastructure more readily permit commuting for employment purposes. These developments not only fly in the face of traditional settlement policies, whereby central authorities have sought to maintain a more widely spread population pattern; they have also created substantial challenges to local authorities. In areas subject to new population pressures there has been a pronounced need for investments in basic social infrastructure and the provision of social services, whereas in areas experiencing depopulation there is often a shortage of qualified labour for provision of public services and, quite ironically, a surplus of abandoned public facilities.

On a more secular note, the Nordic societies have also been subject to forces that have brought about a shift in fundamental orientations not unlike that found in other countries. Contributing to this change is what has been termed the transition from Fordism to post-Fordism – that is the introduction of new production techniques based on high technology and on individualized commodities, new business paradigms and forms of labour organization, new consumption patterns and an increased emphasis on the individual as consumer (cf. Stoker 1990). In an apparent extension of this transition, citizens also now display a more pronounced consumer orientation to local government than has traditionally been the case (cf. Hellevik 1996; Montin and Elander 1995; Rose 1999).

Developments in local government – major reforms but no revolution

These changes in the environment have contributed to a number of developments that, if not constituting an outright revolution, have at least altered the organization and operation of Nordic local government. These developments may be summarized under four headings: (1) pressure for structural reform and reallocation of responsibilities; (2) changes in organization; (3) changes in the modes of operation; and (4) changes in policy perspectives.

Pressure for structural reform and reallocation of responsibilities

One of the most prominent developments has been renewed pressure for the restructuring of local government or, in the absence of this, a reallocation of responsibilities and competencies for providing selected public services. Initially this was most apparent in Norway and Finland, but over time the same tendencies, if perhaps in a slightly different form, have been observed in all four countries. Already in 1989 a public commission was appointed in Norway with a mandate to evaluate the appropriateness of the existing division of local authorities. In its report, submitted in 1992 (NOU 1992: 15), the commission recommended that municipalities should as a rule have a minimum of 5,000 inhabitants, a recommendation which, if enacted, would have implied the elimination of just over 50 per cent of all municipalities. Enactment of even a watered down version of this recommendation was prevented, however, when parliament subsequently passed a resolution specifying that no amalgamation should be imposed against the wishes of a majority of residents in the municipalities affected, but this action did not remove the pressure for restructuring Norwegian local government. In subsequent years central authorities have sought to induce mergers by covering the costs of evaluating the consequences of mergers and offering a financial 'carrot' to municipalities that voluntarily decide to merge. A similar inducement approach has been employed by Finnish authorities. The result has been a slow reduction in the number of municipalities in both countries, but there are clear signs of impatience on the part of central authorities, especially in Norway.

The question of restructuring local government has not solely been an issue in Finland and Norway, the two countries where a large number of relatively small municipalities have existed, nor has it only been concerned with municipal amalgamation. In Sweden, for example, there have even been a few instances in which new municipalities have been formed by splitting older units apart. Thus, whereas there were 248 primary municipalities in 1990, by 2000 there were 289. In Denmark, on the other hand, the number of municipalities has been reduced from 275 to 273 during the course of the 1990s, and pressure to reduce the number still further is highly apparent. To this end the Danish Ministry of Interior has commissioned several inquiries into size related effects in the municipal sector. Results contained in one major report issued in 2000, however, were mixed, showing that for some types of services there is a curvilinear relationship with costs, whereas in other instances the evidence was inconclusive (Indenrigsministeriet 2000). Despite these results, yet another commission was appointed in 2002 with a mandate to evaluate the structure of local government anew, including whether or not there is a genuine need for county government (*amtskommer*) in Denmark. On the basis of the commission report submitted in early 2004, the government has negotiated a proposal which, if adopted, will result in the abolition of all counties and the creation of fewer larger regions and municipalities by the beginning of 2007.

The Danish debate highlights an important facet relating to the question of restructuring local government – namely the role of the intermediate or regional level of government in all of the Nordic countries. Major metropolitan areas, and in particular the capital cities of Copenhagen, Helsinki,

Oslo and Stockholm, have all been under substantial pressure due to the influx of population and their encapsulated position *vis-à-vis* surrounding authorities. This situation has led both local and central authorities to raise questions about the need to find new forms of government for these areas, either through municipal amalgamation or by means of establishing more binding types of intermunicipal cooperation. Again Denmark offers a good example. In 1994 a public commission was created with a mandate to investigate alternatives for reforming county level government in the capital region. This commission considered four alternative models and finally ended up recommending a choice between two possible solutions based on a modified county government model (Hovedstadskommissionen 1995). The issue has yet to be resolved, but a new council for intermunicipal cooperation within the capital area has been created to which members are appointed (Sandberg and Ståhlberg 2000: 77). A comparable council also exists in the Helsinki region in Finland.

Similar developments have occurred in Norway. Oslo has long struggled with problems arising from its encapsulated location, and in 1995 a public commission was appointed to consider options for dealing with this situation. In its report, submitted in 1997 (NOU 1997: 12), the commission was divided in its viewpoints on what was the best alternative for the future, but it did offer concrete recommendations for greater coordination among local authorities in specific areas of activity such as healthcare, transportation and physical planning. Here again, however, no formal decision has yet been reached.

One of the reasons why efforts to achieve territorial restructuring are controversial and have not born much fruit is the fact that it is an issue closely linked to the question of how responsibilities are to be allocated among public authorities. During the course of the 1990s attention has shifted more to this latter question, which all of the Nordic countries have taken up in one manner or another. Public commissions were appointed in both Denmark and Norway, and the reports submitted by these commissions are currently under consideration. Sweden has considered setting up a commission with a comparable mandate, and in Finland similar assessments were made in relation to the Region 2000 reform proposal – a proposal suggesting drastic amalgamation of county-level authorities and the creation of new state authorities at the regional level with responsibility for economic development policy.

The most important regional development to have taken place to date, however, is a regional experiment undertaken in Sweden. As a consequence of this experiment, two 'super-counties' – one in southern Sweden, the other in western Sweden – were created through amalgamation of the former counties within the regions. These new entities have directly elected regional councils and were given special responsibility for regional cooperation and development in their respective areas. But it is important to note that even without special experimental status, cooperation between regional and municipal authorities for purposes of developmental tasks has been established throughout Sweden.

In Finland, new joint municipal boards at the regional level introduced in 1994 have also been given developmental responsibilities. This model, which has long been known in Finland, is now being viewed more favourably in the other countries as well. Denmark in particular has exhibited a flexible attitude regarding a sharing of responsibilities among local authorities both at and between the municipal and county levels. One noteworthy exception to this general trend, however, is the recent decision in Norway to remove responsibility for the operation of hospitals from county governments and to place it instead in the hands of the state, which has created a set of new 'hospital regions' for this purpose.

Changes in the organization of local government

A philosophy of greater flexibility is a prevalent characteristic of new legislation regarding local government passed in Finland, Norway and Sweden during the 1990s. In many respects these legislative acts bore the imprint of the free commune experiments conducted earlier. Rather than requiring the creation of specific bodies, new legislation granted local authorities considerably greater discretion to determine their own internal organization. The overarching principle endorsed was that local authorities should accomplish the tasks assigned to them; how they chose to organize themselves was less critical. To be sure, there are still guidelines regarding the existence and composition of certain bodies, such as municipal or county councils and executive boards, but the number and character of many other bodies were made a matter of local prerogative. The new law on local government in Norway even opened the possibility for local parliamentary democracy as an alternative to the traditional alderman model (a model in which the municipal council elects an executive committee according to proportional representation) which had prevailed earlier and which did not permit a vote of no confidence. A form of local parliamentary government had been in practice in Oslo since 1986 (cf. Baldersheim 1992), but to date this alternative has been adopted by only a few other municipalities. In Finland and Sweden, by comparison, particular attention has been paid to enabling municipalities to choose appropriate forms of intermunicipal cooperation.

At the same time there have also been experiments, particularly in the largest municipalities, with various forms of decentralization – both administrative and political (cf. Bäck *et al.* 2004). In part these developments have been motivated by a desire to achieve an organization better suited to the activities of local government, but there has also been a hope that these arrangements would facilitate and stimulate increased citizen involvement. In Oslo there have even been experiments with direct election to district councils (Klausen *et al.* 2002).

In the wake of new legislation, the number of internal committees and boards has otherwise been reduced in most local authorities. In some cases bodies were eliminated totally, in other cases bodies were combined in attempts to streamline local government. Delegation of authority to lower bodies has also been commonly employed, particularly in connection with a desire to set clearer boundaries between 'politics' and 'administration'. Under a view that has achieved wider currency in recent years, politicians are to concentrate on strategic management decisions, turning the details of implementation and day-to-day operations over to administrative bodies. This philosophy, embodying a strong emphasis on management by objectives, has been especially prevalent in Finland, Sweden and Norway (cf. Haugsjerd and Kleven 2002; Naschold 1995; Øgård 2002), and has in its own right implied a number of restructuring decisions.

The past decade likewise saw increased interest in new types of local government bodies. Particularly important in this respect was the possibility of creating municipal companies. The use of municipal companies has been seen to offer special advantages in areas where there is a combination of administration and business activity, such as is the case with respect to sanitation services, transportation and public housing. Developmental activities have likewise been a new field for the creation of municipal companies.

Moving a step beyond these municipal companies, many municipalities have also sought to establish public–private partnerships. Whereas the former have been seen as especially relevant for authorities pursuing local development policies (cf. Kahila 1999), public–private partnerships have been used in connection with a wider spectrum of activities (cf. Lundqvist 1998; Pierre 1998). It is important to stress that such partnerships, both with private and third-sector actors, are not entirely new (cf. Eikås and Selle 2001). What is new is the degree of interest in exploiting such arrangements in a variety of additional areas where they are now considered feasible.

Changes in the modes of operation

As these last remarks suggest, there has also been a marked change in the modes of operation within Nordic local government during the 1990s. Many, but certainly not all, of these changes can be placed under the umbrella concept of New Public Management. In part this shift is a result of larger national and international trends relating to deregulation and increased competition. Rather than having municipal electric companies holding monopoly status for providing electrical services, for example, residents are now able to shop around for electricity providers. More characteristic of the new situation and mindset, however, is the fact that elements of competition and choice are to be found in areas where local authorities previously were the sole provider *and* producer of goods and services (cf. Klausen and Ståhlberg 1998). Outsourcing and adoption of purchaser-provider models have become quite commonplace. Among the factors contributing to this development have been EU regulations that force local authorities to open for tendering in many areas of activity that were previously a closed domain. Thus, the idea of separating the provider and producer roles has spread throughout the Nordic area, albeit at a somewhat uneven tempo. In many respects Finland and Sweden have been leaders in this regard, while Denmark, and even more so Norway, have been a bit slower on the uptake (Øgård 2002: 49).

The apparent 'wildfire' spread of these practices in the Nordic countries is nonetheless a bit deceptive. Given an almost total absence of such practices up through the mid-1980s, it does not take much change to produce what appears to be a dramatic shift, whereas in reality many local authorities have been reticent to abandon older, more familiar operating practices. In many instances strong employee organizations have also placed a brake on the speed with which these new practices have spread, particularly during the years of economic recession in the early 1990s.

The implementation of New Public Management measures, however, extends beyond those practices or arrangements mentioned so far. A variety of quality-control techniques have been tested and adopted in different settings. Most salient in this respect is benchmarking, but systematic evaluation and quality-control inventories are also commonplace (Baldersheim and Ståhlberg 1999b). Central authorities have been active participants in this connection (cf. SOU 1993: 74), especially with regard to social welfare services mandated under national legislation.

Another facet of the NPM philosophy that has been increasingly evident is a strengthened consumer orientation. To varying degrees local governments have developed citizen charters for selected services, carried out customer surveys and instituted other mechanisms to ensure feedback regarding service satisfaction. The use of more general citizen surveys and in some instances citizen panels or juries has also been evident, although these, and the use of voucher schemes, are still much less common than other NPM practices.

One area in which Denmark, and to a lesser degree Sweden, have made a special mark with regard to a consumer orientation has been in the introduction of user boards in connection with selected local government activities. Most prominent in this respect are user boards for schools where parents of schoolchildren are granted special representation and powers. The intent of these boards is actually twofold. On the one hand they are intended to give users a greater voice in decisions regarding service production and delivery; on the other hand it is also thought that they may provide an arena for learning more about the dynamics of democracy and stimulate additional local involvement. Evaluations of experiences with these boards to date, however, suggest that the results have been mixed, particularly on the latter count (cf. Andersen 1997; Floris and Bidsted 1996; Kristensen 1998; Sørensen 1998), and so far this practice has not to any significant degree been emulated in the other Nordic countries.

Use of new information technology, both as a means of informing local residents and as a means of stimulating citizen involvement, has also had relatively limited distribution and utility to date. A few local authorities have made concerted efforts to exploit these opportunities, often with backing from external sponsors, but these are exceptions rather than the rule. To the extent these technologies are more widely implemented, there appears to be a positive (albeit weak) relationship with the size of the local authority, and the most common forms of technology used are internet home pages and electronic mail, technologies that are well-known in all four countries. For internal purposes, however, IT is very widespread, and the end of the 1990s has been a period of rapid expansion that is likely to continue, providing greater benefits for the public at large in the near future (cf. Christensen and Aars 2002; SKTF 2002).

Changes in policy perspectives

The developments described up to this point are interwoven with two fundamental changes in policy outlooks on the part of local authorities in the Nordic countries. One of these changes concerns internationalization. Local governments had by no means operated in isolation from the international environment previously, but the 1990s was marked by a notable increase in the international orientation of local authorities. This is evident in many respects. For example twinning relations with local governments in other countries have been (re)vitalized and expanded, both in numbers and geographic diversification. The majority of such relationships continue to be with other local authorities within the Nordic area, but an increasing percentage involves local authorities outside the Nordic area. This applies in particular to Finland and Sweden, where local authorities in both countries have been active in establishing twinning relationships with local governments in the Baltic countries and Russia. In addition to this, local authorities in all four countries have established relationships with sister authorities in countries throughout Europe and elsewhere (cf. Sandberg 2000).

It may of course be argued that twinning relationships are largely symbolic, often being based on little more than exchanges of school orchestras, citizen groups or municipal delegations, without having much substantive content. But in most instances these relationships are backed up by a series of other actions that serve to underline a more pronounced international outlook and a genuine interest in learning through more systematic exchange of experiences. Evidence of this is found in strong participation in various EU-sponsored projects, a sharp increase in memberships reported in European and international organizations for local and regional governments, and the development of planning documents containing a solid international component (Ståhlberg 1999; Sandberg 2001). Local authorities have in particular been interested in best practices and bench-marking schemes which may provide ideas for their own activities. International activities of this sort are quite strongly related to the size of local authorities, being most commonly reported by larger municipalities, but examples are also readily found in smaller municipalities (cf. Baldersheim and Ståhlberg 1999c: 136).

The second noteworthy change in policy outlooks of Nordic local governments is a shift in emphasis from a primary concern with service delivery to a greater focus on local economic development. In part this is apparent in the projects of international cooperation and cross-border alliances just mentioned (cf. Baldersheim and Ståhlberg 1999a). Even more significant, however, are the new constellations and activities to be observed at the municipal, intermunicipal and regional levels. One example in this regard is the use of public–private partnerships in the creation of competence centres within such high tech fields as information and biotechnology. Public–private partnerships have also been used for other purposes, including the realization of athletic facilities, cultural events and the building of roads. A stronger developmental orientation among local government leaders, which is revealed by attitudinal surveys (cf. Sandberg and

Ståhlberg 2001), has also led to a variety of intermunicipal and regional-level agreements regarding cooperation for developmental purposes. All of this is not to say that the role of local authorities as important providers, if not actual producers, of a wide range of services has been forgotten. The point is merely that there has been a clear and noteworthy shift in the relative priorities of many local authorities.

Prospects for the future – local governance or still local government?

On balance, how should the situation in the Nordic countries be judged? Has it been a case of movement from local government to local governance, or does local government still reign? Considering developments of the past decade, a fair assessment would be that the evidence is mixed (cf. Gidlund and Jerneck 2000). At the local level there has been a slow turn in the direction of local governance, evidenced by a stronger emergence of partnerships around a variety of programmes and projects involving both private and third-sector parties. These partnerships are closely linked to the shift towards a more prevalent developmental policy orientation, but they are also related to more traditional service provision. Local governments have also shown a willingness to adopt many of the practices associated with New Public Management in their approach to service provision. The essential characteristics and structures of local government nevertheless remain largely intact.

At the intermunicipal and regional levels, by comparison, features of governance have clearly been strengthened (cf. Baldersheim *et al.* 2001). This is most readily seen in the growth of partnerships and joint ventures in connection with developmental activities. More generally, however, multi-level governance seems to be an appropriate frame of reference for understanding a range of practices that have become more common – practices involving among other things network building and negotiation, cross-level project management, and international cooperation and European lobbying, some of which bypass national authorities (cf. Baldersheim and Ståhlberg 2002). The strengthening of intermunicipal cooperation, often working closely with authorities at other levels, is also indicative of this trend.

At the bottom line it is nonetheless important to emphasize that Nordic developments bear witness to gradual change, not revolution. The fundamentals of the Nordic model – the unitary state, universalism as a principle of service provision, tax-based financing and the redistribution of resources – have not only prevailed, but have even shown their robustness in a period of severe trials (cf. Kautto *et al.* 1999, 2001). Developments in the sphere of local government within the Nordic countries have been interpreted as offering a genuine 'third way', solidly anchored between hierarchical steering and market liberalism (cf. Klausen and Ståhlberg 1998). Municipalities as well as regions have in several instances been active in initiating structural innovation in the Nordic countries, facilitating the change from an industrial to an information age. The success of the Nordic model is also evident in the rapid and successful adaptation of Finland and Sweden to multi-level governance within the setting of the European Union. Nordic regions seem in this respect to have been rather more active than many of their continental European counterparts in recent years (Baldersheim *et al.* 2001).

Despite this overall positive picture, local governments face serious challenges as they begin the new millennium. Demographic shifts, stronger competition and market pressures (both national and internationally), and the erosion of traditional social solidarity are keywords in this regard. In dealing with these challenges, it is likely that many of the developments already observed will be further reinforced. Local cooperation among municipalities will probably become even more important, especially as an alternative to amalgamation, there will be a stronger emphasis on the 'new economy' of the information age, with further development of competence centres and networking, and the uneven distribution of resources will stimulate a further pooling and sharing of those resources that are available. In all of these respects one may suggest that the pragmatic evolutionary movement from local government to local governance will continue in the Nordic countries in the years ahead. Whether the result will still warrant being perceived as the 'Promised Land' of local government, however, is impossible to foresee.

7 Poland: a time of transition

Paweł Swianiewicz

To suggest that the legal and economic environment of local government in Poland has undergone rapid change since 1990 is an understatement. Recent years have witnessed a fascinating quest for a totally new model of local governance. If the present condition of local government is compared to the situation before 1990, it is fair to say that almost everything has changed. But even when the present situation is compared with the more recent 'early period' of democratic local government (1991–92), there are few similarities.

The chapter starts with a brief description of institutional changes, the details of which are treated more extensively in other sources (see, for example, Baldersheim *et al.* 1996; Kowalczyk 2000; Regulski 1999; Swianiewicz 1992). This description provides a framework for understanding more comprehensive changes in how local governments operate and are managed. These changes are discussed in subsequent sections, and the chapter concludes with a general assessment of developments within the past decade. Although the initial section describes developments relating to all tiers of sub-national government, the primary analytical focus of the chapter is on the lowest (municipal) level of local government.

Institutional change – local revolution in two stages

Before 1990, the highly centralist doctrine of the communist period left no room for local self-government; local administration was subordinated to higher tiers and branches of central government, and local discretion to decide on financial issues or modes of service delivery was next to none. The dominant constitutional position of the Communist Party kept reforms aimed at real democratization of local politics to a minimum. The inefficiency of the centralist system, however, had been widely recognized for many years. The Polish Communist Party tried to introduce some forms of decentralization (for example in the Acts of 1983 and 1988), but these minor reforms did not alter the doctrinal base of the centralist state, so they could hardly result in more democratic or effective local government.

The turning point was the roundtable meeting between 'Solidarity', the opposition movement, and the ruling Communist Party in 1989. Reform of local government was one of the topics on the agenda, yet it is noteworthy that this was the only topic on which no final agreement was reached. Nevertheless, the main direction for future reform was already traced out by 'Solidarity', and local government reform was one of the main priorities for the first post-communist government formed in September 1989. Quick but intensive preparations allowed for passage of a new Local Government Act in March 1990, which was followed by local elections in May 1990 and a radical decentralization of financial regulations in January 1991. The 1990 reform introduced elected local government at the municipal level (*gmina*).

This solution was seen as provisional. It was assumed that new, elected regional governments would be introduced, and that territorial divisions at the county and regional levels would be reformed. The introduction of a regional tier, however, was postponed for several years. Advocates of reform realized that the regional reform was going to be politically difficult and that it would require lengthy discussions. They therefore opted for a less controversial alternative to achieve a further step towards the decentralizing Polish government – namely a reform of county (*powiat*) government. Hence, a proposal to introduce self-government in over 300 counties was ready in 1993.

Implementation of this reform was begun in 1994 with a 'pilot programme', the idea of which was to transfer county functions to the 46 largest cities (those with more than 100,000 inhabitants). Outside these urban centres county reform was to be implemented the following year. Before the pilot programme was actually implemented, however, new parliamentary elections dramatically changed the political scene. The elections were won by the Post-Communist Party (SLD), a party that was rather sceptical to the reform of local, county and regional government, and which, along with the Peasant's Party (PSL), composed the new coalition government. It soon became clear that reforms not introduced during the 1991–93 period would have to wait much longer.

The new government retained the pilot programme but delayed county reform for an indefinite period. Opponents of the county reform argued that a new tier of government was unnecessary since functions too demanding for individual municipalities could easily be accomplished through voluntary cooperation of neighbouring local governments. But for reasons ranging from psychological motives (for example a desire to maintain freshly achieved organizational autonomy) to the lack of financial incentives for cooperation, intermunicipal cooperation never really worked in practice. Against this background, the pilot programme, inherited from the previous governing coalition, was changed into a permanent Act in 1996, granting additional functions to the largest cities.

Another sign that the climate of opinion had changed was the new government's decision to stop the decentralization of responsibility for primary schools to municipal governments. Originally such a transfer was scheduled for the beginning of 1994, but Prime Minister Pawlak decided to delay it until 1996. It was only one of the first proofs that at least one party of the new government coalition (the PSL) was very sceptical about further decentralization. Despite a large number of governmentally organized seminars, discussions and published papers, no single decision on the future of decentralization was made between 1994 and 1997.

Parliamentary elections held in 1997 brought about another political turn; government power was taken over by a coalition between a newly formed rightwing alliance (AWS) and the Freedom Union (UW). At the end of 1998 this new government decided to change the territorial organization of the state and to introduce new (upper) tiers of government. Meanwhile the municipal level remained unchanged both in terms of territorial organization and in terms of the allocation of primary functions.

There are some striking similarities between the implementation of the reforms in 1990 and 1998. Much as was the case in 1990, preparations for the reforms in 1998 were very short. As in 1990, moreover, the 1998 reforms were only meant to be provisional. The government and parliament agreed that substantial revisions would be necessary one or two years after the new system came into operation, but once again, temporary regulations were extended well-beyond the period initially intended.

Current structure and functions of local government

As a result of this process, there are currently three tiers of territorial governments consisting of almost 2,500 municipalities, 308 counties (plus 65 cities with county status) and 16 regions that replaced 49 smaller units. Authorities at both the municipal and county level are based on principles of self-government. On the regional level, by comparison, there is a dual structure: on the one hand the structure is based on regionally elected officeholders; on the other hand the governor, who has a distinct administrative staff, is appointed by the prime minister. The functions of the elected and the appointed officials at the regional level are clearly separated and there is no hierarchical subordination between them.

The most recent reform placed responsibility for a wide range of functions in the hands of municipal governments. They are responsible for pre-school and primary education, most utilities (such as water and sewage services, central district heating and gas), solid waste disposal, city public transportation, local road construction and maintenance, municipal housing, numerous social welfare tasks and culture. The list of county functions is much shorter, with primary functions being secondary education, healthcare, county roads, employment policy, natural disaster protection, consumer protection and public safety inspections. The aggregate county budget is only a small fraction (about one-quarter) of aggregate municipal budgets.

The goal of the recent reform was to separate functions and policy areas between the different tiers of sub-national government clearly and to eliminate hierarchical dependency of the lower tier upon a higher tier. This objective was largely achieved. Obviously municipal, county and regional levels cooperate in some areas (in economic development policies for example), but in terms of specific service delivery the separation is close to perfect. Relations between central and local government, by comparison, are much more complicated. In some cases, such as education or some social welfare benefit programmes, nationwide regulations are so strict that local government's role is essentially reduced to that of an agent of central government, merely implementing central policies.

In part such a division of functions is possible because of the relatively large size of municipal units in Poland. Page and Goldsmith (1987), for example, have noted that the territorial organization of the state is very much related to the allocation of functions to local units. Small (fragmented) local governments are usually considered to be unable to take over responsibility for many services, which are therefore passed on to upper tiers of government. Contrary to many other countries in the region such as the Czech Republic, Hungary or Slovakia, Poland avoided radical territorial fragmentation at the beginning of the 1990s. As a consequence the average *gmina* has about 16,000 inhabitants and 125 square kilometres. Polish municipalities, in short, are quite big when seen in a comparative European perspective (cf. Martins 1995). Although Polish municipalities are much smaller in population terms than British or Swedish units, they are on average about as large as Danish or Dutch units and much larger than

Table 7.1 *Distribution of Polish municipalities by size of municipality, 1999*

Population size	Number	Per cent
Under 2,000	7	0.3
2,000 to 5,000	573	23.0
5,000 to 10,000	1,064	42.7
10,000 to 20,000	506	20.3
20,000 to 40,000	199	8.0
40,000 to 100,000	94	3.8
Over 100,000	47	1.9
Total	2,490	100.0

Source: Data from official statistics.

Czech, Slovak, Hungarian, French or Italian municipalities. The distribution of Polish municipalities by size is shown in Table 7.1; only few of them are smaller than 2,000 and none of them has less than 1,000 inhabitants.

As of 1999, the three tiers of local governments spent 10.5 per cent of Polish GDP or 36 per cent of total government expenditures. This is a clear increase from the 7.4 per cent of GDP and 16 per cent of total government expenditure spent by local governments in 1991. Almost 80 per cent of all local self-government budgets are spent at the municipal level (including big cities having a county status), 15 per cent at the county level and only 5 per cent by regional self-government (*Statistical Yearbook of Poland* 2001: 90).

Local governments are financed by a mixture of self-collected revenues (mostly local taxes which are set within limits defined by law and collected by local governments), shares of the central income tax collected within the local unit's territory, and transfers by central government. In 1999 the proportion of self-collected revenues was significant (33 per cent), though the largest source of municipal revenue was central grants (34 per cent from general and 15 per cent from specific grants). Though central government has paid lip-service to the principles of financial decentralization, most new municipal functions are financed by central government grants. As a result, municipal government has become increasingly dependent on state grants over time (see Figure 7.1). This situation is particularly obvious in small, rural communities; in municipalities having less than 5,000 inhabitants, 60 per cent of the municipal revenues came from state grants in 1999.

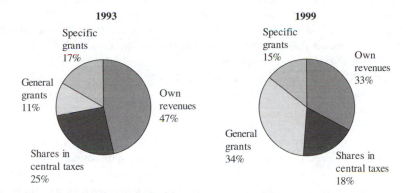

Figure 7.1 *Sources of Polish municipal government revenue, 1993 and 1999*

Source: Calculations by the author based on local government financial reports available from the Polish National Statistical Office (GVS).

The politics of local government

The electoral system used for municipal council elections differs between small and large municipalities:

- In municipalities with fewer than 20,000 inhabitants there is a majority system. The municipality is subdivided into a number of electoral wards, and from each ward one to five councillors are elected. In most such municipalities there is in practice one councillor for each ward.
- In municipalities with more than 20,000 inhabitants there is a system of proportional representation. Here, too, the municipality is subdivided into wards. Up to 10 councillors are elected in each ward, and seats are distributed in proportion to the number of votes cast for each list of candidates in the ward. These lists are submitted by political organizations – usually parties.

Until recently it was not unusual that councillors and mayors were also acting members of the national parliament. A recent amendment, however, abolished this possibility.

The role of the chairman of the council (who has no executive responsibilities and is separate from the mayor of municipality) is to call and chair council meetings. Everyday council work, however, is largely conducted in functional committees – committees for education, economic development, and so forth. The number of committees, their responsibilities and membership depend entirely on decisions made by each council. The only committee which is obligatory for all municipalities is a scrutiny committee, the primary function of which is to control execution of the budget. Since the 2002 elections all political groups represented in the council have to be represented in the scrutiny committee.

Until 2002, municipalities were managed by the executive board, which was elected by the council and consisted of the mayor, a maximum of three deputy mayors and ordinary members. The mayor could be selected from among the councillors, but could also be selected from outside the council. In 2002 about 50 per cent of the mayors in rural local governments and 20 per cent in large cities were 'outsiders'. The system of collective executive boards still operates on the county and regional levels, but 2000 brought a reform leading to direct, popular election of city mayors. These mayors may appoint deputies but do not need to share power with a collective board. The Polish electoral system, however, does not guarantee that these mayors will have the support of a majority in the local council. Among 42 cities with more than 100,000 inhabitants, only seven mayors recently had support of a 'friendly' council majority. Others needed to rely on more or less stable coalitions. In some major cities (such as Łódź, Bydgoszcz and four other cities with more than 100,000 citizens) the situation is quite contrary; a majority of the council is in opposition to the mayor. This is a situation which raises serious doubts about the effectiveness of decision-making in those cities (Swianiewicz and Klimska 2003).

The first democratic local elections in 1990 attracted numerous candidates with no previous political experience; almost 80 per cent of the elected representatives had no prior council experience. In cities over 40,000 turnover was even larger; over 90 per cent of the councillors were new to their job (Baldersheim *et al.* 1996). Similarly, in the major cities virtually all of the mayors were novices, whereas in smaller municipalities cases of continuity were more common.

This situation reflected the fact that party politics had a limited role in the 1990 local elections. Just a few months after the fall of the communist regime, there was simply not enough time for new parties to organize themselves. Moreover, the 'old' parties (established during the communist era) were compromised and had very little electoral support. In this setting it is hardly surprising that merely 7 per cent of all mandates were won by party candidates, and only a minimal fraction (0.2 per cent) were won by the post-communist party (*Statystyka wyborow do rad gmin* 1990: 320–2). In small municipalities with a majority electoral system, the major beneficiaries were independent candidates. In big cities with proportional representation systems, on the other hand, *ad hoc* groups of candidates organized by the Solidarity movement in so-called 'civic committees' were victorious.

But Solidarity candidates were by no means united in their political opinions. In subsequent years new parties emerged from the 'civic committees' movement. Many councillors first elected in the 1990–94 period, however, have never joined a political party, and have rather preserved their status as an independent local activist or expert.

This initial non-partisan period, with thousands of councillors who were essentially on their own without the institutional and political support of a party organization, was bound to be transitional. Each of the two subsequent municipal elections marked a new stage in the development of local party systems. The 1994 local election campaign is best described as a 'hidden partisan' campaign. Small rural municipalities remained the hunting grounds for independent candidates, although the role of the Peasants' Party (PSL) increased considerably. But in urban areas local councils gradually became arenas for party competition. The principal reason why parties rarely used their official names in the 1994 campaign was a general disillusionment with party politics. To avoid this stigma, candidates quite often hid behind not-very revealing names of electoral committees. In Kraków, for example, the elections were contested by lists named 'Your City', 'Alliance for Kraków' and 'Self-Governing Kraków'.

The 1998 elections marked a further step in the advance of political parties in municipal politics. In the country as a whole almost 60 per cent of the mandates were still won by independent or local coalitions (Kowalczyk 2000). But it must be remembered that about two-thirds of all councillors are elected in small rural communities, and a further 30 per cent in relatively small towns (below 20,000 inhabitants). In urban local governments, however, the 1998 election was definitely dominated by political parties, which now openly used their official names. In cities with over 50,000 inhabitants (where 40 per cent of the population lives) independent candidates had almost no chance against party candidates. Elections in most big cities, moreover, were dominated by two major political blocs – the rightist Electoral Action Solidarity, which gained over 16 per cent of mandates throughout Poland, and the leftist Alliance of Democratic Left, which obtained 14 per cent of all mandates. The share of council seats won by these two blocs was much higher in large municipalities and as a consequence they won over 80 per cent of mayoral positions in all cities, frequently replacing the incumbent non-partisan or centrist mayors.

To a large extent the increased importance of party politics explains a very high turnover among urban mayors after the 1998 elections. Even for locally popular urban mayors the prospects for reelection were poor unless they were supported by one of two major parties. Only in rural municipalities did a majority of mayors (61 per cent) survive. In municipalities with over 10,000 inhabitants the majority of mayors was replaced. In cities over 40,000 over two-thirds of the incumbents were not reelected and in the largest cities (over 300,000) only one mayor 'survived' the 1998 elections. All in all turnover among mayors in 1998 was considerably higher than in 1994 (Swianiewicz 2001).

Local elections in 2002, in which mayors were directly elected, brought slightly lower turnover. Among all urban governments the rate of reelection was around 40 per cent. Although most mayors are leaders of local branches of political parties, it was not uncommon, even in big cities, that winning candidates were only loosely connected to their parties, and sometimes were running against the will of their political bosses.

Stabilizing the executive – changes in the mayor's position

It should be clear that the mayor's position before the 2002 reform was not very secure, and job security for mayors was further jeopardized by the possibility of replacement during the four-year term. At the beginning of the decade the position was especially insecure, since mayors could be replaced by means of a council resolution passed by a simple majority. This meant that mayors could lose their positions almost instantaneously as a result of a very short and emotional discussion and a subsequent rash vote of non-confidence. To strengthen administrative stability in local government, replacing mayors had to be made more difficult. Under stipulations subsequently passed, a vote of non-confidence can now only take place two weeks after its introduction and it requires the support of 75 per cent of the councillors. If a mayor wins the vote of confidence, a further vote of non-confidence cannot be proposed within the following six months. But despite these stabilizing changes, mid-term replacements of majors are not rare. In 2000, when the tenth anniversary of democratic local government was celebrated, only 12 mayors in almost 2,500 local governments had survived the whole 1990–2000 decade.

A more radical change in the mayor's position – based on the introduction of direct, popular elections – has been on the political agenda for some time. Surveys showed broad public support for this proposal, and in the spring of 2002 the change was finally approved by parliament, becoming effective as of the elections held in October 2002. Presently, the only method to recall the mayor is through the popular referendum, in which turnout needs to be higher than 30 per cent of the eligible electorate.

Local government and local service delivery

As previously noted, Polish municipalities are responsible for the provision of a wide range of municipal services. Before 1990 municipal services were provided by budgetary units and enterprises operating on the basis of public law, and such units were accountable to local branches of the state administration. In the late 1980s there were over 800 such enterprises. Some of these were organized on the basis of a specialized functional unit for a particular service, but in many cases, especially in smaller towns, services were provided by multi-branch enterprises. Hence, at the beginning of the 1990s, such multi-sector entities constituted over half of all entities in the municipal-sector, although they employed only 30 per cent of all municipal-sector employees.

After 1990, local governments were granted substantial discretion in deciding on new forms of service delivery (cf. Swianiewicz 1997). Available options included inhouse production by a municipal department, a company owned by local government, partial or full privatization, and contracting the service out to a private-sector company. Initially municipalities most often chose the form which seemed the safest – that is, inhouse production by a municipal department. But with the passage of time the alternatives chosen varied, depending to a substantial degree upon the type of services to be provided. Three categories of services can be distinguished in this regard:

- Central heating, water provision and sewage systems. These services are examples of natural monopolies and require careful regulation.
- Public transport, street cleaning, road maintenance, conservation of green areas, funeral services and distribution of bottled gas. These services are more open to market competition.
- Maintenance of municipal housing. Until recently legal regulations (including centrally regulated and very low rents) required that this sector be considered separately because these regulations made housing management unattractive for private companies. Recent reforms in this sector, however, make this activity more like those services open to market competition.

Available data suggest that local governments have been quite careful in implementing changes in those services which are natural monopolies and in the case of housing where prices were centrally regulated. Enterprises in these sectors were usually transformed into budgetary units, and privatization was only rarely selected as an option. The case of the Gdańsk sewage system, which was privatized, is a rare exception. But in services more open to market competition, by comparison, transformation was much faster and cases of privatization were much more frequent. Some services, such as bottled-gas distribution and funeral services, have now been almost entirely privatized.

It is also important to mention numerous new entities (both public and private) that entered the market for provision of municipal services after 1990. A survey conducted by Aziewicz (1994) suggests that almost half of the entities active on the municipal services market should be classified as private enterprises. Only one-fifth of these private firms was created as a result of privatization processes, while the remaining 80 per cent were newly created on the initiative of private businessmen. Another 30 per cent of all entities delivering municipal services should be classified as municipal (owned by local governments) and the remaining 20 per cent as others (state-owned, church-owned or NGOs). The role of private entities should not be overestimated however. A significant portion of these entities – 70 per cent – consists of very small firms while municipal enterprises are usually much larger.

At the beginning of the new millennium it seems that the framework for a new system of service provision has been established. Market solutions in municipal services, including the presence of private companies in the competitive market for many municipal services, are now widely accepted. But even more striking is the diversity of choices for models of service delivery selected by different municipalities. It is not difficult to find examples both of cities with a very traditional approach, based on publicly owned entities closely controlled by town hall, and of cities that have gone a long way towards privatization and contracting-out, leaving for themselves only the roles of regulating, procuring and controlling the provision of services on behalf of the local community.

Local government and the local economy

Although dealing with the condition of the local economy is not an obligatory function of municipal government, it has nonetheless been a prominent concern for municipalities. Most Polish municipalities not only conceive of themselves as service providers, but also feel responsible for the overall welfare of their community. During the last decade there has been a noteworthy change in local governments' approach to local economic development, in particular with respect to opinions on direct involvement of the local public sector in economic activity.

Before 1990 government pervaded all sectors of the Polish economy, and numerous public enterprises were dependent on local authorities. Shortly after the 1990 local government reform many local politicians saw no reason to withdraw from economic activities such as running hotels and small production firms. Proponents of continued broad involvement of local governments in economic activities advanced the following arguments (for details, see Aziewicz 1998 and Wojciechowski 1997):

- economic activity of local government would help to cope with unemployment;
- profits from such economic activities would increase the capacity to finance other important tasks; and
- local government is able to provide goods and services which are not delivered by anyone else.

The last argument was particularly relevant at the beginning of the 1990s when local government involvement was advocated because in some areas the market was very weak. Yet many others indicated the danger of unfair competition between municipal and private companies. More generally speaking, what they were suggesting was a conflict between two roles of local government – one being as entrepreneur, the other being to represent interests of the local community.

Discussion over the legal limits of local government economic activity lasted several years. In a law enacted in 1990 it was stipulated that local government would be allowed to engage in all forms of economic activity if 'the public interest would so require'. But only two years later a law was enacted restricting local government economic activity to public utility tasks. This limitation, however, was introduced without a clear definition of the term 'public utility'. The most important Polish local government association suggested that local governments' participation in profit-oriented companies should not be narrowly circumscribed; they claimed that the interpretation of the term 'public utility' should be left to individual local authorities.

In subsequent years discussion over the proper realm of local governments' business activities has lost most of its practical relevance. Together with the development of the market economy and a gradual decrease in support for direct involvement of the public sector in economic life, the willingness of local governments to directly enter into business activity has in practice decreased dramatically over the last few years. Rather, municipalities have increasingly emphasized a strategic approach to local economic development. At the beginning of the 1990s the idea of preparing a local development strategy would have been considered an exotic idea, but by 1999 about one-third of all local governments had such a document. In 80 per cent of the cities with over 100,000 inhabitants a written strategic plan was endorsed by the city council (Swianiewicz 2000). Whether such a strategy is actually implemented is of course another story. In some cases these documents are treated only as a formality, something needed only for presentations to potential donors (both domestic and international) who may offer grants for local investments. In general, however, it is fair to say that the awareness in local government of the importance of the strategic approach, as well as the readiness to implement such a strategy, has increased substantially over the last decade.

There is also an increasing understanding of the competitive environment in which cities and municipal governments operate. Some local authorities even overestimate their role and responsibility for economic development. A good example is provided by reactions to the results of a regularly published 'ranking of cities' investment attractiveness' (Swianiewicz and Dziemianowicz 1999). Even though the municipal impact on this attractiveness is very limited, local political actors treat the results of the ranking as a summary evaluation of the quality of the work of the local executive. Despite these developments, the skills of an average local official to work with local business are far from being sufficient, or at least are not seen as satisfactory by local businessman (Swianiewicz 2000).

Relations with citizens and non-government organizations

During the last decade public interest in local government and local democracy has not been very impressive. Turnout in local elections has been quite low (42 per cent in 1990, 32 per cent in 1994 and 47 per cent in 1998) and always considerably lower than in national elections. Moreover, Polish citizens do not perceive their local government as very important. In 1994 just over 40 per cent of citizens felt that local government decisions had a significant impact on their lives whereas 16 per cent saw no impact at all. Both turnout levels and the perceived salience of local government are considerably below the scores in some other countries of Central and Eastern Europe, such as the Czech Republic and Slovakia (see Swianiewicz 2001).

At the same time, the level of trust in local government is relatively high, and is, for example, substantially higher than trust in central-level political institutions (cf. Figure 7.2). Trust in local governments increased dramatically in 1990 together with local government reform, rising from about

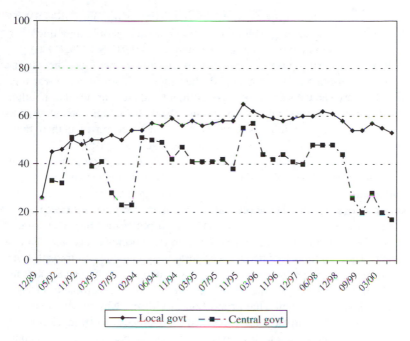

Figure 7.2   *Trust in central and local government in Poland, 1989 to 2000*

Sources: Data for 1989 are taken from Pelczynska-Nalecz (1998), while other data are from regular surveys conducted by the Centre for Public Opinion Surveys (CBOS).

25 per cent in 1989 to over 45 per cent in 1990, and has slowly grown to a level of 50–60 per cent since then. The proportion of citizens disapproving of local governments' activities, by comparison, has been relatively stable and relatively low (between 20 and 35 per cent).

In such circumstances it is not surprising that throughout most of the last decade, a majority of Polish citizens have supported further decentralization. In 1994 only 5 per cent of the respondents considered that local powers were too extensive, while almost half thought they were too narrow (Centre for Public Opinion Surveys [CBOS] 1994). A majority of the respondents also supported decentralization of responsibility for primary schools to municipal governments, the introduction of new tiers of self-government, and some other decentralization reforms. This relatively positive picture, however, is spoiled by an increasing conviction among citizens that local governments in Poland are corrupt. In a 1995 CBOS survey, for example, many people thought that corruption was mostly a problem of the central level and of the state administration (CBOS 1995). But surveys conducted in 1999 and 2000 show that people now think it is equally widespread at the local government level (CBOS 1999, 2000).

It is noteworthy that the conditions described here are not found uniformly throughout the country. Rather, there is a strong and clear relationship between the size of local government and citizens' level of involvement and trust. On each of the issues discussed above, opinions of citizens living in small communities have been much more positive than those expressed by inhabitants of large cities (Swianiewicz 2001).

Survey results also show that the vast majority of Polish mayors consider being informed about citizens' preferences, talking to people and supporting various forms of bottom-up activities to be among the most important tasks of local governments. These official claims, however, have not been consistently reflected in citizens' perception of local policy-making. The number of people who think they have no impact on local policy decisions is in fact larger than the number of people who think they can have an impact. Even so, while shifts in attitudes have been slow, changes in this respect are one of the most interesting trends to be observed in local government throughout the last decade. Thus, the proportion of citizens who believe that they can influence local matters has increased markedly, rising from 15 per cent in 1992 (Swianiewicz and Bukowski 1992) to 31 per cent in the January 2000 CBOS survey. Over the same period, the proportion of claiming 'no influence' dropped from 85 per cent in 1992 to 67 per cent in 2000.

It is important to stress in this connection that some participatory opportunities for local residents are prescribed by law. Among others these include the obligatory consultation of citizens in the case of certain local decisions, such as land-use plans. Such consultations are to take place before the final vote in the municipal council, but these consultations are merely advisory; they are not binding for the council. There are also rules to ensure public access to local council meetings.

In addition Polish law permits local referenda to be organized on certain issues. The most frequent type of such referend is about whether or not to dissolve the municipal council in mid-term and to call new local elections. For this particular type of referendum it is required that over 10 per cent of the electorate sign a petition, and at least 30 per cent of the electorate must actually vote for the results to be valid. Between 1992 and June 2000, over 200 referenda of this type were held, yet only 27 of them were successful. There is, however, a clear increase in the number of successful referenda of this type in recent years. Other local referenda usually concern one of the following issues: location of controversial infrastructural facilities such as solid-waste disposal plants, changes of geographical borders (usually division of a municipality into two or more separate local governments), and 'self-taxation' of the local population – that is, introduction of an additional local tax – in order to improve certain local services.

Until recently it was also possible to recruit up to half of the members of the council sector committees (such as the committee for education and the committee for spatial planning) from outside the council. This widely used possibility provided an opportunity to discuss many important issues in a relatively open forum. Even so, two major arguments were advanced against this practice: (1) outside members did not have an electoral mandate to legitimize their position of influence; and (2) participation of outsiders increased the size of representative bodies. In order to improve decision-making processes and reduce the cost of local government operations, participation of outside members was therefore recently abolished. The number of councillors was also reduced for much the same reasons.

Most local politicians in Poland who are concerned about communication with the public concentrate almost exclusively on government policies to inform citizens, not on ways to improve the flow of information in the opposite direction. Nevertheless an increasing number of local governments have recently been trying to improve their communication with the public. Several examples of such innovative approaches are provided in the report summarizing relevant experiences of municipalities involved in the experimental USAID Local Government Partnership Programme conducted from 1996 to 2000 (Wiktorowska 2000). The experimental techniques introduced included website information for citizens and local businessman, introduction of regular meetings of councillors and mayors with neighbourhood and occupational groups, special telephone lines to executive board members, surveys of citizens opinions, survey consultations of budget proposals and programmes of local investments, and mail boxes placed in the town hall and other central places around the town.

Another noteworthy development is the increasing cooperation of municipalities and local NGOs. Before 1990 the number of NGOs in Poland and the scope of their activities was extremely limited, but this sector has expanded dramatically in the 1990s. Cooperation with NGOs in providing many vital services (mostly in social services area) has clearly been a new trend in many municipalities in recent years. Between 1993 and 1996 the proportion of NGOs in Poland receiving support from local governments increased from 16 to 29 per cent (Regulski 2000). An increasing number of politicians are aware that many tasks may be provided by NGOs better and cheaper than by local government inhouse service-delivery units. Despite a very clear trend, however, good cooperation with NGOs still remains more of an innovative approach rather than a rule typical of most local governments.

Internationalization of local government

Much as in other countries, local governments in Poland increasingly operate in an international context. In Poland this internationalization is essentially a phenomenon of the last decade. Previously, internationalization was very limited due both to a weak local government system, and to an ideologically motivated restraint on international contacts. At least four developments in recent years merit mention:

- There is an increasing number of direct contacts between local governments across national borders. This is true both in terms of international travel by local government officials and through formal twinning arrangements with local government in other countries (cf. Baldersheim and Swianiewicz 2002). Another form of direct international contact is provided by 13 Euroregions in which Polish municipalities cooperate with their counterparts in Sweden, Denmark, Germany, the Czech Republic, Slovakia, Hungary, Romania, Ukraine, Byelorussia, Russia, Lithuania and Latvia. Many of these Euroregional activities are subsidized by European Union programmes.
- A distinct form of international contact is the result of technical assistance programmes run by foreign donors in Poland throughout the last decade. In a 1997 survey, 15 per cent of the mayors reported that they had used the assistance of foreign experts at least once. In the same survey half of the mayors agreed that experts' work had been useful for the development of their municipality. The largest programmes have been financed by the European Union (mostly through the PHARE programme), but also by individual governments (American USAID and the British Know-How Fund being the largest).

The other two developments relate to the impact of European integration on local governments in Poland. This impact is twofold and may be characterized as both a 'carrot' and a 'stick':

- *The carrot.* European integration increasingly provides for opportunities to apply for European funds targeted at local development and infrastructure. This is not only an opportunity to accelerate development, but also an occasion to learn and to implement new techniques of project preparation and evaluation. Many of the European Union and the World Bank programmes formally require analysis of how investments impact on social and economic life, something which was never undertaken by Polish local governments previously. Initially local staff used to learn new skills only in order to prepare better applications for foreign institutions, but presently more and more local governments also try to employ these skills in their own investment planning.

- *The stick*. Although there is no separate section of European law related to local governments, many EU regulations pertain to local government procedures and standards of local service provision. Polish local governments are increasingly aware of obligations arising from the necessity to meet European standards in environmental protection, employment practices and so forth. It has an impact not only on their investment programmes but also on management practice.

Conclusion – from local government to local governance?

During the last decade Polish local government has been characterized by changes and discontinuities rather than continuities. The main reason for this is the establishment of a previously unknown system of local self-government. But apart from these very important institutional changes, it is reasonable to ask if there has also been a more subtle change in the style of local management and government? Has there been a Polish equivalent of a shift from local government to local governance and the rise of new public management that is currently so widely discussed in many Western democracies?

Most Polish local governments would probably feel attracted to a broad definition of their role as guardians of the overall well-being of their communities, an idea implicit in the notion of governance. This is quite evident from the results of surveys among local officials and by changes in the scope of local government activities and interests. On the other hand, the relatively weak skills and willingness to enter into comprehensive cooperation with the private sector, NGOs or neighbourhood groups mean that most local authorities remain within a more traditional paradigm of local government.

Ideas of New Public Management have been quite widely discussed by Polish local politicians and top executive staff. It is telling that Osborne and Gaebler's (1992) book *Reinventing Government* was translated into Polish by the one of the former top executives of the city of Gdańsk. It is also characteristic that one of the well-known progressive local politicians – the former deputy mayor of the city of Krakow – has been promoting the idea that managing a city is identical to the management of a large private company in lectures delivered throughout Poland.

Any generalization based on this evidence, however, would be an over-simplification. There is enormous and probably increasing variation found among local governments in Poland, and in recent years the distance between innovators and laggards has tended to increase. The number of innovators has been quite limited, although for obvious reasons they have been much more visible and their activity has been widely publicized. These variations present themselves in at least two ways. First, there are obvious differences in local management styles *between* municipalities. Some municipalities are managed in ways that are clearly reminiscent of features found within New Public Management and other related ideas, but many other municipalities have concentrated their focus on a traditional model of public provision of public services. The former type is more frequent among mid-sized and large cities, although occasional examples of innovations might also be found in small towns and rural local governments. Second, there are also major variations *within* many local governments. These variations refer to the large gap existing between the vanguards – a relatively small group of top innovators – on the one hand, and the rest of the municipal politicians and administrative staff on the other hand. In some small municipalities this is simply a gap between one innovative mayor and the rest of the staff, which lags behind.

It is difficult to assess to what extent new ideas and new tendencies have been inspired by foreign consultants and by other forms of international contacts. It is not difficult, however, to predict that the progress of European integration will continue to strengthen innovative tendencies within Polish local government in the future.

8 Germany: A new type of local government?

Oscar W. Gabriel and Susanne Eisenmann

At the beginning of the 1990s, a mood of reform spread over the debate regarding the future development of local government in Germany. Seeking to optimize the goals of citizen participation, responsiveness, innovation and efficiency, local political leaders initiated large-scale reforms of the existing local government structures. These goals have in particular been pursued by introducing so-called New Public Management measures and by increasing citizen participation in the local political process. In part these innovations were facilitated by the need to establish a democratic system of local government in East Germany, in part they have resulted from the trend towards an increasingly internationalized system of governance that has also permeated the local level. Political innovation has also been promoted by political and administrative leaders who have felt that existing structures no longer met the standards of modern local government.

The focus of this chapter is on two main topics of discourse concerning the reform of local government in Germany:

- the reform of local political institutions and processes, particularly the implementation of New Public Management measures and e-government; and
- the impact of new types of institutionalized and non-institutionalized citizen participation on the existing system of local government.

In the first part of the chapter we provide a short summary of the administrative and political structures of local government in Germany before and after the reforms of the 1990s. We then turn to the practice of local politics and government. Particular attention is given to the efforts to implement two leading principles of the reform movement – namely enhancing administrative efficiency and broadening citizen participation. In concluding we assess to what extent goals set by the reformers have been achieved so far.

Local government in the German federal system

Administrative organization

Irrespective of fundamental changes in the environment of the political system, the territorial organization of the German State and the functions allocated to various tiers of the political system have remained basically unchanged since the late nineteenth century. Similar to other federal systems, state authority and related political functions have traditionally been attributed to the federal (*Reich, Bund*) and state levels (*Länder*). Local government as a third administrative and political tier consists of local municipalities, counties, county-free (larger) cities, associations of small villages and various kinds of special purpose units (*kommunale Zweckverbände*) (cf. Gunlicks 1986: 32ff).

After German reunification in 1990, the highly centralized administrative system of the former GDR was replaced by the West German model of federalism and local self-government. Since then, Germany has consisted of 16 states (*Länder*) with strongly varying population sizes, social structures and levels of economic development. Hamburg and Bremen have a double status as both state and local government, the same as has applied to Berlin since 1946. In total, the local tier consists of 323 counties, 116 county-free cities and 14,199 municipalities with a large share of small rural villages in East Germany and a predominance of medium-sized cities in the Western part of the country (see Laux 1999: 181; and Table 8.1). The difference in

Table 8.1 *Distribution of local governments in East and West Germany by size of municipality, 1999*

Population size	West Germany		East Germany		Total	
	N	Per cent	N	Per cent	N	Per cent
Less than 500	1,530	18.0	2,351	41.4	3,881	27.3
500 to 1,000	1,309	15.4	1,326	23.3	2,635	16.7
1,000 to 2,000	1,539	18.1	830	14.6	2,369	16.7
2,000 to 5,000	1,785	21.0	750	13.2	2,535	17.9
5,000 to 10,000	1,042	12.2	207	3.6	1,249	8.8
10,000 to 20,000	744	8.7	115	2.0	859	6.0
20,000 to 50,000	401	4.7	81	1.4	482	3.4
50,000 to 100,000	93	0.2	14	1.1	107	0.8
100,000 to 200,000	39	0.5	4	0.1	43	0.3
200,000 to 500,000	20	0.2	7	0.1	27	0.2
More than 500,000	12	0.1	0	0.0	12	0.1
Total	8,514	100.0	5,685	100.0	14,199	100.0

Source: Data from Statistisches Jahrbuch deutscher Gemeinden (1999: 102f.).

size is a result of the varying strategies of territorial reform pursued by the West German *Land* governments in the 1970s on the one hand and the legacy of the GDR on the other hand. Each of these local authorities represents a particular type of public administration, guided by bureaucratic as well as democratic standards and exercising considerable discretion in performing their functions. This especially applies to the county-free cities that are endowed with the whole range of competencies attributed to municipalities and counties elsewhere.

Contrary to many other Western democracies, in Germany there has been no perceived need to decentralize administrative structures and, consequently, to transfer state responsibilities to the local level. The reason for this is that the notion of subsidiarity has long served as a guiding principle for handling public affairs in Germany. Insofar as state and federal authorities are not explicitly entitled to deal with a particular political matter, local authorities are seen to be the relevant agencies. However, real political life does not fit neatly into this ideal picture, since a complicated system of joint-planning, financing and legislation of federal, state and local authorities (*Politikverflechtung*) has developed over the years (see Scharpf *et al.* 1976; Zintl 1999).

The tasks of a local government and how they are financed

A complicated pattern of policy-making competencies corresponds to the territorial organization found in Germany. Although each of the existing tiers is endowed with legislative and administrative powers, the federal government exercises primary *legislative* authority, while *implementing* federal laws within a relatively wide margin of discretion constitutes the most important function for the *Länder* and local governments. From a policy perspective, the responsibilities shared by the federal, state and local authorities may be grouped into three broad categories: planning, service delivery and regulation. Local government institutions exercise a broad scope of competencies in such policy areas as social services, land planning and energy supply (see Gunlicks 1986: 84ff).

The range of functions actually performed differs from one local authority to another depending on the actual needs of the local community, on its spatial, economic and social characteristics, its historical traditions, and on the political and administrative leaders' views of what is necessary. The involvement of private associations, clubs or enterprises in social or cultural affairs may also relieve a local authority of some of its tasks. Spurred by enduring fiscal stress and recent efforts to revitalize the idea of a 'civic community', such a transfer of responsibilities from the public sector to

voluntary associations and neighbourhood groups has in fact been consciously pushed by political leaders at various levels of the political system.
A similar, but nevertheless not identical, approach consists in transferring
some service functions, such as sewage collection, energy and water supply,
to private enterprises.

Local authorities do not have complete freedom in performing their tasks
however. Some tasks are mandatory functions assigned to local authorities
by state legislation, while others are voluntary and can be pursued almost
entirely free from state influence and supervision. Some of the most important mandatory tasks are as follows:

- general education,
- welfare for the young, including the provision of kindergarten places
  for every child older than three years of age,
- subsidized housing construction,
- construction and maintenance of local roads,
- sewage disposal, and
- maintenance of a fire brigade.

Whereas mandatory duties are the result of special legal obligations
imposed by state authorities, voluntary tasks are based on a general provision of the German Basic Law which endows local communities with the
right to plan and regulate all local matters not explicitly exempted from
their jurisdiction. The following are examples of voluntary tasks:

- building and promoting athletic and leisure facilities,
- financial support for cultural amenities,
- care for the elderly, including provision of leisure time amenities, and
- public utilities run by local authorities.

The large number of mandatory tasks enumerated above does not come by
chance. Rather, it reflects a secular trend in the development of a modern
welfare state in which the principle of equal access to public services is
strongly emphasized. At present a far larger part of local activity consists in
performing duties set by state laws. The impact of this development on
local autonomy has been strongly criticized by local representatives.

Restrictions on local authorities in the performance of their tasks are not
solely a matter of the attribution of competencies however; in addition
financial resources necessary to perform these tasks are strongly dependent
on factors beyond the control of local decision-makers. General principles
regarding the distribution of public revenues are laid down in the German

Basic Law. In order to equalize great variation in local economic resources, particularly between West and East Germany and, to a lesser degree, between south and north German states, the Constitution provides for a mixed system of local finance. This system is comprised of taxes levied by the local authority itself – primarily property taxes (*Grundsteuer*) and trade or sales taxes (*Gewerbesteuer*) – and the participation of local political authorities in 'tax associations' in which local authorities share income and value-added taxes and receive allocations from the Land's share of the taxes apportioned between the states and the federal government. Local authorities also obtain funds from several other types of resources, including state grants and fees.

In terms of local autonomy and performance, local taxes are a cornerstone, particularly insofar as local authorities may set the tax rate. In the 1990s, however, taxes amounted to no more than a third of total local revenue, with almost half of this accounted for by local income taxes. And although the share accounted for by income taxes has risen by 10 per cent from 1970 to 1995, the share of genuine, freely set local taxes – sales and property taxes – has dropped. Moreover, the share of total tax revenue accounted for by local taxes declined during the same period (Karrenberg and Münstermann 1999).

At present two developments are regarded as constituting a threat to local autonomy. The first is the huge gap between West and East Germany, particularly regarding the low tax share of East German local authorities, which makes them strongly dependent on subsidies from state grants and transfers financed by West German states and local communities. The second threat is a decline in genuine, freely-set local revenues and local participation in an opaque system of revenues jointly accessible to federal, state and local authorities. Not only are local authorities strongly dependent on decisions on local revenues made at the federal and state level, the system of grants has become so complicated that local administrators, not to speak of politicians, sometimes do not even know what types of special grants are available to them.

Faced with an overload of responsibilities and limited financial resources, over the last few years local authorities have developed several strategies in order to maintain or increase their discretion in performing various tasks. The simplest, but not most satisfying, strategy consists in reducing or even cancelling the delivery of local services. More frequently, however, local authorities have decided to establish a variety of public–private partnerships (PPP). The models employed include the following:

- Outsourcing tasks that do not necessarily need to be performed by the public sector and providing private agencies with a high degree of discretion in terms of the production and delivery of services.

- Retaining responsibility for service production and delivery in the public sector, but transferring parts or the entire package to private enterprises acting under the direction and control of local authorities.
- Establishing systems of cooperation between public and private agencies which in part are formally regulated with respect to the specific tasks to be performed by the respective partners.
- Establishing arrangements for leasing and facility management, with public authorities acting as customers in competitive markets.

The policy areas in which systems of PPP are found are as diverse as the formal arrangements described above: urban planning, water and energy supply, sewage disposal as well as social and cultural services are all policies implemented cooperatively by public and private agencies with great variety in the division of labour (see Heinz 1999).

The structure of local self-government before reunification

Since the German Basic Law contains only a few general rules on local politics and government, more detailed provisions are traditionally laid down in the state constitutions and municipal charters. Up to the time of German reunification in 1990, a rich variety of institutional arrangements was found, mostly reflecting well-established regional traditions going back to the nineteenth century (for details see Gunlicks 1986: 5ff.). The existing types could nevertheless be grouped into four basic categories – the South and the North German Council Constitutions, the Magistrate Constitution and the Mayor Constitution respectively (Gunlicks 1986: 67ff.).

Irrespective of the particular provisions of the community charters, the differentiation of political and administrative functions followed roughly the same pattern. The council acted as a legislative body endowed with the right to decide on all key political issues, including the budget, local regulations, the scope of services, planning, and so on. The other important institution was the administration led by a mayor in some states and a city manager in others. The administration was in charge of preparing and implementing the decisions of the council as well as performing the functions delegated to local government by federal and state authorities.

Apart from this basic division of labour, the interplay between the council and the administration differed considerably between the various local regimes. Grauhan (1969) described the basic difference between various types of government as that between 'legislative' (north German council type) versus 'executive' leadership (south German council and mayoral types), while the magistrate type did not neatly fit into these categories. The notion of executive leadership serves to describe a strong predominance of the local administration, particularly the mayor, in the decision-making system. This pattern was even more marked in the council than in the mayoral type. The north German council type, by comparison, was characterized by an extraordinarily strong position of the city council which exercised a final say in all matters, even those regarding local administration. A comparative empirical study of four middle-sized cities conducted by Derlien and associates (1976) demonstrated that the difference in the distribution of power not only existed in the written constitution, but also in political reality.

The structure of local self-government after reunification

The new constitutional framework

Demands for a standardization of municipal charters had been placed on the political agenda several times in modern German history, but prior to reunification in 1990 ensconced regional traditions served as a bulwark against fundamental change. Even so, the efficiency and responsiveness of local government have long been debated in political as well as academic circles. A strong preference for one of the alternative types did not initially exist. Supporters of the north German model emphasized the democratic achievements of the system, particularly the broad dispersion of power among political and administrative institutions and actors and the strong position of the council and its committees in the local political process. The south German model, by comparison, was mainly praised for its emphasis on strong leadership, which was seen as producing coherent and efficient local policies, particularly in the fields of budgeting and planning (Banner 1989). The assumed strengths and weaknesses of the models, however, were never systematically validated by empirical research.

The strong preference of some leading executives of the German Association of Cities for the south German council model eventually led to a 'victorious advance of the Plebiscitary Mayoral System' (Bovenschulte and Buss 1996) immediately after German reunification. The basic elements of this model were implemented in almost all other German states. With the exception of Hessen, the new model now prevails in all the German states either as a pure type or with some minor modifications.

It approximates the traditional system of Baden-Wuerttemberg and exhibits the following characteristics (see Figure 8.1):

● A directly elected mayor acts as a representative of the municipality and chairman of the local council as well as of council committees. In addition, the mayor is a chief executive officer responsible for the implementation of federal and state policies delegated to local authorities. This broad range of competencies forms a genuine, not delegated, domain of mayoral responsibility and can only be modified by a revision of the community charter. As head of the council, the mayor prepares the council's agenda and chairs the council meetings. As chief executive officer, he is in charge of implementing the council's decisions on all relevant local policy matters. With the exception of Hessen, where the magistrate is still the leading administrative agency, but

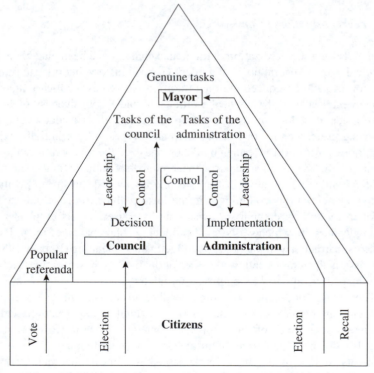

Figure 8.1   *The German plebiscitary mayoral system of local government*

Source: Knemeyer (1999: 117). Translation by the authors. Reproduced by permission from Leske & Budrich, Oppladen.

headed by a popularly elected mayor, introducing elements of collective leadership does not disperse administrative power.

- The city council is elected according to a system of proportional representation and is endowed with the formal right to decide on all basic self-government affairs, including the budget, planning, regulation, type and scope of services, and so on. Moreover, the council exercises control over the administration, including the mayor.
- As implied in the principle of popular sovereignty, citizens are another important force in the political game. Not only do they have the power to elect the council and the mayor, but in most *Länder* they may also call for popular referenda.

Irrespective of these broad common characteristics, some differences between the municipal charters have persisted. Among those are the length of the electoral terms of the council and the mayor, the possibility of recalling elected representatives, the type of electoral systems, the internal organization of the administration and the council, and the formal requirements and restrictions applying to initiatives and referenda.

The impact on political practice

If the analysis is shifted from formal institutional arrangements to the 'real' processes of interest articulation, aggregation, policy-making and policy implementation, the variety of local political life becomes more apparent. Although most empirical studies about the distribution of influence in the local decision-making process are outdated and do not refer to the situation after unification, they nevertheless point to a gap between formal institutional arrangements and real local political life. Most importantly, local government in Germany cannot be adequately described unless the strong position of political parties is considered. At least in most medium-sized and big German cities, politics is characterized by party competition, coalition building, bargaining between top political and administrative leaders, and in some instances other relevant sectors of the local society, such as voluntary associations and the business community. Local councils and administrations controlled by a broad, coherent and long-persisting party coalition or even a strong majority party will act in a different way than unstable and shifting majorities in the council and a fragmented political-administrative elite or a leadership coalition including only a small segment of the local political community. Whether a consensual or a conflictive style of interaction prevails between the various segments of the local elite may also be more important for local political life than formal institutional arrangements.

Other elements shaping the local political process are the prevailing mass culture and the type and level of political activity. Apart from political authorities and actors in a narrower sense, such actors as social notables, economic leaders or activists in the voluntary sector may play an important role in setting the local agenda and making or blocking local decisions, and certainly the same applies to the local mass media. Moreover, people and institutions who are influential in a particular domain are not necessarily so in another (see Walter-Rogg 2002).

Evaluation of the reform

The question of whether and how far the reform has contributed to more efficient and open local government cannot be definitively answered. One result, however, is quite obvious: formal political power has shifted from the municipal council to the local administration and the citizenry as a whole. A directly elected mayor not only enjoys a basis of legitimacy of his or her own, but in many respects has also become largely independent of the majority parties in the council. Although proposals submitted by the administration will not automatically be approved by a majority of councillors, the power of the political branch of local government has decreased considerably. Finally, if a deadlock between the political and the administrative leader of a community was a weakness of the 'old' north German council model, a similar – and possibly more severe – deadlock may arise in the new system. In some instances, for example, the majority party in the council will not support a popularly elected mayor belonging to one of the minority parties. Under these circumstances there is a need for permanent consensus building. Such a situation will not necessarily produce serious problems if party loyalty does not matter greatly in the political process and if a consensual style of policy-making prevails in a community. However, if a strong polarization along party lines is typical and controversial political issues are at stake, finding efficient decisions on local policies in the new system can be an extremely difficult task. The situation in the city of Frankfurt is a good illustration of the respective shortcomings. After her electoral victory in autumn 2000, Lord Mayor Petra Roth (CDU) experienced substantial problems in building a party coalition in the city council, and decisions on important issues proved difficult.

The position of the council in the local political system has been weakened in another respect as well. The institutionalization of initiatives and referenda as instruments of direct citizen participation in the decision-making process implies a redistribution of legislative and agenda setting power between the council and the citizenry as a whole. Issues that can be decided by the voters directly are no longer under the exclusive legislation of the elected representatives, and roughly the same applies to initiatives. Although the capacity of actors outside the council to place political issues on the local agenda does not completely undermine the agenda-setting function of the elected representatives, their gatekeeping role in a decisive phase of the policy-making process has been undermined by the new institutional arrangements.

Modernization of administration and increased citizen participation – new solutions to actual problems?

In the eyes of many, a more efficient and responsible system of local government cannot be achieved simply by constitutional reform. Further steps need to be taken to modernize local government. In Germany, New Public Management and citizen participation have become magic words in this respect.

New Public Management

As the environment of the local administration has changed considerably in recent years, the gatekeeping structure and performance of the traditional bureaucratic system have increasingly been challenged as failing to meet the requirements of an efficient and service-oriented form of modern local government. Regarding local administration, the focus of the debate has been on redefining the scope and type of local services, the principles underlying the interaction between the administrative and political branches of local government and the citizens, and, finally, the optimization of resource allocation and management techniques. On the political side, improving citizen participation in the decision-making process and strengthening the role of the local council are the main goals. The concept of 'New Public Management' is the term under which various attempts to modernize local government have been subsumed (for details, see Bogumil 2001: 168ff; Stucke and Schöneich 1999; and Weiss 2002).

Notwithstanding the rich variety of the models to be found under the label New Public Management, the general thrust underlying the quest for a reform of local government in the German case can easily be singled out and summarized as follows:

- *Orientation towards clients.* The main function of the local administration is no longer seen as implementing given rules, but as reacting in a flexible and efficient way to the changing needs of clients. Consequently, services most frequently demanded by citizens have become bundled in a single agency (*Bürgeramt*) equipped with staff disposing not only of administrative, but also of social skills.
- *Efficiency.* The New Public Management philosophy argues that local performance can be substantially improved by switching from an input to an output-oriented way of producing public goods. This presupposes a precise definition of the number, quality and costs of the goods to be produced by each and every local administrative unit, and the resources needed in order to produce them in an effective way. The entire set of specific products is integrated into a 'product catalogue' serving as a basis of political control of the administration. In addition to being responsible for the delivery of such a 'product' – as has always been the task of public administrations – administrative units are expected to manage the monetary, organizational and human resources allocated to them in an autonomous and efficient way. Consequently, not only the quantity and quality of the products are subjected to political scrutiny, but so also are the resources needed to produce the respective services. Management tools like cost-benefit analysis, contract management and motivational training of the staff are all intended to contribute to the goal of improving administrative efficiency.
- *Decentralization.* Production and delivery of local public services are decentralized as far as possible in a functional as well as territorial sense. Decentralization refers to both resources and products. If public goods can be provided more efficiently by private enterprises, privatization or establishing systems of public–private partnership are regarded as appropriate.
- *Benchmarking.* The new administrative system is not only aimed at contributing to a more transparent and efficient performance of local government tasks, it is also conceived as a basis of institutionalizing benchmarking and best-practice mechanisms. These practices are developed in order to evaluate how efficiently various local tasks are performed by various units of a particular local administration as well as by different municipalities as a whole.
- *Functional differentiation between politics and administration.* Ironically, New Public Management reinvents the functional separation of politics and administration which was regarded as a major shortcoming

of the north German council model and eventually led to its abolition. Since the highly decentralized administrative system stipulates a strong need for integrating, coordinating and controlling the decentralized units, the decision-making and steering system needs to be rearranged. Specification of contracting goals, management by objectives, and exercising general political control of decentralized administrative units are now considered as the prime means available to political decision-makers in steering the administration. The council, moreover, also allocates financial resources needed for the production of services. The administration, on the other hand, works as the implementing agency in charge of carrying out daily administrative routines within the broad framework of goals set by the council. These goals are contracted with the administration and provide the basis for the specification of the products to be supplied by the departments.

For the local council this new division of labour implies a need to confine itself to the making of so-called strategic decisions and to coordinating and controlling the various activities of the administrative agencies. This applies to both the products and the management of resources. Intervention in the conduct of the daily administrative business is no longer seen as an activity of the political branch of the local system. It should be noted, however, that the local council's influence is, at least theoretically, operative in all stages of the budget-making process: planning, deciding, implementing and controlling. The basic aim of this new distribution of competencies is to increase the transparency, efficiency and accountability of local policy-making. By using managerial tools and by granting a broader discretion to the administrative staff, the intent is to improve the competence of the staff. More generally, the objective is that personal, organizational and financial resources should be used more flexibly and efficiently.

German experience with New Public Management

The implementation and success of NPM strategies can be illustrated by the cities of Essen, Stuttgart and Frankfurt am Main, all of which belong to the frontrunners in the development of New Public Management strategies (cf. Berger Roland & Partner GmbH 1998, 1999 and 2000). The NPM system developed in Essen, for example, is based on the organizational and managerial principles of a business enterprise. Its basic aim is the development of a standard 'corporate' planning system, characterized by broad targets considered as binding for all the activities of the local agencies (council and administration). This planning system is intended to enable the administrative management unit – which is comparable to the management board of a corporation – to concentrate exclusively on the task of strategic management. Operative activities in performing daily tasks are left entirely to the subordinate administrative departments. The top administration is thus solely concerned with setting benchmarks and targets, whereas the departments can devote themselves to acting within the broader framework of goals set by the management unit.

The main problem of this approach lies in the basic assumption that local authorities can be equated to a business corporation and that consequently not only the organization as a whole, but also the distribution of competencies and responsibilities among various administrative branches and processes of implementation of local government tasks should be designed according to the model of a business corporation. Due to this overemphasis on the principles of business management, the role played by the local councils and its relevant subsystems is largely neglected.

Neither Stuttgart nor Frankfurt has gone so far as Essen in redistributing the competencies between the administrative and the political branches of local government. In Stuttgart both the local council and the top administrative leaders are involved in a complex process of negotiating the basic goals and benchmarks of city policies. Besides strongly decentralizing the local administrative structure and strengthening the policy-making function of the decentralized administrative units by increasing their discretion in resource management and service delivery, a reporting system has been established in order to integrate and make transparent the activities of various parts of the administration. When combined with the introduction of product oriented cost and result accounting, the foundation for encompassing and continuous political control over day-to-day local government affairs is created.

The focus of the approach to NPM chosen in Frankfurt am Main has almost exclusively been on the development of a comprehensive catalogue of products based on the evaluation of costs and performance. Since the end of the 1990s, the main issues in the implementation of a product-oriented budget are to provide the basis for defining a broad range of rather general administrative goals on the one hand, and a related set of specific sub-goals or products derived from the broader goals on the other hand. As in the case of Stuttgart, these goals are defined and specified jointly by political and administrative bodies during the process of budget-making. Budget decisions made exclusively by the council as a whole, as well as budget-related motions placed on the agenda by one of the parties represented in the council, are to become a thing of the past. In the new system, basic

Table 8.2 *Implementation of elements of New Public Management in three German cities*

Elements of NPM	Essen	Stuttgart	Frankfurt
Catalogue of products	No	Yes	Yes
Contract between administration and council	Yes	Yes	No
Budgetary responsibility of administrative units	Yes	Yes	Yes
Controlling system	No	No	No
Reporting system	No	Yes	No
Broad scale implementation in practice	No	No	No

Source: Data from Berger, R. and Partner GmbH (1998, 1999, 2000).

decisions on the budget as well as the implementation of the budget in administrative practice are left largely to the local administration, which can act with a high degree of autonomy.

As shown in Table 8.2, the allocation of responsibility for an efficient budget management is the only common element of the NPM systems developed for the three German cities discussed here. On the other hand, workable concepts of control are generally missing, and steps towards the implementation of the complete model have not yet been made in the three cities. Stuttgart has developed the most complete concept, while Frankfurt and Essen have not only chosen different approaches, but have also opted for partial solutions.

Political participation and civil society

Modernizing public administration is by no means the only approach to the reform of local government. Traditionally, local government has been regarded as the place where direct citizen participation in the political process may be organized most efficiently and hence where the ideal of an open and responsive government may be more readily achieved. Giving people more say in local affairs is not only conducive to the quality of local democracy, but may spill over into the political system as a whole.

For a long time, participation was equated to casting one's ballot on election day and to carrying out activities related to political parties and campaigns. Up to the mid-1970s, participation in local elections was very high in Germany. Since then, however, electoral turnout has declined in most municipalities. Another type of participation that has also traditionally been widespread and remains so today is membership in voluntary associations. Almost 50 per cent of all German citizens report such memberships, and a considerable part takes an active role within these groups (Anheier *et al.* 2000). In recent decades, however, the repertory of political action has broadened considerably. In particular a variety of so-called unconventional activities such as joining a demonstration, signing a petition or taking part in a citizen action group have become more common. As shown by Kaase (1990), activities of this type are mainly addressed to local institutions and actors.

Influenced by the successful democratic revolution in the former GDR, the municipal charters of almost all states were changed in the 1990s in order to give citizens a stronger position in the local political process. Baden-Wuerttemberg is the only exception, since all forms of institutionalized participation have been available there since 1956. A similarly positive stance on the notion of active citizenry has also been evident in public discourse. Under the heading of *Bürgergemeinde* (community of citizens), a large-scale programme sponsored by the Bertelsmann Foundation has aimed to encourage the concept of active citizenship and to induce local decision-makers to acknowledge citizen participation as an important resource in local politics. Similar initiatives have been taken by the governments of some German *Länder* in order to vitalize the idea of the active community. The following formal and informal activities are examples of the types of participation currently available to the German public (see Wollmann 1999):

- Apart from the municipal councils, the mayors in all German states are elected by popular vote. Moreover, the possibility to cast preferential votes for candidates listed on the party tickets further strengthens the voter's position in the electoral process. In all but two German states (Bavaria and Baden-Wuerttemberg), recalling elected mayors is also a legal right of the citizenry or the council.
- Initiatives and referenda on selected local issues have been institutionalised in all municipal charters. Although the formal requirements vary from one state to another, this option has considerably increased citizen influence in policy-making, at least potentially.
- A large number of consultative institutions have been created. Citizen assemblies, the right to submit proposals on various policies to decision-making bodies, and council hearings are typical examples in this regard.
- A dense network of participatory institutions beyond the formal stipulation of municipal charters and electoral law has emerged in many

municipalities. Roundtables and panels, workshops, planning groups and citizen surveys are integrated parts of local planning and decision-making in many local municipalities, particularly under the heading of Agenda 21.

- An important component of e-government – e-participation – has also been placed on the political agenda. While electronic voting, initiatives and referenda have so far only been practised experimentally and with limited success in some peripheral fields of local government, informal types of e-participation are more widespread.

- Finally, traditional forms of political participation, such as working in a political party or voluntary association, becoming active in a local planning process, have by no means faded away. On the contrary, informal engagement in social activities seems to have blossomed anew during the last few years.

The real motivation for opening the political system to broader citizen participation is not completely clear. Some proponents of participatory democracy hoped that a larger number of citizens would be mobilized, that people who kept their distance from politics would benefit from the new possibilities, that the distance between the governing and the governed would diminish and that necessary political innovation would be more easily accomplished. But as the empirical data show, none of these hopes has to date been fulfilled. Only a minority of citizens engage in forms of political participation beyond voting. It nevertheless deserves mentioning that evidence suggests that a relatively large group of people are willing to become politically active if needed (see Gabriel 2002).

Statistical data on the use of citizen initiatives and referenda provide some additional insight into the reality of direct democracy. These statistics demonstrate that, so far, direct democracy plays a minor role in local political life. In Baden-Wuerttemberg, for example, where institutions of direct democracy have existed since 1956, only 273 initiatives and 139 referenda have been induced by the citizens in a total of 1,120 municipalities. Even in Bavaria, where the instruments of direct democracy are most broadly used, the number of initiatives (623) and referenda (398) held so far is by no means impressive. Contrary to the expectation of some theorists, in short, broad mobilization of people belonging to the inactive stratum of the political community has not been achieved so far. Just as before, well-to-do and well-integrated citizens constitute the core of political activists for all types of activity going beyond voting. Hence, opening new channels of influence has to date increased the power of the already active, but has not contributed to mobilizing the apathetic (Gabriel 2002).

Internationalization and local democracy in Germany

As a consequence of increasing internationalization of social, economic and political life, a new type of 'multi-level government' has evolved in many countries. In addition to national, federal and local actors and institutions, supra-national organizations and actors are now often important participants in the political game. The European Union is of course the most prominent example of this development in most European nations, since many regulatory competencies formerly attributed to the national political systems have now been transferred to European institutions (see Schmidt 1999).

Multi-level government is by no means a new phenomenon in Germany. As described by the term *Politikverflechtung* (Scharpf *et al.* 1976), a close network of policy-making among federal, state and local agencies has existed for many years. In this arrangement, lawmaking is essentially the task of the federal institutions, while states and municipalities are in charge of implementing public policies. However, international systems of multi-level government are in many respects different from the traditional type of *Politikverflechtung*. Most importantly, the inclusion of a new international actor – the EU – has undermined the traditional concept of sovereignty and fundamentally altered the character of interaction between local, state and federal agencies.

For German local government these developments have had some important implications. Compared to most other member states of the EU, the position of local government in Germany is particularly strong in terms of local autonomy. As Goldsmith (1995) has pointed out, autonomy has a twofold meaning. On the one hand autonomy can be understood in the *legal sense* as a high, constitutionally granted, degree of discretion in the fulfilment of local tasks – including the raising of necessary financial resources. On the other hand autonomy in the *political sense* is broader and refers to the capability of local agencies to influence the conduct of state and national policies that are relevant to local political life. While the legal status of local government has not been strongly changed by the process of Europeanization, political autonomy clearly has. This is because associations of German cities, municipalities and counties have enjoyed legally guaranteed access to the policy-making process in federal politics, something which is not to the same degree given at the European level. Hence, the influence of local authorities in the European policy-making process is markedly diminished compared to the traditional system of *Politikverflechtung*.

This decline of influence in supra-local regulations, which is strongly relevant to local policy-making, is reinforced by another difference between the political institutions and processes of the EU on the one hand, and the traditional pattern of German politics on the other. The system of interest intermediation, particularly the strong position of political parties in the political system, has provided multiple points of access for local political actors when they tried to exercise influence on state and national politics. Such a system of interest intermediation, which proved to be very effective in the transmission of local demands into the national political system, is simply lacking at the European level. In large measure the same applies to patterns of representation of local constituencies and party branches at the national and the European level. Regarded from this point of view, the intensification of European integration has been accompanied by a considerable loss of local political autonomy and a diminishing quality of local democracy.

Conclusion

Due to internal changes as well as to challenges arising in its environment, local government in Germany has recently passed through a period of fundamental change. Relevant keywords are German unification, globalization and economic integration, and the modernization of German society with related changes in citizen attitudes towards political institutions, actors and public services.

Political elites have reacted to these challenges by implementing a reform of the municipal charter aimed at increasing administrative efficiency as well as the quality of local democracy. Reallocating the distribution of influence in the triangle formed by citizens, political and administrative leaders respectively was regarded as a first step in the reform process. This was followed by the introduction of New Public Management strategies and new communication technologies. To avoid a situation in which reforming local government would be a matter limited to political elites, citizen participation has been regarded as a cornerstone in the new type of local government pursued since the beginning of the 1990s. While some German cities have made substantial progress on the way to a service-oriented community and to including citizens in the political process so far, others are still lagging behind, and it cannot with any certainty be said what explains the different speed of the innovation process.

In many respects institutional reactions to the ongoing changes have not strongly altered the basic features of local political life. As may be demonstrated in the case of political participation, changing attitudes and behaviours of the people led to institutional change rather than being induced by them. Up to now, the impact of New Public Management on the way local politics operates also seems to be rather limited. But this is only one side of the coin. Broad empirical evidence exists, indicating that the real impact of institutional reforms does not normally become visible immediately after having been implemented. In this respect some frontrunner cities may still induce other municipalities to follow, particularly since 'best practice' and 'benchmarking' have become popular topics in the debate on the reform of local government.

9 Switzerland: reforming small autonomous municipalities

Andreas Ladner

The Swiss political system has long attracted attention from students of comparative politics for a variety of reasons, not the least because of its cultural, linguistic, religious and regional diversity. Yet despite this diversity, the country has managed to achieve a degree of political integration and stability that many have seen as enviable. Just what the 'secret' of this success may be is the subject of a good deal of conjecture as well as scholarly effort (see, for example, Codding 1961; Hughes 1975; McRae 1983; Steinberg 1996). In a recent work Wolf Linder (1998) emphasizes three particular institutional features of the Swiss political system which appear to have been important in allowing the country to achieve the track record it has – federalism, direct democracy and consociationalism. And as Linder aptly notes (1998: 49), local government is 'the foundation stone of the three-staged federal system'. Indeed, municipalities are an important pillar of the political system and political culture in Switzerland. Not only do municipalities form the lowest level of state administration, but they are legally independent public institutions having their own 'constitution', the municipal code, within their sphere of responsibility (Tschäni 1990: 281).

In this chapter the foundation stone of the Swiss federal system is examined more closely. The initial section sets the scene, highlighting the substantial degree of autonomy enjoyed by municipalities as well as some of the difficulties this autonomy has increasingly come to entail. The remainder of the chapter is then devoted to recent developments, especially reform initiatives which have focused on different facets of New Public Management, and concludes with some summary remarks.

Small municipalities, high autonomy and increasing difficulties

During the last 150 years municipalities have been able to maintain a high degree of autonomy within the cantons, similar to the high degree of autonomy the cantons enjoy within the federal state. Three features serve to illustrate this autonomy:

- First, municipalities exercise substantial freedom in determining the organization of their political systems within terms set by cantonal legislation (see Ladner 1991a). Since the degree of autonomy granted to the municipalities and local preferences vary from one canton to another, however, an enormous variety of political systems is to be found. For example, just under 20 per cent of all municipalities have a local parliament whereas the all others still have a local assembly. Usually it is the bigger municipalities (those with 8,000 to 10,000 inhabitants or more) which have a parliament, but in the two French-speaking cantons of Geneva and Neuchâtel all municipalities, even the very small ones, have a parliament. Similarly, nearly 30 per cent of the municipalities elect their local executive with a system of proportional representation (PR), whereas all others use a majority system. And in about one-third of the cantons municipalities are free to choose between the two systems, whereas in all the others cantonal legislation obliges municipalities to use either PR or majority voting. Finally, in many cantons the municipalities are free to choose the size of their executive, whereas in other cantons the size of the executive is linked to the size of the population.
- Second, Swiss municipalities also exercise far-reaching competencies to fulfil their tasks and provide goods and services. Under a notion of subsidiarity, all activities not explicitly assigned to higher political levels remain within the scope of municipal authority. Some of the main responsibilities of municipal government include administration of social security and public health (hospitals), care for the elderly (including construction of homes for the aged), provision of education, waste treatment, electricity, water, gas and local roads. Municipalities are also in charge of local cultural affairs, the appointment of municipal executive and administrative authorities, stipulation of municipality citizenship requirements, and hold municipal property in trust. Here again, however, there are differences between the cantons.
- Third, fiscal autonomy of the municipalities is especially salient (see, for example, Linder 1991; Linder and Nabholz 1999: 129). Municipalities control their own finances and are free to set the local tax rate, which

amounts to more than one-third of the total tax paid by citizens. In poorer municipalities the local tax rate has to be set up to three or four times higher than in well-off municipalities in order to cover all the expenses. Considering the relative importance of local taxes, this leads to important differences between municipalities, something which is only partly corrected by an elaborate system of financial transfers, both horizontal and vertical.

For the most part cantonal legislation treats municipalities equally, regardless of their size. But there are exceptions, such as giving bigger municipalities the possibility of having a parliament or bringing decisions to the polls, or to exercise greater authority in granting construction permits. The most important differences, however, stem from the fact that municipalities of several hundred inhabitants simply do not have to provide the same services as big cities.

Despite what is said so far, in recent years municipalities have increasingly complained that not only do they lack the resources but also the freedom and authority necessary to fulfil their responsibilities adequately. In part this is because they are being confronted with a growing number of tasks of greater complexity. But in addition there is an increasing interdependency of different levels of government, and municipalities have increasingly become executive organs and administrative units of the state (see Geser *et al.* 1996: 292–336).

Even so, the importance of the municipalities' position is emphasized by the fact that the number of municipalities has changed very little over the years. This is rather astonishing since the size of Swiss municipalities is in general extremely small (see Table 9.1). More than half of all municipalities have less than 1,000 inhabitants. Within Europe, only Greece, France and Iceland have on the average smaller local administrative bodies than Switzerland (Conseil de l' Europe 1995). Only a small percentage of the Swiss population lives in these mini-municipalities, yet unlike many of the Northern European countries, few serious attempts were made to amalgamate municipalities until the 1990s. Between 1848 and 2000 the number of political communities only shrank from 3,203 to 2,896, and in the last 10 years there has been only a small number of mergers in a few of the 26 cantons (Dafflon 1998: 125–8).

Increasing difficulties and reforms

In the last few years municipalities in Switzerland have increasingly come under pressure. A survey of all municipalities in 1998 (see Ladner *et al.*

Table 9.1 *Distribution of Swiss municipalities by size of municipality, 2000*

Population size	Number	Per cent	Percent of total population
Less than 250	504	17.4	1.0
250 to 500	492	17.0	2.5
500 to 1,000	566	19.5	5.6
1,000 to 2,000	540	18.6	10.7
2,000 to 5,000	503	17.4	22.2
5,000 to 10,000	173	6.0	16.7
10,000 to 20,000	88	3.0	16.8
20,000 to 50,000	22	0.8	8.8
50,000 to 100,000	3	0.1	3.0
More than 100,000	5	0.2	12.8
Total	2,896	100.0	100.0

Source: Data from official statistics.

2000) showed that many are stretched to the limit of their capabilities. According to their own estimations income support, care for the unemployed and the functioning of the local executive government (recruitment and inadequate managerial facilities) are particularly problematic. Other critical areas identified are care for asylum-seekers, civil defence, sewage treatment and public transport. If these results are compared with a similar survey undertaken in 1994 (Geser *et al.* 1996), it is apparent that difficulties have increased in almost all task areas, particularly with respect to care for asylum-seekers, civil defence, public transport, provision of sports facilities, care for the elderly, integration of foreigners and youth policies.

With the economic recession occurring in the 1990s, furthermore, the financial position of virtually all municipalities worsened, leading to a sharp rise in the debt quota (Federal Finance Administration 2000). Over the period from 1995 to 1997, according to information provided by their local secretaries, 32 per cent of all Swiss municipalities closed their books at the end of an accounting year with a deficit, and 19 per cent have had to increase taxes since 1994. A comparison of the statements of account from 1995 to 97 with those from 1991 to 93 shows that just less than half of all municipalities that closed their accounts with a budget deficit between 1995 and 1997, had also done so between 1991 and 1993. In recent years, in short, there have been a larger number of structurally weak municipalities.

Social change, especially the processes of individualization, pluralization and secularization, are also becoming increasingly apparent in the municipalities. According to results from the survey of local secretaries in 1994, citizens have, on the one hand, become more critical and demanding insofar as the performance of the political-administrative apparatus is concerned. They more often contact the authorities directly and try to turn down unwanted projects by legal means. On the other hand, citizens are less willing to play an active part in serving the municipality, or to stand for political office. Municipalities find it very difficult to recruit enough people for all of the different political functions. It should be noted, however, that due to the smallness of the Swiss municipalities there is an enormous number of public posts to be filled. By one estimate they amount to about 3 per cent of the people entitled to vote, and in some smaller municipalities the percentage rises to 10 per cent or more (see Ladner *et al.* 2000: 23 ff).

Of course not all municipalities encounter the same problems. In the eyes of municipal secretaries it is not necessarily the very small municipalities which are suffering most. Rather, the larger a municipality is the more it appears to have reached the limits of its capabilities. One reason for this is that larger municipalities, as regional centres, also have to fulfil more tasks and there is a greater awareness of problems and possible difficulties that this entails.

In line with the increasing difficulties municipalities have experienced in fulfilling their tasks and the worsening of their financial situation in the 1990s, a reform debate has swept over municipalities. A nationwide survey among municipal secretaries carried out in 1998 revealed that the municipalities were not only reconsidering their position within the canton, but also different forms of cooperation with other municipalities or the private sector, amalgamation with other municipalities and reforms of local government (see Ladner *et al.* 2000).

Changes in scope and position: cooperation and accountability

Reallocation of responsibilities

In recent decades more and more governmental activities have been delegated to municipalities and legal restrictions imposed by higher political levels have been intensified. By the middle of the 1990s a majority of cantons and many municipalities realized that cooperation between the cantonal and the municipal level was far from optimal. It was widely recognized that any major reform of municipal government should first clarify what is to be done by the municipalities and what alternatively is within the scope of cantonal responsibility. Moreover, the flow of financial resources between the two layers has been considered to be opaque, ineffective and inefficient, violating the 'principle of fiscal equivalence' which states that those who decide what has to be done also have to provide the necessary resources. In almost all cantons, therefore, there have been attempts to review and allocate tasks and resources to the different layers of the state more adequately (see Ladner and Steiner 1998: 24 ff).

Most of the reforms subsequently introduced follow the principle of 'fiscal equivalence', and build on two central ideas: first that transfers to the local level should be made on the basis of the municipalities' possibilities of raising their own resources, and second that fiscal transfers should be given in the form of block grants rather than being tied to the provision of specific tasks (earmarked grants).

The philosophy behind the reallocation of tasks to the different layers of the state comes very close to the concept of New Public Management (NPM). However a variety of problems remain to be solved: which tasks can be left entirely in the hands of municipalities; what is an appropriate financial adjustment between 'rich' and 'poor' municipalities; what kind of goods and services, and according to what standards should be provided by all municipalities; and how can optimal use of municipal resources be assured? To answer some of these questions more transparency is needed with respect to the costs of different services and goods provided by each municipality. To achieve this several cantons are planning an extended benchmarking scheme among the municipalities (see Steiner 2000a).

In general, the principles of subsidiarity and local autonomy have so far not been questioned. In the future, however, local autonomy is most likely to be restricted to an 'operative autonomy', whereas strategic responsibilities will increasingly move to higher state levels. Cantonal authorities will tell the municipalities what to do, and the municipalities will decide how they want to do it.

Cooperation between municipalities becomes even more important

The most popular reform activity among Swiss municipalities at the end of the 1990s is increased cooperation. In a 1998 survey, two-thirds of the municipalities claimed that they had increased the degree of cooperation with other municipalities within the last five years. For all other municipalities the degree of cooperation had remained unchanged. Of course the idea that municipalities should work together to provide certain services more efficiently is by no means new. In the history of Swiss municipalities there have always been some forms of cooperation, which is not astonishing if we consider the smallness of many of them.

The traditional form of intermunicipal cooperation is an administrative union (*Zweckverband*), an association under public law. In recent years, however, municipalities have increasingly cooperated on the grounds of private law, which offers them more flexibility. This is because public law in Switzerland regulates the organization of the state and administration in terms of sovereignty and is necessarily of binding character, whereas private law regulates the relation between organizations and individuals on equal terms and offers the possibility of specification through contracts. In 1998, at least half of all municipalities worked together with at least one other municipality in fields such as schools, medical care, care for the elderly, refuse disposal, water supply, sewage treatment and civil service. In fields such as support for the unemployed, civil service, fire brigade and medical care, cooperation has been especially intensified within the last few years (see Ladner *et al.* 2000). Even so more intensified cooperation remains possible in quite a few areas, including such fields as general administration (computer networks and facilities, accounting and registration offices), provisions for asylum-seekers, planning, construction permits, public buildings, environmental issues, private transport, integration of immigrants, and local executives. Until now, less than 20 per cent of the municipalities work together in these fields.

For intermunicipal cooperation in general, it seems obvious that in larger territorial units quite a few services profit from 'economies of scales'. But cooperation also raises questions of democratic decision-making and control. How can decisions be taken within a union of municipalities of different size, if the principle of 'one-man one-vote' places smaller municipalities at a disadvantage? How can delegates on the boards of a union of municipalities be controlled democratically and how, in the case of cooperation on the basis of private law, are contracts to be formulated and property rights to be regulated?

Public–private partnership, an 'old' solution rediscovered

Cooperation with the private sector is also not a new feature for Swiss municipalities; it has long been a necessity (see Ruegg *et al.* 1994). The smallness of many municipalities has not allowed most of them to have a big administration with many civil servants, and more than 60 per cent of all municipalities claimed in a 1994 survey that they regularly relied on the services of private partners (see Geser *et al.* 1996). Services where public–private partnership is especially frequent are construction and planning, where about half of the municipalities need external help. In addition about one-third seek cooperation in the fields of traffic, legal issues and computer technologies. With the adoption of NPM reforms, privatization and outsourcing have gained additional attractiveness. For some this is because private-sector cooperation is another step in the direction of the neo-liberal minimal state, for others it is because they feel that public services and goods do not have to be produced by the public sector exclusively as long as they remain politically controlled and accountable to the citizens and their representatives.

Amalgamation of municipalities is still not a major issue

Municipal amalgamation has never been a popular issue in Switzerland. Territorial reforms carried out in most Northern European countries in the 1970s had no influence in Switzerland, and there have never been any serious attempts to reduce the number of municipalities. In the middle of the 1990s, however, amalgamations did become more widely discussed, especially in cantons like Fribourg, Thurgau, Luzern, Tessin and Graubünden, where, with the exception of Lucerne, the municipalities are particularly small.

Considering the stability of municipal boundaries it is quite noteworthy that 20 per cent of the municipalities surveyed in 1998 claimed to have been discussing an amalgamation with one or more neighbouring municipalities. However, only 8 per cent of the municipalities, mainly in the cantons named above, seem to have more precise plans and projects. Nevertheless, a large-scale reform seems unlikely in the near future. To bring all municipalities to a minimal size of 3,000 inhabitants, as was recently suggested by authorities in the canton of Luzern, would mean that 80 per cent of the municipalities would be merged. It remains an open question, furthermore, whether there is anything like an optimal size for municipalities, and whether the traditional form of territorial units with a general responsibility for all local tasks will survive. It is likely, however, that there will be some amalgamations of very small municipalities, especially in cantons like Fribourg and Ticino.

New layers of government, centralization or decentralization?

There have also been discussions about forming new jurisdictions such as regions or 'greater city areas', or shifting competences to administrative units (*Bezirke*) which already exist in some cantons, but up to now have been of minor importance. Yet having a tight network of administrative units with 26 cantons and about 2,900 municipalities for only seven million people, there is not much enthusiasm for introducing new layers of government. In the case of rural municipalities the question is whether such regions could really cover a wider range of local tasks and how democratic decision-making would be organized. As in the case of amalgamations, the idea of a partial integration of well-off municipalities is met with reluctance since these municipalities would have to pay more tax and loose political influence. For certain tasks (for example public transport), however, extended city areas seem to be appropriate.

With its 26 cantons and roughly 2,900 municipalities, Switzerland is already a very federalist and decentralized country. Given this situation, it is quite obvious that there is no trend towards more decentralization. What is needed is a more adequate concept of local autonomy and federalism, assigning financial responsibility and accountability wherever possible to one layer of the state only, and, for tasks where such a division is not possible or desirable, to distinguish between strategic functions situated on the higher level, and operational freedom attributed to the lower. To balance structural differences between municipalities, as well as between the members of the federal state, however, a system is needed which assures equal standards as far as public goods and services are concerned, and which does not induce local authorities to behave uneconomically in order to obtain more transfers from higher state levels. In the current reform of inter-governmental relations the concept of minimal standards for services seeks to reduce differences due to federalism and municipal autonomy without infringing too heavily on the discretion of smaller units. Reforms also aim at making financial adjustment more directly based on standard costs for the services provided and giving municipalities more possibilities to allocate their resources by moving away from subsidies towards global transfers.

Politics and administration: decision-making and New Public Management

Attempts to strengthen executive leadership

In the face of changing circumstances, municipalities have on their own initiative undertaken a variety of reform measures. As a general trend, the survey carried out in 1998 (Ladner *et al.* 2000) reveals that many municipalities have tried to make decision-making easier and more efficient by shifting competences from the citizens or the legislatives to the executive, and from the executive to the administration or to the different specialized commissions (for schools, planning, construction and so on), as well as by reducing the number of commissions or by reducing the size of all these bodies. In some cases they have extended the administration or transferred services and tasks to the private sector. Reforms of the political system have been more seldom. There is a slight tendency to replace majority voting with proportional representation (PR) voting as far as the electoral system for the local executives is concerned, although there are also examples of shifts from PR to majority voting. Yet regardless of the voting system adopted, all important parties are usually represented in the executives due to the so-called '*freiwilliger Proporz*' (voluntary proportionality). A shift from majority to PR voting should therefore not necessarily be considered as a change from 'concentration of power' to 'power sharing', but rather as a for-malization of an informal rule for power sharing. Municipalities with rather large executive bodies, furthermore, have tended to reduce the number of seats. However, all these changes can be considered as minor reforms, hardly likely to increase overall municipal performance. Of greater signifi-cance in this regard is the spread of New Public Management measures.

The spread of New Public Management in Switzerland

Internationally, New Public Management (NPM) is a label referring to comprehensive reform of the public sector aimed at the administration as well as the political side of local government. The idea that NPM means everybody is doing more or less the same thing, however, has rightly been questioned (cf Pollitt 2000: 184). Not all countries have started from the same point, either in terms of the shape of their public sector or in terms of what they think about the role and character of the state. Nor do all gov-ernments possess the same capacities to implement reform – note, for example, the difficulties of federalist countries. And finally, many OECD countries have welfare-state organizations that are not organized along strict bureaucratic lines. State schools, hospitals and social and community services agencies have a variety of forms in which autonomous profession-als and not bureaucrats are the key actors (Clarke and Newman 1997). This last observation is particularly true for Switzerland.

In the Swiss case, the wave of New Public Management swept over the country in the course of the 1990s. Some initial pilot projects were first launched in the mid-1990s in municipalities within the cantons of Bern, Basel-Land and Zurich (Haldemann and Schedler 1995: 100), and since then the number of NPM reform projects has risen considerably. Thus, a survey of cantons conducted in 1998 showed that NPM reform projects were underway in 24 out of 26 cantons (Ladner and Steiner 1998: 23), and a survey of municipalities at the end of 1998 revealed that over a third had already considered NPM reforms (Ladner *et al.* 2000: 128f). Although it cannot be said that NPM is an issue throughout Switzerland, NPM theory has been received favourably in practice. Approximately a quarter of the municipalities claim that not only have they considered NPM reforms, but that they have even taken the first steps towards implementing NPM measures.

Among the municipalities claiming that they have taken the first steps, however, only a small portion have already implemented core elements of NPM, such as product definitions, global budgets, performance agreements and contracts (see Figure 9.1). These elements are essential to operate a

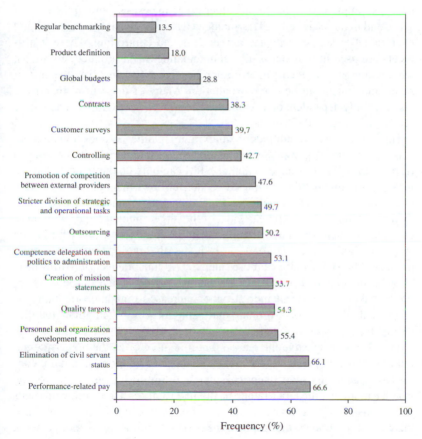

Figure 9.1 *Elements of New Public Management implemented in Swiss municipalities with NPM reform projects (N = 590)*

Source: Local secretary survey 1998 (see Ladner *et al.* 2000).

municipal administration in a performance- and outcome-oriented fashion (Schedler and Proeller 2000: 121–2). More popular in Swiss municipalities are changes in the human resources area (elimination of the civil servant status, performance-related pay, and personnel development measures). This is related to the goal of adjusting working conditions in the public sector to those of the private sector. Alongside human resource management, normative strategic management is also gaining in importance, a trend that can be seen in the creation of mission statements and the delegation of operational tasks from the political to the administrative sphere.

It is interesting to note, moreover, that the few municipalities that have already defined products (less than 20 per cent of all NPM municipalities) have also implemented numerous other NPM measures, both in the narrow sense and in the wide sense. This includes a stricter division of strategic and operational tasks, performance agreements and controlling. These instruments are used in four out of five municipalities with product definitions, which supports the theory that comprehensive NPM involves the instruments that enable an outcome-orientation. Many of these instruments are also mutually dependent on one another: contracts, for example, make more sense with product definitions.

Having such a large number of small municipalities as does Switzerland, it is interesting to know to what extend small municipalities are able to respond to NPM reforms, or whether NPM can only be implemented in the few larger municipalities. Empirical evidence shows that up to now NPM is not widely spread in the smaller and medium-sized municipalities with less than 5,000 inhabitants, whereas most of the larger municipalities with more than 5,000 inhabitants have already taken the first steps with NPM in one form or another (cf Figure 9.2). It is worth highlighting that among municipalities with a size of more than 20,000 inhabitants, four-fifths have already implemented initial NPM elements. As far as the introduction of product definitions as an indication of increased outcome orientation is concerned, the data show that small and medium-sized municipalities hardly use this at all.

In a Swiss perspective the reason that it is more often the bigger municipalities which implement NPM is not so much to be found in a more conservative, generally more sceptical approach to reforms on the part of the smaller municipalities, but rather in the nature of the larger municipalities and towns with bigger and more complex administrative structures, and their need to bridge the gap to the general public, to simplify work processes and to optimize the task of administration generally. On the other hand, it seems likely that only the larger administrations can afford to implement NPM, because in contrast to small municipalities, they have the

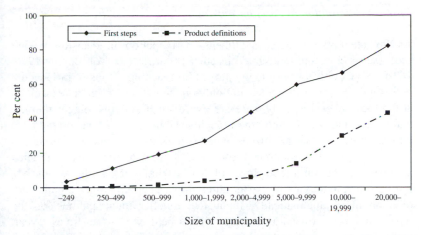

Figure 9.2 *First steps with New Public Management and the implementation of product definitions in Switzerland by size of municipality ($N_{min} = 30$, $N_{max} = 569$)*

Source: Local secretary survey 1998 (see Ladner *et al.* 2000).

necessary human and financial resources, as well as the necessary know-how. Reforms are in this sense very likely driven by a combination of need and resources.

What has led the municipalities to start NPM reforms? Empirical evidence shows that it is certainly not only the lack of resources or financial problems. There are obviously municipalities that turn to NPM reforms in reaction to their difficult financial situation (budget deficits), but others (with budget surpluses) introduce NPM for other reasons. These latter municipalities may be thought of as proactive rather than reactive, taking advantage of the resources they have.

Within the individual language regions, the portion of the German-speaking municipalities implementing NPM is the largest (more than one-third). While 13 per cent of the Italian-speaking municipalities state that they have some practical experience in NPM, the figure for the French-speaking municipalities is less than 10 per cent. This cautious attitude to NPM on the part of French-speaking Switzerland is quite surprising. One reason may be that the Swiss advocates of NPM (Ernst Buschor and Kuno Schedler) are German-speaking, and German-speaking Switzerland has traditionally been far more open to innovations from Germany, Holland and Anglo-Saxon nations. French-speaking Switzerland, by comparison, is more strongly oriented to France, a country in which NPM is not yet very widely spread (Steiner 2000b).

Citizen participation in decision-making

As for attempts to increase citizens' participation in decision-making processes such as those observed in other countries (see Von Beyme 1996: 162ff), Swiss citizens have long enjoyed far-reaching means of influencing political decisions. This applies not only on the national level but especially at the local level. Basically there are two distinct systems: bigger municipalities and many of those in the French-speaking part of Switzerland have a local parliament where citizens have the possibility of undertaking initiatives to change the communal code and to initiate (optional) referenda against projects and decisions of the parliament or the executive. Furthermore, in the case of expenditures above a certain limit, a compulsory referendum is (automatically) mandated. Smaller municipalities, on the other hand, have a local assembly which is held two to four times a year, where citizens are entitled to vote on the proposals put forward by the executive. In the course of the assembly they also have the possibility of altering the content of those proposals. Citizens in most of the municipalities with assemblies also have the possibility of launching initiatives by collecting signatures, to seek a referendum against proposals and decisions of the executive, and sometimes even against decisions of the local assembly (see Ladner 1991b; Lafitte 1987).

Given existing possibilities for citizen influence, in short, the idea of introducing or increasing direct democracy is not an issue in Swiss municipal reforms. If there are changes, they are aimed at making compulsory (financial) referenda optional. This implies a reduction in the number of referenda to be held: if no opposition against a project arises, no ballot has to be held. However, there have been attempts to increase the involvement of citizens in local politics, particularly with the aim of committing people to a project and preventing a failure at the final decision stage. In a survey conducted in 1994, almost two-thirds of the municipalities claimed that they more often organize meetings to inform their citizens and try to integrate them in the planning process for municipal projects. By comparison, only about 15 per cent claimed that they had increased the scope of initiatives and referenda. Additionally, New Public Management reforms also oblige authorities to find out whether their 'customers' agree with the quality of the goods and services they provide, and increasingly push them to conduct surveys. Goal-oriented political steering needs to know what goals are to be achieved. Ideally these goals have to be defined jointly with citizens and fixed with a mid-term perspective in a municipal development or legislature programme.

Conclusion – similar but different

At the end of the twentieth century, Swiss municipalities have experienced a wave of reforms and institutional changes. It is interesting to note that the different reform activities at the local level are closely connected to each other, and that the philosophy behind NPM (at least in its steering orientation rather than a purely economic version) serves as a blueprint for almost all reform activities. Any reorganization of local government has to make clear first which goods and services remain the prerogative of local authorities, where cooperation with the private sector or other municipalities makes more sense, and which layer of the state is accountable. With the idea of strategic political decisions and operative freedom, with global budgeting on the bases of contracts and facilities to control output, perspectives are offered which can be applied not only to the reorganization of local governments but also to the different forms of cooperation, outsourcing and contracting-out and the repartition of tasks between the different layers of the state.

Despite all these reform activities, it is impossible to foresee at the moment what local government in Switzerland will look like in future. A large-scale amalgamation of the numerous very small municipalities seems very unlikely, not only because it would be met by strong political resistance, but also because different tasks need different territorial boundaries. Intensified cooperation among municipalities, public–private–partnerships and better clarification of cooperation with higher levels of the state along with reforms of local government seem to be more promising.

Compared to what is happening in other countries, the question is whether Swiss reform activities give support to the idea of Switzerland as a special case (*Sonderfall*), or whether the developments follow a pervasive international trend? According to Naschold's meta-analysis of various local authority reform programmes throughout the world in the mid-1990s, the following reform trends can be observed internationally (Naschold 1997: 15–48): internal modernization of the public administrations involving the elements of performance control, budgeting and human resource management; 'democratisation' of the municipalities (opening up of the decision-making procedures, transfer of public tasks to the municipalities); a stronger market orientation of municipalities (benchmarking, outsourcing, performance agreements, legal independence and privatization); and an ongoing decentralization (see also Lane 1997; Dente and Kjellberg 1988; Stoker 1996; Wollmann 1998).

As far as NPM is concerned, Switzerland has followed the same development as other countries, perhaps with a time lag of a few years. Market orientation is currently being intensively discussed and first attempts are apparent, but necessary instruments such as benchmarking and performance agreements have only been introduced in the larger towns so far. But Switzerland does not follow the international trend when it comes to democratization and decentralization of the administration in the sense of decision-making procedures and task distribution. Indeed, in numerous important task areas (welfare, schools and hospitals for example) the role of the cantons is being confirmed. The Swiss municipalities are being given more organizational autonomy (operational freedom), but they are seeing a decline in material and task-specific autonomy. This may have something to do with the fact that on an international scale Swiss municipalities are small and have a relatively large amount of autonomy with a broad task profile. Similarly, there are only very few attempts to increase the already far-reaching means of direct democratic participation. On the contrary, there have been attempts to limit ballots solely to more important questions. In these respects then, Switzerland is still not completely in line with other countries.

10   The United Kingdom: an increasingly differentiated polity?

David Wilson

Elected local government in the UK is now but one part of a complex mosaic of agencies concerned with community governance. In the last two decades its role as a *direct* service provider has declined markedly. Partnerships at local level have increased: elected local authorities now 'share the turf' with a wide range of non-elected agencies conventionally known as 'local quangos' – quasi-autonomous non-governmental organizations – including health authorities, police authorities, learning and skills councils. The once dominant position of elected local government has been challenged by the 'quango explosion' and by the increased involvement of voluntary agencies and private-sector bodies in service delivery. As Jim Bulpitt (1989: 57) observed, local government used to rank as one of Oakeshott's subjects of 'unimaginable dreariness'. In the last decade, however, it has become high profile, even exciting!

The Conservative governments of Margaret Thatcher and John Major saw local government at a low ebb. Stoker (1999a: 1) provides a good summary of the situation:

> What happened to British local government during the period of Conservative government from 1979 to 1997 was in many respects a brutal illustration of power politics. The funding system was reformed to provide central government with a considerable (and probably unprecedented) level of control over spending. Various functions and responsibilities were stripped away from local authorities or organised in a way that obliged local authorities to work in partnership with other public and private agencies in the carrying out of the functions.

After 18 years of Conservative rule, a Labour government was elected in 1997 having stated in its election manifesto that 'local decision-making

should be less constrained by central government, and also more accountable to local people'. At the same time, however, the erosion of local
authorities as direct service providers did not seem likely to be suddenly
or dramatically reversed. Indeed Prime Minister Tony Blair warned
(1998: 20):

> The government will not hesitate to intervene directly to secure improve-
> ments where services fall below acceptable standards. And, if necessary,
> it will look to other authorities and agencies to take on duties where an
> authority is manifestly incapable of providing an effective service.

Under 'New Labour', in short, there was to be no return to local authorities
being near monopolistic service providers. Throughout the postwar period
local authorities have never been the sole governmental actors within localities, but the advent of local governance has resulted in patterns of behaviour that are far more complex than even a decade ago. In this context
Rhodes' (1997) differentiated polity model, which sees governance as a
series of exchange relationships, is a helpful frame of reference for understanding the situation existing in the UK, although it underplays the continuing importance of the centre.

Local governance at the beginning of the 1990s

To understand UK local government it is essential to grasp the basics of its
historical development and evolution. As Keith-Lucas and Richards emphasize (1978: 35), local government 'was not evolved to provide a coordinated system of administration for a logically defined range of services; it
emerged, piecemeal, in answer to a succession of separate needs and
demands'. There was no blueprint; rather, pragmatism has been the dominant driver of change. Local government evolved largely in response to
pressures produced by urbanization and problems generated by the
Industrial Revolution.

The major features of local government in England and Wales were laid
down by the 1835 Municipal Corporations Act and by three statutes at the
end of the nineteenth century: the Local Government Acts of 1888 and
1894 and the London Government Act of 1899. With some modifications,
notably in London, the structure lasted until the Local Government Act of
1972 ushered in a new pattern of elected local government which became
operative from 1974. Further change was to follow rapidly under
Conservative governments with the abolition of the six metropolitan county

councils and the Greater London Council in 1986, and of the Inner London Education Authority in 1990. In Scotland, too, the 'modern' structure of local government dates from the late nineteenth century, although there was extensive revision in both 1929 and 1973. The 1972 Local Government (Northern Ireland) Act replaced 73 local authorities with 26 single-tier district councils in Northern Ireland – a structure that has survived to the present day.

Local government authority and responsibilities

Traditionally, local councils have only been able to do what statute permits – a doctrine known as *ultra vires*, a Latin term which translates 'beyond the powers'. If a local council does something or spends money that is not statutorily authorized, it is deemed to have acted *ultra vires*, that is beyond its powers, and therefore illegally. This has been a severe impediment to innovation at the local level. The Local Government Act of 2000 goes some way to providing local authorities with a new, less restrictive, legal framework by introducing a more general power of 'well-being' which gives scope for innovation across service areas. There are limitations, however. The new power is *not* directly equivalent to the 'power of general competence' possessed by local authorities in most other European countries. Most significantly, it cannot be used to raise money. The Act's accompanying guidance is nevertheless positive and expansive. There is now much more scope than ever before for local authorities to become engaged in joint action in policy areas where previously councils would have had to check that they had specific powers. This applies to issues such as tackling social exclusion and improving local environmental quality for example (see Wilson and Game 2002: 367).

While local government in Britain rests on a constitutionally weaker base than it does in many European countries, local authorities are still responsible for literally hundreds of different services. In general terms, unitary authorities in England, Scotland and Wales provide all major services, as do English metropolitan districts. In London services are shared between the boroughs and the new Greater London Authority (which has a largely strategic role). Within the remainder of England services are shared between two major tiers of local government – county councils and district councils. Major services such as education and social services are the responsibility of larger county councils, while the smaller district authorities oversee functions such as social housing, leisure/recreation and waste collection.

The structures of local government

As Leach and Percy-Smith (2001: 60) note, 'Demands for improved integration of services and for larger authorities to realize economies of scale
underpinned a succession of projected and realized reorganizations of local
government from the 1960s through to the 1990s.' The battle was between
those who wanted services split between districts and counties – sometimes
with different party political control – and those who advocated unitary single-tier authorities. At the beginning of the 1990s a mixed system was still
firmly in place in Scotland, Wales and the shire counties of England, with
unitary authorities restricted to London boroughs and urban England,
plus Northern Ireland (whose district councils had relatively few powers).
Table 10.1 provides a non-hierarchical representation of elected local government structures in the UK in 1990. Outside London and the provincial
metropolitan areas it reveals a tiered system with all the attendant tensions
inherent in such divisions: competing mandates, the blurring of lines of
responsibility in service provision, resource jealousies. The system was to
undergo further change in the 1990s with the advent of more unitary
authorities, but given the rise of local *governance* (especially the increased
importance of other non-elected agencies in providing services) such unitary authorities were only to have responsibility for some (not all) local
functions. Fragmentation was the order of the day in 1990, and it still is.

The size of local authorities in 1990 (as today) varied enormously *within*
each category. Counties varied from 100,000 (Powys) to 1.5 million
(Hampshire); district councils within the counties varied from 18,670
(Radnor) to 433,000 (Bristol). Populations in the 36 metropolitan districts
ranged from 172,000 (South Tyneside) to almost 1.1 million (Birmingham).
Within these authorities the great majority of the 25,000 elected councillors

Table 10.1   *The structure of local government in the United Kingdom, 1990*

London	Rest of England/Wales	Scotland	Northern Ireland
32 London boroughs plus City of London Corporation	47 Non-metropolitan county councils	9 regions	26 district councils
	333 Non-metropolitan district councils	53 district councils	
	36 metropolitan district councils	3 'most purpose' island authorities	

in 1990 were (and still are) elected under the labels of national or national-ist political policies, although in the more rural areas the picture was, on occasions, very different with high proportions of non-partisan councillors, many of whom stood as Independents. The best examples of complete non-partisanship in 1990 were the three unitary or all-purpose Scottish Island authorities: Orkney, Shetland and the Western Isles.

The organization of local government

The way in which local authorities in Britain have traditionally been orga-nized is through committees of councillors serviced by professional officers located in departments. Committees can be seen as a council's workshops, where councillors' local knowledge and their political assessment of local needs are brought together with professional and expert advice of officers to produce, ideally, policies that are both democratically responsive and able to be implemented. In 1990 some large authorities had up to 100 com-mittees, sub-committees, working parties and panels. There was invariably some kind of central management committee, often chaired by the leader of the majority party, for which the primary task was to coordinate the work of specialist committees and to provide the council with overall policy leadership. Committees have traditionally enabled councillors to acquire specialist knowledge and thereby hopefully produce more informed decision-making. Nevertheless, they have been widely criticized for length-ening the decision-making process, often by networks of sub-committees. Councillors can also become narrowly focused and fail to appreciate the work of the council as a whole. As will be seen later, such criticisms were central to Blairite proposals regarding the strengthening of executive leadership.

While the formal authority of elected councillors has long been apparent, the importance of local government's non-elected, paid workforce has not. In 1990 the UK workforce was about 26 million, of which almost 3 million worked for local authorities. In short, local authorities provided about 11 per cent of all full and part-time jobs. The professional knowledge and expertise of senior officers, moreover, frequently meant that they exercised a good deal of influence in shaping policy. Councillors, by comparison, were unpaid and part-time. This left a void which paid professionals were frequently keen to fill. Even so plenty of leading and long-serving council-lors, such as past and present committee chairs and leaders of party groups, had the experience, knowledge, authority and political skill to assert them-selves in any confrontation with officers.

Local government finance

Local government finance has constituted a constant source of tension between the localities and central government. Central government has controlled local authorities by two means: first by regulating the amount of money that they can spend locally and, secondly, by scrutinizing the way in which that money is spent. Until 1990 (1989 in Scotland) a property tax called the rates provided local authorities with limited taxation powers to meet some of their spending needs. In 1984 the government took powers to limit (cap) rates in an attempt to prevent rate rises beyond a predetermined level. Each year from 1985–86 to 1990–91 a limited number of the highest spending councils, usually between 12 and 20, had their budgets capped. Not surprisingly, most of the selected authorities were Labour-controlled. By using this capping mechanism, Conservative central-government ministers in effect controlled local budgets and prevented excessive increases (that is those above the parameters established by the centre).

Over time revenues generated by local taxation gradually declined as a proportion of a local authority's net expenditure, and local authorities became increasingly constrained by the centre. From 1990 to 2002, for example, this proportion declined from 53 to 19 per cent. The latter figure is much lower than in most other Western European countries. To 'ease' the situation, a new local tax – the community charge, or poll tax – was unleashed on an unsuspecting public. Its introduction, however, further undermined the financial independence of local authorities. Dependence on the centre had never been greater, especially as further central controls were placed on borrowing for capital projects. Local financial discretion had become increasingly illusory.

In 1993 the community charge was replaced by the council tax. Whereas the rates were a tax on property and the community charge/poll tax was a tax on the individual, the council tax is a combination of the two. Although a number of 'localist' initiatives have been undertaken since 1997 under New Labour (for example, some relaxation of capital funding controls and the introduction of a power to promote 'well-being'), central–local government relations have continued to be characterized by central government insisting on retaining control. Nowhere has this been clearer than in the financial arena.

Despite policies pursued by the Conservatives, local government remained big business in 1990, accounting for 26 per cent of total government expenditure. Nevertheless, times were changing. Nicholas Ridley, when Environment Minister in the Conservative government, argued that the 1989 Local Government and Housing Act completed the framework whereby local authorities became 'enablers and regulators rather than providers of services'. The stage was set for greater involvement by private-sector firms, voluntary bodies and non-elected organizations in providing services; the so-called 'enabling authority' had arrived.

Continuity and change

From 1990 up to the present there has been a variety of reforms, the most noteworthy being structural and financial reform. Thus, in England, outside London, a total of 46 new unitary authorities came into existence between 1995–98, replacing five counties and 58 districts, whereas in Wales 22 new unitary authorities replaced the existing 45 counties and districts, and in Scotland 32 unitaries replaced the 65 former regions and districts. There was no change in Northern Ireland where the 26 district councils remained intact, albeit with substantially fewer functions than their counterparts in mainland Britain. These changes were largely driven by the quest for economies of scale; the number of local authorities decreased dramatically over a relatively short period of time, and the average size of local authorities increased accordingly. Table 10.2 sets out (again in non-hierarchical format) the structure of UK-elected local government in 2002. In 1974 (before reorganization) there were 1,855 local councils with an average population of 29,000. By the 1990s this had been cut back to 521 with an average of 106,000 inhabitants, and by 2002 there were only 442 local authorities (a figure which included the newly created Greater London Authority which came into being in 2000) with an average population per council of some 128,000 – 4.4 times larger than the position in the early 1970s. As a result

Table 10.2   *The structure of local government in the United Kingdom, 2002*

London	Rest of England	Wales	Scotland	Northern Ireland
1 Greater London Authority	34 Non-metropolitan county councils	22 Unitary councils	32 Unitary councils	26 District councils
32 London Boroughs plus City of London Corporation	238 Non-metropolitan district councils			
	46 Unitary councils			
	36 Metropolitan district councils			

the UK now has significantly bigger local authorities and far more inhabitants per elected member than all other European countries.

The Conservative years (1979–97) saw not only a sharp reduction in the number of elected local authorities (and hence elected councillors); they also witnessed the rapid growth of non-elected or indirectly elected bodies at the expense of directly elected councils. Service responsibilities were removed from local authorities and given to central government appointed agencies such as Training and Enterprise Councils (TECs), Housing Action Trusts (HATs) and Urban Development Corporations (UDCs). This trend led Jones and Stewart (1992: 15) to remark that:

> Government is being handed back to the 'new magistracy' from whom it was removed in the counties more than 100 years ago. Elected representatives are being replaced by a burgeoning army of the selected – the unknown governors of our society.

Those services that remained with elected local authorities became subject to greater national direction and control; constraints upon local councils were particularly severe. Compulsory competitive tendering (CCT) became the order of the day. As Rhodes (1997: xvii) notes, in the 1990s British government adopted a strategy of 'more control over less'. It increasingly bypassed elected local authorities for special-purpose bodies.

This shift from traditional bureaucracies to fragmented delivery systems highlights the shift from government to governance. During the 1990s appointed agencies (conventionally known as quangos) became increasingly central to the formulation, implementation and delivery of local public policies. According to Weir and Beetham (1999: 192), 'executive quangos moved under the Conservatives from the "arms length" margins of government to become major agents of government policy and actions'. Hall and Weir (1996) identified some 6,425 quangos, 4,653 of which had a local focus. Such bodies take decision-making responsibilities out of the direct ambit of democratic institutions. They were, however, crucially important elements of local governance, reflecting the managerialist priorities of successive Conservative administrations in the wake of an increasing number of local authorities controlled by opposition parties. By 1997 the Conservatives controlled only 23 authorities out of 441 (5 per cent). In such an environment appointed quangos were particularly useful as a means of bypassing the increasingly hostile world of elected local government: they facilitated the centre's policy priorities taking root at local level.

Local democracy and citizen involvement

Given the advent of a fragmented pattern of local governance in which councillors have a less direct operational role, it can be argued that it is not unreasonable for there to be fewer authorities and fewer councillors. Indeed, are more councillors necessarily a solution to what has been termed a 'democratic deficit' if, once in office, they have relatively little influence on policy formulation? There is, for example, a good deal of evidence that local elites of senior councillors and senior officers exercise disproportionate influence in shaping policy (see Wilson and Game 2002). So simply to increase the number of elected councillors from the 22,300 in office in 2004 might not affect the distribution of power very much at all (especially given the subsequent rise of executive leadership at the local level). This argument does not hold sway with the traditionalists, however. Jones and Stewart (1993: 15) maintain that local government is enhanced as *local democracy* by the closeness of council members to those they represent: 'A greater number of members serves to embed local government into the grass roots. They make local government more responsive to the local community and understanding of its wishes and needs'. Nevertheless, the reality is that in the 1998 and 2000 local elections only 29 per cent of the electorate voted. Subsequent years saw a slight increase, but representative democracy at local level was hardly buoyant.

Rather than through electoral participation, the mode of citizen involvement most assiduously developed by Conservative administrations was in relation to service use: citizens were first and foremost seen as customers and consumers, not as voters. The primary role of citizens was in terms both of assessing service quality (through, for example, satisfaction surveys and charter initiatives) and contributing to service management (for example through more powerful school governing bodies and forms of tenant management). The customer was treated as being sovereign. The empowerment of citizen customers was seen as a means of disciplining local politicians who were self-interested and out of touch.

While the subsequent Labour government has recognized the value of participation in relation to service quality, enhanced citizen involvement is also part of an explicitly *political* agenda incorporating broader issues of democratic renewal. Whereas the Conservatives sought to recast local government in terms of efficiency or 'value for money', New Labour sees interaction between local authorities and communities as equally important. This was stressed in the 1998 consultation paper, *Modernising Local Government – Local Democracy and Community Leadership*: 'Increasingly, the degree to which an authority is engaged with its stakeholders may become a touchstone for the authority's general effectiveness' (DETR 1998b: 23). Given the intermittent nature of local elections, public involvement is seen as crucial to the health of local democracy. New methods of consultation such as citizens' juries, citizens' panels, and visioning exercises have emerged to work alongside more traditional mechanisms such as public meetings. The Blair government has not jettisoned the traditional Conservative consumer orientation; it has developed it, but at the same time retained a strong emphasis on service delivery. There has also been a growing emphasis upon the local delivery of national priorities based on increasingly powerful inspection regimes.

Central to the Labour government's modernization agenda is a commitment to electronic service delivery. This was first signalled in the 1999 Cabinet Office White Paper *Modernising Government*, which argued that all public services should be made electronically available by 2005. As part of the process, all local authorities were obliged to develop 'implementing electronic government' (IEG) statements by 2001, setting out their plans to achieve the 2005 target. Only 6 per cent of these plans were deemed 'unsatisfactory' by the government, although there appears to be considerable disparity between the IEG statements and the reality of achieving electronic service delivery (Pratchett 2002).

A fundamental problem associated with e-governance is that while approximately 40 per cent of households now have some form of access to the internet, its use is predominantly among the better educated and wealthier sections of society. Yet at grassroots level many services, such as social housing, are targeted at groups that have low access and less willingness to use new technologies. Closing neighbourhood offices and other outreach facilities is less of an option for local authorities than it is for commercial organizations. Despite such obvious problems the 2005 target remains. As Pratchett (2002: 340) observes, managing the transition to electronic services requires careful planning, but the problems are not insurmountable. Indeed, many argue that careful implementation of electronic services through a range of different technologies will enhance access rather than undermine it.

CCT, Best Value and inspection regimes

Of all the changes introduced by the 1979–97 Conservative governments, probably the most far-reaching were those associated with compulsory competitive tendering (CCT), particularly if it is seen as one dimension of the 'New Right' privatization or contracting-out strategy of those governments. Essentially the process required a comparison of the costs of continuing in-house provision of specified services with those of any interested private contractors and an expectation that the contract would be awarded to the most competitive bidder – in effect, invariably, the *lowest* bidder. CCT owed much to New Right 'think tanks' such as the Adam Smith Institute. The argument was that contracting-out of services, formerly provided monopolistically by local government, would lead to both improved service provision and reduced costs. It would lead to less and smaller government. Ironically, however, CCT did not spell the beginning of the end of local authorities as direct service providers; indeed, in one way it had the reverse effect. For, in presenting authorities with the challenge of winning contracts in-house, it encouraged them to streamline and strengthen their management systems so that they would be better able to compete.

CCT was but one part of the broader restructuring of the UK public sector carried out by the Conservative administrations of 1979–97, using tools from the New Public Management toolkit. Central to this restructuring was devolution of powers and responsibilities to service departments on a contract basis, 'freeing managers to manage', and the introduction of performance-related pay. As Pollitt and his associates observe (1999: 40), these themes 'were most powerfully combined and exemplified in central government's attempts to create a series of self-managed local service delivery organizations'.

At the heart of the Conservatives' New Public Management strategy, Labour had opposed CCT from the outset. In its place Labour introduced 'Best Value'. After an initial period with a series of pilot authorities, the full Best Value (BV) regime came into operation for all authorities in England from April 2000 and in Wales three months later. It was one of the early priorities for the new government and received statutory backing in the 1999 Local Government Act. Under the Best Value scheme each local authority is obliged to assess its priorities and produce Best Value Performance Plans. What have become know as the '4Cs' are central to performance reviews. Each review must: (a) *challenge* why and how a service is being provided; (b) invite *comparisons* with others' performance across a range of relevant indicators; (c) *consult* with local taxpayers, service users and the wider business community in setting new performance targets; and (d) embrace fair *competition* as a means of securing efficient and effective services.

It soon became clear to local government that, while it would be rid of the deeply unpopular CCT regime, BV would prove every bit as centrally prescriptive and potentially even more interventionist. It applied, moreover, to every single service and function. The evaluation report (DTLR 2001) was revealing. On the positive side it concluded that the BV framework had the potential to facilitate service improvement and it provided several examples from the pilot authorities of both improvements and cost savings:

- Camden's productivity gains helped provide an extra 70,000 hours of extra social care over five years at no extra cost;
- Portsmouth Council was able to teach twice as many dyslexic children as before and to a higher standard; and
- Lewisham LBC made efficiency savings of £500,000 in its revenue and benefits service.

However, the evaluation report also highlighted some serious difficulties. Pilot authorities proved far better at comparing and consulting than the other two Cs – challenging and competing. Few were found to have thoroughly examined the underlying need for a service. Similarly, competition was problematic for the authorities strongly committed to in-house provision, who hoped that the disappearance of CCT had seen the end of having to compete constantly with the private sector (see Wilson and Game 2002, ch. 17).

By the time the Audit Commission's first annual report on the new regime – *Changing Gear: Best Value Annual Statement 2001* – was issued, the Commission had undertaken 500 inspections, covering a wide range of services. Each of these services was scored on a three-star rating system, in which a no-star rating represented a poor service and three stars represented an excellent service. Analysis of its 500 inspections showed that 63 per cent were considered fair (one star) or poor (no star); only 2 per cent achieved a three-star rating while a further 35 per cent achieved a two-star rating. Overall, 8 per cent were considered to be poor. As Pratchett (2002: 338) notes:

> Of those that were considered to be fair or poor, less than half were considered likely to improve. While identifying some examples of good service provision, the Best Value inspection process also identified some significant failings within local government services.

There has long been government-appointed inspectors for particular services: the Fire Services Inspectorate, Social Services Inspectorate, HM Inspectorate of Constabulary, the Benefit Fraud Inspectorate and the Office for Standards in Education (OFSTED) are classic examples. By 2001, though, those already in existence had expanded and they had been joined by a whole new army of best-value inspectors. The estimated annual cost of all the inspectorates scrutinizing local government is around £600 million. In addition, there are numerous 'opportunity costs' to local authorities such as staff time, the stifling of experimentation and innovation, and the damage to staff morale (see Davis *et al.* 2001).

The schools inspectorate, OFSTED, is an example of an inspectorate whose work has expanded in both scale and significance. Its several thousand visits to schools each year now form the basis of ministerial judgements about whether a school has 'serious weaknesses', requires 'special measures', or is failing so fundamentally that it needs a completely 'fresh start'. The Department of Education's Standards and Effectiveness Unit claimed by 2001 to have closed some 130 'failing' schools and 'turned round' nearly 800. In addition to dealing with schools, OFSTED now undertakes inspections of whole Local Education Authorities (LEAs), LEA-funded youth services, early years childcare and education, education action zones, and many other areas besides. Under New Labour the inspection regime became increasingly oppressive, something recognized by DTLR minister Stephen Byers in a LGA Conference speech in July 2001 following Labour's second election victory: 'Local authorities are suffering from inspection overload. This can divert valuable personnel and staff from the top priority which must be the provision of high quality services.' He promised to reduce this burden, and deregulating measures have included the abolition of 84 consent regimes – a significant lull in the relentless centralization of the previous two decades.

Strengthening executive leadership

In July 1998 the Blair government published a White Paper entitled *Modern Local Government: In Touch with the People* (DETR 1998a) which outlined three models of executive leadership, as set out in Exhibit 10.1. One factor behind the drive towards strengthening executive leadership was the government's disenchantment with the traditional committee system which, as the White Paper observed (1998a: 25) led 'to inefficient and opaque decision making'. These service committees (for example education, social services, housing), according to the government's critique, resulted in councillors spending too much time, unproductively, in too many meetings, while real policy decisions were being made elsewhere, in party groups, behind closed doors, and with little if any public input. Dynamic executive leadership at local level was what the Labour government was seeking to achieve through its proposals. The danger, however, was that such proposals (especially the directly elected mayor options) could lead to more elitist decision-making, non-executive councillors being increasingly marginalized.

Exhibit 10.1   New Labour's models of executive leadership

Option 1   A *directly elected mayor with a cabinet*. The mayor to be directly
elected by the whole electorate and to appoint a cabinet from among
the councillors.

Option 2   A *cabinet with a leader*. The leader to be elected by the council; the
cabinet to be made up of Councilors whether appointed by the leader
or elected by the council.

Option 3   A *directly elected mayor with a council manager*. The mayor to be
directly elected by local people, with a full-time manager appointed
by the council to whom both strategic policy and day-to-day
decision-making would be delegated.

Source: *Modern Local Government: In Touch with the People* (DETR 1998a).

The Local Government Act of 2000 confirmed the three options set out
in Exhibit 10.1 but, following pressure in the House of Lords, the government added a fourth option for small local authorities of 85,000 inhabitants
or less (21 per cent of councils) – namely retention of a revamped committee system if, following consultation (usually via a postal questionnaire)
such a system was desired by the local population. Executive leadership
has, therefore, become the norm in the UK, although by June 2004 only
11 local authorities (along with the separately elected Greater London
Authority) had chosen the government's favoured option, the directly
elected mayor scenario. The leader and cabinet model (the least radical
option) turned out to be the preference for over 95 per cent of local authorities. This result is hardly surprising since the elected mayoral options were
not popular amongst the bulk of councillors who feared being sidelined if
such a radical change took place.

Greater London was treated separately. The Greater London Authority
Act 1999 provided for a directly elected mayor and a separately elected
assembly, each chosen for four years. The GLA represented the first substantive move towards a new form of local governance in Britain, with clear
separation of powers between the directly elected mayor and a small
London Assembly of 25 members. Elections were held in May 2000 with
the Authority becoming operational in July 2000. The Labour Party han-
dled the process of candidate selection ineptly. It was determined to prevent
Ken Livingstone, a Labour MP and former Leader of the radical Greater
London Council, from being adopted as the party's official candidate, the
end result being that Livingstone stood as an Independent and easily
defeated all opponents, including the 'official' Labour candidate, Frank

Dobson. As Travers (2003) notes, the mayor's huge electorate and the GLA's strategic role suggested devolved regional government, like the Scottish Parliament, but in practice the financial rules and close continuing central government control made the GLA look more like local government. There is executive leadership, but the parameters have been tightly drawn by the centre.

Democratic consultation

The Local Government Act 2000 required all local authorities to consult their communities before selecting a new political management structure. Invariably this was done by means of a postal questionnaire. In a small number of authorities there were also referenda to determine whether authorities were to go ahead with the directly elected mayor option. As noted earlier, enhancing public participation was a major theme of New Labour's first term in office (1997–2001), but political interest nevertheless remained low. The Blair government attempted to tackle this problem on two fronts: first by devising ways of boosting voting turnout and, secondly, by advocating new methods of participation and consultation. In the context of the former, the Representation of the People Act 2000 allowed a small number of councils (32) to experiment with new voting arrangements in the May 2000 local elections. Among the experiments undertaken were the use of different voting days, electronic voting, weekend voting, mobile polling stations, early voting and blanket postal voting. Results from these experiments (and similar experiments, including e-voting, in 2002) suggested that only blanket postal voting had a major impact, with turnout in some wards being doubled. Overall, however, turnout in local elections remained low, around the 30 per cent mark.

Partly in the light of the shortcomings of *representative* democracy, the Labour government has attempted to enhance *participatory* democracy as part of an explicitly political agenda incorporating broader issues of democratic renewal. Under New Labour, participatory schemes have become integral parts of the local government landscape, yet in their own right, no matter how elaborate or innovative they might appear to be, they do not necessarily result in any policy impact. Such schemes guarantee nothing – other than making the relevant local authority look progressive! New Labour has constantly espoused 'participation' as one of its watchwords, but as Beetham (1996: 33) reminds us, the term 'participation' is too vague a concept to serve as a proxy for 'democracy' in the absence of any specification of participation in what form, by whom, or to what effect.

Beetham recalls that the most participating regimes of the twentieth century 'were communist systems, so-called people's democracies; yet that participation delivered little popular control over the personnel or policies of government'. Likewise, Parry and his associates (1992) emphasize that a participatory democrat will not seek only to maximize participation but to equalize it. Ironically, the same Labour government that is keen for councils to actively promote public participation is also insisting upon more elitist executive leadership in all but the smallest local authorities.

Regionalization and the impact of international forces

In the UK the issues of regionalization and intermunicipal cooperation do not have the same importance as in much of the rest of Europe. The relatively large size of UK authorities means that they have the resources to carry out most statutory services themselves, although there has been a growth in partnerships between local authorities and the private/voluntary sectors in recent years (see Sullivan and Skelcher 2002). The establishment of the Scottish Parliament, the Welsh Assembly and the Greater London Authority, moreover, has clarified service responsibilities that were previously divided among several fragmented bodies, thereby sharpening democratic accountability.

It should be noted, however, that the Regional Development Agencies Act passed in 1998 created eight (nine with the addition of one for London in the following year) new Regional Development Agencies (RDAs) for England – ministerially appointed bodies charged with improving the economic performance and competitiveness of their regions. At the same time, a matching set of regional chambers, often referred to as 'assemblies', was set up to oversee the RDAs and supposedly secure some form of local political accountability, despite the fact that they are nominated and appointed, rather than elected. A White Paper on directly elected regional government in England, '*Your Region – Your Choice': Revitalising the English Regions*, was published in May 2002 (Cabinet Office 2002). But if regional government is to attain greater prominence, it is likely to do so only where it is supported by the local population in a referendum. While regional loyalties are strong in some parts of England (notably the north-east), they are weak elsewhere. Another patchwork of authorities is likely to emerge, following the referenda in three English regions scheduled for October 2004.

In this context the European dimension of UK local governance requires recognition, and two points are to be made in this regard. First, at a basic level, an extra dimension to central–local relations emerges. As Peter John observes (2001: 65) 'Rather than being bipolar, central–local relations become just one of the dyads between the three levels of government. The already dense networks that join levels of government within nation states become even more complex as a result of Europeanization'. While true, it is also useful to be mindful of what Bache (1998: 155) has termed 'flexible gatekeeping' and the 'extended gatekeeper' with respect to regional policy development in the European Union. By these terms Bache refers to the control exerted by the nation state. While sub-national actors may participate, Bache argues (ibid.) that 'multi-level governance needs to take greater account of the gate-keeping powers of national governments across all stages of policy-making, over time and across issues'. An excessive focus on the numbers of sub-national agencies 'consulted' on EU policy issues, in short, can lead to an underestimation of the underlying power of central agencies to utilize their considerable resources in shaping policy outcomes.

Much UK local authority interest in Europe has focused around securing EU finance. Indeed the UK is the country with the largest number of offices in Brussels, largely because of its fragmented structure of government at the sub-national level and (in the case of England) its lack of regional units. Indeed, the lack of clear regions (in comparison with much of the rest of Europe) has been a significant hindrance for some parts of England securing EU funding. In essence, local governance in the UK now has a clear EU dimension. This changes the scene of intergovernmental relations, but as John notes (2001: 92), this 'does not radically transform central–local relationships; moreover, Europeanization and sub-national mobilization are patchy'. It is a dimension of local governance that changes in importance both over time and from issue to issue – part of a complex mosaic of influences.

Conclusion – is the centre too powerful?

Central–local relations have been a particular source of interest since the Labour government came to power in 1997. Both academics and practitioners have pointed to tensions within the government's reform agenda – between a 'top-down' and 'bottom-up' approach; between a drive for national standards and the encouragement of local learning and innovation; and, as noted above, between strengthening executive leadership and enhancing public participation. Labour's modernization strategy has clear elements of a top-down (or hierarchist) approach (legislation, inspectorates, white papers), but there is also a significant 'bottom-up' (or localist) element (a variety of zones, experiments and pilots). While there is certainly far greater dialogue between central and local government than during the Conservative years, this should not be seen as a proxy for policy influence. As has been observed elsewhere, 'multi-level participation should not be mistaken for multi-level governance' (Wilson 2002: 2).

In Labour's second term, a key early document was the December 2001 White Paper, *Strong Local Leadership – Quality Public Services*. It acknowledged (DTLR 2001 paras. 4.2–4.4) how stultifying central government controls had become. It promised that in the future central government would shift its focus from controls on inputs, processes and local decisions to assuring delivery of outcomes through a national framework of standards and accountability. The White Paper sets out rewards and incentives for local government – a system of 'earned autonomy'. Some rewards and incentives are common across local government, providing opportunities for all authorities – such as the reduction in the number of plans that authorities are obliged to produce – but many of the incentives are concentrated upon rewarding high-performing authorities by relaxing financial restrictions and improving their operational environment.

Despite government rhetoric, what emerged, as 'earned autonomy' was anything but liberating. Councils are divided into five bands ranging from poor to excellent following their Comprehensive Performance Assessment (CPA) by the Audit Commission. Of the 150 authorities that underwent their second CPA in 2003, 26 rose by at least one category while 9 went down. Overall, some 27 authorities were deemed 'excellent'. There is still, however, a need to convince government that such councils can be trusted with greater freedoms and flexibilities. Indeed, this is against a backdrop of central government's threat in 2004 to 'cap' the council tax of both 'good' and 'excellent' councils. Essentially the government's message to local authorities remains: organize yourself to deliver what government wants and you could be rewarded; fail to deliver what the government wants and your days will be numbered. The resource exchange emphasized by Rhodes (1997) in his differentiated polity model therefore remains heavily loaded in favour of the centre.

In his Foreword to the 2001 White Paper, Tony Blair observed: 'I want to see central government and local government working together in a constructive partnership to deliver the high quality public services that local people have the right to expect'. Deregulating measures were set out – and implemented – which included the removal of many of the specific policy areas for which central government consent is required before local initiatives are permitted. The regulatory concessions to local government in the 2001 local government White Paper contrast sharply with the Education Bill before Parliament in 2001 which gave the Secretary of State for

Education and Skills important extra regulatory powers. In 2004 the Office of the Deputy Prime Minister (ODPM) – the newly designated local government ministry – remained but one element of a complex Whitehall universe, the constituent parts of which remain culturally and operationally diverse (see Marsh *et al.* 2001).

The Local Government Act 2000 gave local authorities major new powers. They now have a community leadership role with powers to promote and develop social, environmental and economic well-being. The same Act gave local councils a new role in the context of collaboration with other agencies; they are now expected to lead the search for solutions to the range of crosscutting social, economic and environmental problems in the locality. The Health and Social Care Act 2001, for example, gave overview and scrutiny committees of major councils powers to publicly scrutinize the health service. A purely hierachist interpretation of UK local government is, therefore, a distortion of reality, but without an adequate local financial base it will be difficult to make community leadership real. It is, as Lowndes (2002) observes, an increasingly disaggregated local arena characterized by a complex web of crosscutting and hierarchically arranged relationships. Given the diversity of local partnership bodies and the variety of front-line service-delivery institutions, central–local relations might be more appropriately seen in terms of multi-level governance. In a similar vein, John, in his work on local governance in Western Europe (2001: 175), emphasizes that there 'is no uniform pattern. There is a massive variety of political arrangements and practices across and between local political systems'. Local governance in the UK clearly exemplifies this.

11   New Zealand: a quantum leap forward?

Graham W.A. Bush

In 1990, local government in New Zealand had just emerged from its most radical restructuring since first being established nearly 150 years earlier. Once safely reelected for a second three-year term in 1987, the Labour government embarked upon fundamental reforms across an expansive range of governmental and private activities. While many actors in a somewhat complacent and conservative system of local government initially felt that it neither needed reforming nor would fall into the reformers' clutches, it soon became apparent that virtually no sector of governmental activity would be immune, and that retaining the status quo would not be an option.

Notwithstanding extensive rounds of consultation, restructuring was centrally imposed and closely conformed to principles underlying the reform process throughout the wider public sector. At the heart of the reforms were the goals of achieving responsible management of publicly-owned resources and a high standard of accountability and transparency in governing each locality (Anderson and Norgrove 1997: 118). Explicit priorities were operational efficiency, managerial separation of commercial, regulatory and service-delivery functions, transparent trade-offs among objectives, and clear and strong mechanisms for assuring accountability. What this portended in practical terms for the Local Government Commission, the government's executive instrument, was a system of local bodies which were: (1) much fewer in number; (2) multi-purpose; (3) based on current rather than historical communities of interest; (4) functionally efficient and effective; (5) more responsive to local inputs and needs; and (6) technically and managerially more robust (Bush 1995: 85).

To understand the sweeping impact of the reforms, it is useful to highlight some of the most prominent features of local government before and after the 1989 watershed. Following this, developments during the 1990s and up to the present time, including passage of a new Local Government Act in 2002, are presented and discussed in greater detail.

Reshaping and reprogramming local government

Through legislative fiat and mandatory reorganization schemes, the structure of local government was drastically altered in 1989. The number of regions was reduced from 22 to 12, 205 territorial local authorities (TLAs) – the heartland of New Zealand's local government with general responsibility for governing a defined geographical area – were slashed to 74, and the special-purpose-board sector was virtually abolished, their functions either being subsumed into the surviving units or transferred to publicly-owned companies (see Table 11.1). At the same time, a sub-stratum of community boards was given greater emphasis. Although not uniform throughout the country, these mixed appointed-elected boards were subordinate to the TLAs and were intended to bridge the widened gap between citizens and their much enlarged local bodies. Labour's vision of regional councils forming the embryo of true regional government was not shared by the National Party, however, and one fallout from the National Party's victory in the 1990 general election was the restriction in 1992 of regional units to a planning role for the management of natural and physical resources. The special problem existing in Auckland, New Zealand's principal city, was resolved by creating a directly elected services trust, to which all the Auckland Regional Council's commercial enterprises were transferred.

While the structure of local government was changed dramatically by the 1989 reform, fundamental issues of local government functions and finance were essentially untouched, the idea being that these were to be dealt with later. The principle of *ultra vires*, by which local authorities were restricted to activities for which express statutory permission existed or could be obtained, was left in place, reflecting a strongly centralist vein in prevailing political philosophies about the role of government. The practical consequence of this has been that major social spheres of public activity such as health, welfare, policing and education have never lain within local government's domain. Some 60 separately identifiable functions that fall within six broad sectors of activity were nonetheless within the sphere of competence of territorial local government at the beginning of the twenty-first century. These six sectors are community improvement, planning, utilities, regulation, nuisance control and (very limited) social welfare respectively.

The functional picture is very different for regional councils and community boards. Whereas the former have their roles tightly defined as managing the natural environment, transport planning, harbour control and civil defence (Bush 2001: 160), the functions – and to a large degree even the existence – of community boards are entirely dependent on the discretion of the parent council. Consequently, the pattern varies from the delegation

Table 11.1 *The structure of local government in New Zealand before and after the reform of 1989*

Level of government	Before March 1989		After November 1989	
	Type of structure	Number	Type of structure	Number
Regional	● Regional councils	3	● Regional councils[a]	14
	● United councils	19	–	–
	total	*22*	total	*14*
Territorial	● Municipality	106	● City councils	14
	● County	67	● County council[b]	1
	● District	31	● District councils[a]	59
	● Town District	1	–	–
	total	*205*	total	*74*
Community	● District community councils	13		
			–	–
	● Community councils	118	● Community boards	159
	total	*131*	total	*159*
Special purpose	● Energy boards	38	● Energy boards[c]	37
	● Hospital/Area health boards	29	● Hospital/Area health boards	14
	● Licensing trusts	28	● Licensing trusts	28
	● Pest destruction boards	61	–	–
	● River/Land drainage boards	27	–	–
	● Catchment boards	17	–	–
	● Harbour boards	15	–	–
	● Miscellaneous	20	● Miscellaneous	7
	total	*235*	total	*86*
Grand total[d]		593	–	333

[a] Includes one authority which has both regional and territorial status; [b] Chatham Islands regarded as needing special administrative arrangements; [c] ongoing separate reform converting certain types of elected energy boards into power companies; [d] excludes local quangos and other bodies not normally classified as local authorities – for example 22 District Road councils, 10 Education boards, 34 Airport authorities and so forth.

Source: Data from Department of Statistics (1990: 84–94).

of almost every function legally possible to the delegation of almost no responsibilities at all, relegating the boards concerned to virtual talking-shops. A 1995 survey revealed, for example, that of 44 functions that theoretically could be delegated, in 40 per cent of the cases the community board had an advisory role, in 10 per cent a decision-making role, in 6 per cent a combined role, while in 33 per cent the council retained all authority unto itself (Department of Internal Affairs 1995: 1).

The reform also left most aspects of the local electoral system – which had long been based on the principle of direct popular elections with a first-past-the-post rule – intact, but several changes were undertaken. First, the directly elected mayor model became mandatory for all TLAs; second, the casting of ballots by post became effectively universal; third, the requirements for candidates to have a residential tax rating or electoral connection with their local authority area was abolished; and, fourth, from 1992 the practice of multiple office-holding (being a member of a regional council and a TLA or a community board concurrently) was prohibited. In addition, 15 months before each election local authorities are required to complete a review of representation, with attention being given to the number of councillors and whether they are to be elected by wards.

Aside from these changes, the 1989 reform did not alter the basic system of political control and command. Legal power has always been vested in the majority of the elected councillors and board members who attend duly constituted meetings. Power to make and execute policy resides at the political level, but solely with the collective body, not the mayor or any other titleholder. In the management realm, however, the 1989 reform did initiate one revolutionary change. Previously, all acts were done in the name of the council, and the council – that is the political majority – was the fount of all authority. The council was the legal employer of all staff and could, and often did, issue detailed instructions about the implementation of policy and the provision of services. 'Interfering in administration' had been the rule, rather than the exception.

1989 ended this legal monopoly on power. In accord with the principle of 'letting the managers manage', the new legislation decreed that the political arm's rights with respect to management was limited to the appointment of the chief executive officer: for all other positions the employer was deemed to be the chief executive officer. He or she has the obligation to ensure that the local body enjoys the human and other resources necessary to ensure that policies are properly implemented, although the elected members retain responsibility for vetting and approving the supporting budget. Reinforcing this transfer of managerial power was the liberalization of service-delivery methods. Implicit was greater use of contractors and other private-enterprise mechanisms, local-authority trading enterprises, and cooperative arrangements with other local bodies. The era of dominant in-house provision, in short, was ending.

Compliance with much tougher accountability standards also became mandatory. A new category of local authority – the Local Authority Trading Enterprise (LATE) – was created, and all councils had at least to consider the organization of all relevant activities in such enterprises. At the same time the establishment of separate service-delivery centres was formally encouraged. Led by the Society of Local Government Managers, local government staff strode towards true professionalism and embraced components of the new managerialism. For elected members the greatest impacts came through obligations to separate the oversight of regulatory and service functions, and to prepare comprehensive annual plans and reports, the former being subject to community consultation.

The Labour government's grand goal of achieving a comprehensive but staged local government reform package was ultimately frustrated, and this was due to more than just its electoral defeat in 1990. Three items in particular were destined for the 'too hard' basket. One was the idea of according local government a power of general competence, but this was soon blunted by its extraordinary constitutional implications. A second was how to accommodate in such a package the aspirations and interests of the indigenous Maori people, guaranteed certain rights under the 1840 Treaty of Waitangi. This was bound to be politically explosive, and was earmarked for later attention. Third and equally intractable was the reshaping of local government's revenue base. A discussion document on the subject raised sufficient furore that this issue was also put on hold (Bush 1995: 99–100).

Central government dominance and tolerance

Local government did not tamely or passively acquiesce in its ordeal, but did accept that in the end it had no alternative. Throughout the intense and prolonged reform process the primary focus was on the fate of both individual and classes of local bodies. Typical questions were 'Why was our local body to be abolished?'; 'Was a rash of community boards really needed?'; or 'Would the ongoing task of pest destruction be properly ensured?' Attracting much less attention was an accompanying set of extremely fundamental edicts about operational forms, the making of policy, and managerial practices and ethos. The explanation for this lies in the nature of local government's subordinate position in New Zealand's governmental apparatus. There is no written constitution, no upper house of Parliament, and there is no tradition of the courts playing a protective overtly 'political' role, all of this leading one observer to describe New Zealand as an 'elected dictatorship' (Mulgan 1994: 91). Rather, the basic canons of democracy are safeguarded by commitment and their incorporation in statute.

Theoretically, this places local government in a parlous position, its very right to exist depending on the will of the government through its control of Parliament. The extinction of local government may be completely inconceivable, but whole classes of local bodies have been abolished in the past. More immediately, it is the centre which determines local government's structure, role, funding and prerogatives. This is reinforced by the *ultra vires* doctrine (Bush 1995: 170–3). Since 1989, furthermore, the Minister of Local Government has had a right to review any local body in the event of a significant failure to meet obligations or of mismanagement of resources, and, in certain circumstances, to dismiss its mayor and councillors.

Casting local government as a hapless creature of central government, however, would grossly distort the actual nature of the relationship. Admittedly, local bodies are most accurately envisaged as machinery devised for effective government at the sub-national level, and local bodies have at times been on the receiving end of government edicts. Formal legal sovereignty cannot be shared. Yet in practice local government's playing field is usually quite congenial; neither Parliament nor government has ever been concerned with minutely prescribing local government's behaviour, nor with treating its members as servants or agents of the Crown. A state of mutual interdependence is recognized, not least because, until recently, about half of all MPs had been mayors or councillors. Even more tellingly, the tolerance or even *laissez faire* attitude typically exhibited by central government towards its 'junior partner' emanates from the associated facts that local government has no responsibility for education, mainstream social welfare, health, or law and order and, except for roading, consequently derives very little of its income from government grants or transfers.

Notwithstanding the huge burst of changes forced through in 1989, both central and local government tacitly acknowledged that in two crucial respects, reform was uncompleted. First, it needed to be made to work in practice and to achieve the gains in efficiency and effectiveness that its architects promised. This included further adaptations and modifications as experience proved were desirable. Second, and quite separately, aspects that had been deferred or not addressed during the 'white heat' phase had to be returned to the agenda and resolved. So the prevailing sentiment was a subtle intermixture: while support for returning to the *status quo ante* rapidly dwindled, the plea was to accord local government an assurance of genuine stability. The new system needed time to work into its optimal shape and absorb the further instalments of change which were pending (Bush 1995: 101–5, 310–12).

Post-1990 changes in the context and system of local government

Faced with a plethora of demands arising from the system's restructuring, local government was fortunate during the 1990s that central government was essentially willing to stand back and let things settle. Until 1999 the National Party was in power either on its own or in coalition, and despite its fulminations when in opposition against Labour's strategy, National's attitude on assuming office was much more pragmatic. What National *did* do included making the process of reconstituting abolished local bodies theoretically (but less so in practice) easier to attain, reducing regional government's role, abolishing one regional council and converting its constituent TLAs to unitary authorities (combining both territorial and regional functions), passing Labour's Resource Management Act, and advancing reforms in the health, transport and energy sectors along lines more in accord with philosophies of the economic Right.

What National declined to engineer was a wholesale undoing of the reform package. It labelled as autocratic and antidemocratic the means by which it had been imposed, but the contents and outcome were treated as a platform for further improvement. Reinforcing this was National's predisposition to let local government look after itself. It even spoke effusively about forging a stronger and more vibrant partnership with local government, although its actions scarcely measured up to this ideal. Overall, National honoured its undertaking to permit local government a reasonable period of grace in which to get the reformed system into an effective working mode.

In some sensitive areas, though, the National government's policies were definitely adrift of what Labour's would probably have been. The National Party was ideologically averse to local bodies competing with private enterprise in the provision of 'commercial' services and commodities, especially when the playing field was tilted in local government's favour. Downgrading regional councils was one measure in this connection. Some initial encouragement was also given to other areas that were campaigning for regional councils to be replaced by unitary authorities, but nothing tangible occurred. To deal with Auckland's special status, in 1998 the National government vested in an appointed body – Infrastructure Auckland – port company and other shares, and charged it with funding transport, roading and stormwater projects. Very predictably, National refused to tackle the issue of the relationship between Maori and local government, leaving in place rights of consultation accorded local tribes on transport and resource management but ruling out any other accommodation. Finally, isolated sniping at the community board model may have been a forerunner to a more serious assault, but its defence by local government's own lobby, Local Government New Zealand, negated that prospect.

Organizational, operational, managerial and fiscal changes in the 1990s

Undoubtedly, the deepest and most enduring changes wrought by the 1989 reform have been along the operational–managerial axis rather than the structural–functional axis. Some were already in use, reflecting shifts occurring beyond New Zealand's shores. Others were either statutorily embedded by the reform, or given substantial additional impetus. In breaking new ground by venturing into delineating the purposes for which local government exists, the 1989 legislation specified two purposes – the operation of competitively neutral trading undertakings, and the efficient and effective exercise of functions and duties – which directly bore on the how, rather than the what and why, of local government (Bush 1995: 125).

Evidence of this can be gleaned from monitoring studies conducted by the government agency responsible for local government, the Department of Internal Affairs (Anderson and Norgrove 1997: 171–2), enquiries of the Controller and Auditor-General into financial management and operational accountability (Bush 1995: 180–1), and independent analysis (Anderson and Norgrove 1997: 163–6; Boston *et al.* 1996b: 183–202). What these investigations confirmed were trends towards managerial innovations, consultation, performance measurement, development of strategies, sharpened financial management and alternative methods of service delivery. Broadly expressed, local bodies were taking tentative steps from being primarily service-delivery agencies towards focusing on ensuring effective governance of their communities.

Service delivery

One of the prime targets trained in the sights of the reform architects was the traditional propensity for TLAs to deliver services in-house. Henceforth, the acid test was efficient and effective outcomes, not fidelity to one form of discharging responsibilities. Continuing to use its own forces was not formally prohibited, but the local body also had to consider the advantages of contracts or arrangements with the Crown or another local body, setting up a Local Authority Trading Enterprise (LATE), or contracting out the function to a person or organization. Regional councils were prohibited from using their own staff unless they were formally satisfied that it was the most advantageous option. Underlying this framework was the assumption that in-house departments, virtually being guaranteed a monopoly and resources, had become lax and too little concerned with performance, and needed a salutary dose of competitiveness. The model espoused was that applying to road construction and maintenance, which, under other legislation, was already subject to competitive pricing procedures (Anderson and Norgrove 1996: 146).

Despite intermittent agitation by sector groups such as Federated Farmers and monetarist think-tanks like the Business Roundtable, true privatization (with local authorities completely exiting from an activity in favour of the market) has made relatively modest inroads into local government. An attempt in the late 1990s to open the water-supply business to the private sector encountered overwhelming public opposition. A variant which made bigger headway was the dogma that 'local bodies had no business being in business'. Not only was private enterprise supposedly inherently able to provide the service more efficiently, but it was unethical for local bodies to compete from their privileged, protected position against local businesses which were substantial contributors to the local body's revenue.

Three principal outcomes can be ascertained. First, there is now extremely little 'head-to-head' commercial competition between local bodies and the private sector. Being able to choose between the two in purchasing a commodity or a service to all intents and purposes no longer applies. Public transport, for example, is almost completely privatized. Second, among local bodies the gamut of contracted-out services has steadily widened (Controller and Auditor-General 2002a: 12). To traditional activities such as refuse collection, legal services, roading and drainage have been added engineering, inspecting, aspects of resource and property management, parks maintenance and public relations. Third, a similar trend has occurred with respect to the arm's-length Local Authority Trading Enterprise. Originally conceived to subject trading activities like water and power supply to commercial rigour and practices, it has been utilized for non-commercial functions like works (roading and drainage). The most enthusiastic exponent, Dunedin City Council, has its forests, tourist railway and even treasury managed by LATEs.

This shift in the service-delivery regime is anything but cosmetic, although many local bodies still seem insufficiently customer-focused (Controller and Auditor-General 2002a: 29–30). Whatever the shift, the explanation is not overt compulsion exerted by central government. Central government's strategy has consistently been limited to using statute and regulation to decree how local bodies should resolve the issue of delivering services. For each activity, they have to establish clear objectives, ensure that its performance is regularly measured, maintain oversight and ensure separate management of regulatory functions. However, discretion over the choice of delivery modes was retained by the local bodies.

To the extent that a shift has occurred, the causes are multiple and intertwined. First, boosted by rightwing economic resurgence and the new managerialism, a general climate emerged which extolled private-sector models of service provision. Second, there was a growing awareness of the desirability of limiting or transferring risk. Third, from 1996 onward a statutory obligation to fund depreciation of assets was introduced, a policy that jolted local bodies steeped in the expediency of expenditure deferral. Fourth, there was a belief that commercial disciplines would result in least-cost services. Fifth, varying but mounting ratepayer pressure to reduce rate burdens arose. Finally (as regards the formation of LATEs), operational activities were removed from political interference.

Imposition of comprehensive policy planning

Prior to 1989 systematic planning was completely foreign in nature to most local bodies and the policy process was poorly understood (Bush 1995: 226–8). Yet driven by both efficiency and accountability goals, the reform forced local authorities to embrace planning as a fundamental process. Initially this comprised the statutory preparation of annual plans and reports. In the mid-1990s an entirely new raft of financial planning instruments was added, while near the end of the decade strategic planning arrived on stage unprodded.

For the ensuing year in detail and the next two in outline, the local body now must annually prepare in two stages (draft and final) a plan which states its intentions regarding significant objectives and activities, performance targets, indicative costs, sources of funds and rating (land tax) policy. Later it has to report in detail on how the plan fared, including a comparison between projected and actual performance. The report is then audited by the Audit Office, an agency of central government. Notwithstanding some lingering resentment among local bodies about the time, cost and consultative aspects of the planning process (see below), it has exerted a salutary discipline on the sector. It compels councillors and officers to cooperate, confronts the former with their policy-making obligations, heightens external accountability, and makes it more difficult to deliver words and promises but no action.

Inasmuch as financial management is a servant rather than an autonomous spirit, its ultimate concerns must be with larger purposes of the local body. Hence, endeavouring to plan financial strategy inevitably implies venturing into general goals and objectives. As of the 2002 general election, however, Parliament had yet to make the preparation of strategic plans mandatory. In the mid-1990s about 40 per cent of TLAs had voluntarily embarked on the shaping of a strategic plan stretching over a 10-year horizon (Bush 1995: 224), but official concern was subsequently expressed about insufficient effort being devoted to producing such a document (Controller and Auditor-General 2002a: 16).

Compulsory consultation frameworks

One of the cornerstones of the 1989 reform was enhanced accountability, and this was defined as a two-way process – the local body rendering an account to the community of its record, but also having to ascertain the community's views and preferences. Thus an integral and novel part of the annual planning process was to present the local body's intentions to the citizens, and then afford them the opportunity to indicate their reaction.

The legislative provisions established a Special Consultative Procedure (SCP) under which the local body was required to publish its proposed annual plan, seek community opinion (both written and oral), take these into account in reaching decisions, and then advise participants about the fate of their submissions. It was envisaged as the way of the community's collective vision being translated by the key formal players (the councillors and staff) into reality. The SCP also applied to other actions such as a local body's intention to divest itself of a significant undertaking. Another vital piece of legislation, the Resource Management Act 1991, also laid heavy emphasis on public consultation: on matters affecting the *tangata whenua* (local Maori groups) it is compulsory. The array of financial management measures (such as funding, investment and borrowing policies) introduced in 1996 was also tagged with consultation obligations.

What difference this avenue for participation made is problematical (see Cheyne 2002; Cheyne and Comrie 2002; Lynch 2002; and Reid 2002). Citizens were more explicitly to be made partners in planning and development strategies. Generally, however, submissions were sparse (one or two per thousand electors in 1995) and of mediocre quality, and as a result effecting only sporadic minor changes in draft plans. NIMBY-ism lurked everywhere and some of the populist submissions were obviously orchestrated. As the community became accustomed to the process, there is some evidence that both the quantity and quality of submissions improved, and in turn the local bodies accorded it more status, most notably by campaigns to encourage participation (Boston *et al.* 1996b: 195). Subsequently, a survey revealed that the average number of annual plan submissions (339) received in 2000 more than quadrupled the comparable figure for 1992.

Going down the consultation path so determinedly was not just pursued as an end in itself (Controller and Auditor-General 1998: 10); permeating the stand was a belief that local bodies, which existed to meet their community's needs, should have to hear what the community was thinking. The 1989 reforms, which increased the size of TLAs, widened the perceived gap between the local body and the citizen, and two-way accountability was therefore promoted as a bridging mechanism. It was also argued (though little proven in practice) that more responsive and efficient policies would be achieved. Finally, while retaining the model of representative democracy, it introduced a moderate leavening of participation.

The new orthodoxy of internal accountability

Of all the changes emerging from the 1989 reform, none has had greater consequence than that in the relationship between the elected councillors and the administrative arm. According to new stipulations, the CEO is now appointed by the council (often assisted by employment consultants) on a performance-based five-year contract, and is at the fulcrum of authority. Passing the buck is not an option: the council decides and the CEO is responsible for ensuring successful execution (Boston *et al.* 1996b: 190–1).

Local government, however, is a political arena, and in the real world relationships can never be that clean-cut or explicit. Two of the CEO's statutory roles are to provide advice and to ensure the proper management and planning of the local body's activities. These tend to breach any formal policy-administration dichotomy. Likewise, policy outcomes depend very heavily on implementation, and elected members can chafe at being legally impotent in this regard. Ideally, what should prevail is an atmosphere of productive mutual trust and recognition of interdependence, but that is not easily fashioned or maintained.

Unable or unwilling to shed old ways, many councils in the 1990s retaliated against the only part of the managerial instrument still accessible – the CEO. By 1994, 36 of the 86 TLAs and regional councils had replaced their CEOs, the overwhelming majority because of perceived unsatisfactory performance, the desire for fresh leadership, or serious breakdowns in relationships (Boston *et al.* 1996b: 191). The manner in which several councils exercised this right was so unsatisfactory that the Controller and Auditor-General drew up guidelines to assist in a more professional fulfilment of the employer role (Controller and Auditor-General 2002b). Recently there has been isolated grumbling from elected members for whom the possession of political-administrative power is a zero-sum game which 'their side' has lost. Any campaign for the restoration of the pre-1989 status quo, however, would be utterly futile. Strains in the relationship between the CEO and elected politicians nevertheless still do manifest themselves and bring the risk of 'suspicion and insular behaviour', thereby placing in jeopardy a local body's most crucial working relationship (Controller and Auditor-General 2002a: 7).

The forces of financial management

Insofar as the 1989 reform addressed local body financial practices, it did so chiefly from the angle of upgrading accounting standards. Borrowing, auditing, investing and expenditure were treated similarly, with the annual plan and report being the overall mechanism of financial control. But the revolution in financial management was still to occur. Encouraged by Audit Office disquiet over the lamentable level of ignorance in local bodies about the condition and value of their infrastructural assets, this came about with the passing of the Local Government Amendment Act No. 3 in 1996 (Anderson and Norgrove 1997: 159–60). With the sector's tacit endorsement, what was imposed on every local body from 1998 on was a comprehensive strategic framework within which financial affairs had to be conducted.

Incorporated as principal components of this framework were a long-term financial strategy along with funding, investment and borrowing management policies (Anderson and Norgrove 1997: 177–82). These had to comply with a series of specified principles, such as prudence, provision for expenditure needs, assessment of benefits and costs of options, balancing of the books, and a responsible debt-level regime. The fulcrum was the long-term (a minimum of 10 years) financial strategy, which had to identify and explain estimated expenses, propose sources of funds, estimate cash flows and commitments, and significant risks.

Most of the principles would be endorsed by the economic and accountancy professions, but some trespassed into fields of subjectivity. 'Matching funding sources to functions' can be translated as 'user-pay' and on this issue there has been deep division among and within local bodies. The obligation to start funding the depreciation of infrastructural assets also initially caused considerable consternation because of its impact on rating levels. One consequence of applying even more rigorous standards of transparency could be exposure of just how subjective and complex – and hence quasi-political and legally challengeable – funding decisions may be (Controller and Auditor-General 2002a: 11).

Despite proving a hard taskmaster, the 1996 measure has on balance appreciably lifted the general quality and sophistication of local-authority financial management. Stewardship is more sober, asset management is progressing, generally accepted accounting standards are being met, and financial strategies have become more insightful of, and relevant to, local body purposes. Yet, as befits a vigilant auditor, local government's responses have not been unreservedly approved. Among the problems identified, those referring to insufficient infrastructure information, perfunctory non-financial reporting, indigestible and unwieldy public documentation, and the demands being posed by the implementation of the Local Government (Rating) Act 2002 have the weightiest implications (Controller and Auditor-General 2002a: *passim*).

Impact on inter-local authority cooperation

Historically, local authorities cooperated in a highly pragmatic fashion. Sometimes functions were run cooperatively; sometimes one provided a function on behalf of others, usually overseen by a joint committee (statutorily allowed); sometimes by a separate legal entity. Occasionally one local body would provide staff for another; sometimes an officer would be employed by two local bodies. Likewise a town planning scheme would occasionally be jointly produced. Such cooperative practices were very common between a moderate-size rural borough and its surrounding county, whereas urban local bodies tended not to cooperate so closely.

The advent of quasi-regional local bodies from the late 1970s added another layer of complexity, because most were not allowed to provide their own staff or services, which were supplied by the principal constituent territorial authority. Relationships between the two independent regional bodies (Auckland and Wellington) and their constituent TLAs were often quite frigid. Also pre-1989 relationships between TLAs and *ad hoc* special-purpose bodies (for example hospital, harbour, power boards) were convoluted and almost impossible to easily unravel.

The 1989 reform did not formally prescribe the basis of relationships; rather, it added yet another layer of complexity – namely the relationships between a TLA and any LATEs it chose to create. The wholesale consolidation of TLAs put an end to most geographical local-body associations, although sometimes these were replaced by informal mayoral forums. Confrontation between regional bodies and TLAs over land-use planning matters was as common as was conciliation. In carrying out works and functions, any local body could enter into an arrangement or contract with, *inter alia,* any local authority or LATE. Similarly, a LATE owned by several local bodies was legally permitted. The picture of inter-authority cooperation, in short, has remained extremely variable according to the region, but is usually dominated by an air of pragmatism.

Towards an appraisal

In the late 1980s the international community of public managers, experts and academics became aware that something remarkable was happening to the New Zealand public sector. Slightly later, the realization that a similar phenomenon was occurring in its local government counterpart resulted in the arrival of a steady stream of specialists seeking to understand the reform's objectives and methods (see for example Phoenix Rising 1993). They observed the ongoing application of a heady mixture of insight, ideas copied from both abroad and the private sector and dogma. It was neither pure orthodoxy nor was it universally embraced by local authorities, but there was a broad consensus that, taken altogether, the changes were enhancing the capacity of local bodies to respond to their communities' preferences and needs more efficiently and effectively. The 1989 reform and its aftermath has been characterized as 'a renovation which has resulted in the system's rejuvenation' (Bush 1995: 317). Confirmation of a 'leading-edge' status came in 1993 when Christchurch City Council was adjudged cowinner of the prestigious international Bertelsmann Prize for innovative and democratic local self-government. In a sense Christchurch stood for the local-government sector's achievements generally, and New Zealand was charitably referred to as 'the world leader' in local government effectiveness.

Despite this recent international acclaim, it is important to emphasize that the reform was essentially top-down rather than bottom-up. Local authorities were, at least at the outset, largely in a position of being grudging recipients, reacting more than being active innovators and initiators. Globalization, in short, has first and foremost had its impact on local government in New Zealand indirectly, through policies adopted by national authorities, more than it has through direct experience or awareness of overseas developments among local authorities.

Meanwhile an authoritative and comprehensive benefit–cost analysis of the reforms is, over a decade on, still waiting to be undertaken. This, however, betrays more the paucity of capable analysts than the worthiness of the subject. There have been several tentative and intermediate assessments (Anderson 1993; Elwood 1995; Boston *et al.* 1996a, 1996b; Anderson and Norgrove 1997; Forgie *et al.* 1999), and the Controller and Auditor-General and his office have produced an invaluable series of reports on financial and operational aspects of the reenergized system. On two intertwined matters the assessments are unanimously in accord: (1) notwithstanding some minor slips, local government has accomplished a quantum leap forward, and (2) a return to the *ancien regime* would be an enormously retrograde step.

After the leap – what does the future hold?

Once the restructured system found its feet in the early 1990s there were pleas from a wide spectrum of stakeholders that it be allowed a period of stability in order to prove or disprove itself. A crucial designer of the reform, Brian Elwood, the chairman of the Local Government Commission, opined that it needed two terms (six years) breathing space to optimize its potential. Governments of both centre-right and centre-left orientation have heeded such pleas (the 1996 financial management legislation was regarded as an integral element of the original package, as were parallel reforms in the transport, health and energy sectors).

Although assurances of a calmer setting were honoured, they were never intended to mean that for local government, reform had been relegated to history. The sector itself, for example, has pressed for a thorough review and consolidation of its governing legislation, which was declining in utility as it was growing in volume. Another controlling statute that had visibly aged, the Local Elections and Polls Act 1976, received an overdue review in 2000, with its refitted successor (Local Electoral Act 2001) containing a mandate to ready the electoral process for the electronic age. Much less compressed was an unavoidably laborious examination of the funding powers possessed by local bodies, which were acutely sensitive about political and legal challenges to the basis of funding decisions. Eventually, legislation was enacted in 2002, its principal promise being improved guidance and protection for local authorities against legal challenges in their taxation role rather than sanctioning the baking of a bigger 'rate cake'.

Fundamental reshaping and repositioning notified

Transcending all other current issues for local government is how implementation of the Local Government Act 2002, which came into force in July 2003, will shape its future. The potential implications for local government's role, machinery and processes are almost impossible to exaggerate. Some themes in the legislation are linear developments of concepts originating in the 1989 reforms and others are expressions of particular priorities, but a few are quite novel. In no way is the Act merely a consolidation of a basic statute amended nearly to extinction in the course of 25 years. The very process of its formation – involving local and central government officials working collaboratively on an equal footing – was itself without precedent.

Whereas the purposes of local government as elucidated in the 1989 reform were rough-hewn prescriptive principles, by 2002 these had been refined into '[enabling] local decision making and action, by, and on behalf of, communities, and promote the social, economic, environmental, and cultural well-being of communities in the present and for the future' (Local

Government Act 2002, Section 10). The strategic vision of local government is unashamedly expansive, participatory, and embraces a philosophy of governance that prefers the local body at the centre of advancing community goals rather than just as a service-provider and regulator. Reinforcing this are requirements to cooperate and collaborate with other relevant bodies and for all local bodies within each region to negotiate protocols for communication and coordination.

The emphasis on consulting the community is dramatically strengthened and formalized, and principles relating to the supply of information, due process and appropriateness are prescribed. There is an even tougher regime in the form of the special consultative procedure (SCP) introduced in 1989. Already mandatory for developing the annual plan, the SCP has been extended to cover a new instrument, a long-term council community plan (LTCCP), and also decisions on a whole sheath of what are termed 'significant proposals' such as the sale of strategic assets, commencing or ceasing a function, or changing its mode of delivery. In sum, the overriding goal is to involve the community across the policy-making spectrum far more meaningfully. A lobby group, Business New Zealand, has estimated that the welter of consultation requirements will add 15 per cent to rates bills.

The vexing issue of local-body obligations to Maori is also partly addressed. Processes that provide opportunities for Maori to contribute to decision-making are mandated, an option to create Maori wards (TLAs) or constituencies (regional councils) was created in related legislation and circumstances under which Maori must be consulted are specified. The Minister of Local Government's existing powers with respect to reviewing and replacing a local authority by a commissioner or ordering an early election have similarly been modernized. Sprinkled throughout the enactment are both principles and policies with which the local body must respectively comply or develop.

Legislation regarding local government finance was also belatedly enacted in 2002, but it was only concerned with re-honing the rating instrument. Constraints on borrowing have been progressively loosened since 1989, but there is no intention that the qualified power of general competence conferred in the Local Government Act 2002 will allow local bodies to determine their own sources of revenue. Indeed, in their financial dealings they have to comply with a raft of specific principles and formally prepare no fewer than six related policies, the foremost being one which deals with revenue and financing, investment, and partnerships with the private sector. Neither history nor the current climate suggest that there is any serious prospect of local government gaining access to another lucrative source of revenue such as a tax on income or goods and services.

Competence to power into the unknown

Considered in isolation, the array of restrictions, policies, principles and compulsions forced on local government by the Act seem perplexing and puzzling, and quite alien to both the traditional freedoms accorded the sector and the fact that one of the Act's stated purposes is to bestow on local authorities powers to decide which activities they undertake and the manner in which they are undertaken (Local Government Act 2002, Section 3). The explanation is that these instruments are not ends in themselves, but in reality the *quid pro quo* for the conferral of something that local government has intermittently advocated but never held any serious expectation of receiving – the power of general competence (PGC). The notion that local government is in principle empowered to do anything that is not statutorily prohibited represents a complete reversal of the *ultra vires* principle that has hitherto reigned unchallenged throughout the system's history (Bush 1995: 172–3, 300).

Just as *ultra vires* has never choked local government's lifeblood supply, PGC will bestow nothing remotely akin to unfettered freedom. It can only be exercised for performing local government's purpose. Local government, moreover, must endeavour to comply with a detailed assortment of principles and processes. Also available for dissidents seeking to ambush frontier extending initiatives by local bodies are the residual measures of injunctions, judicial reviews, ministerial rights of intervention and the general law. That the Audit Office has to certify the key strategic-planning instrument (LTCCP) will likewise be a brake on functional adventurism. Any assertion, therefore, that the environment for local bodies will be one of licentious freedom is quite untenable. Nevertheless, a circumscribed opportunity now exists for local bodies to at least test the waters for carving out a dramatically expanded role.

At this stage any attempt to predict the practical effect of a qualified power of general competence can only be wild speculation. A multitude of transitional arrangements will both mask and delay the impact of the Act's fundamental objectives. By mid-2003, all but eight city/district councils and one regional council had opted for a transitional annual plan in preference to a LTCCP. Constraining any system-wide boldness will be the status quo, the innate conservatism of most local bodies, the obstacles placed by Parliament (including a review of the Act by 2007), the unconcealed hostility of business and ratepayer lobbies, and – perhaps most insidiously – a persuasive feeling that although its legislation was in unquestionable need of fundamental reconstruction, local government itself was not, so why try to fix *it*? The constitutional architects' intention may well be that, through a revised statute, a cautiously crafted power of general competence, and local authorities and citizens working in collaboration, local government will, within the parameters of sustainable development, become truly democratic and effective. The chance is now there to be grasped: if it transpires that many local authorities do prove capable of fulfilling such grand expectations, a revolutionary new era will have arrived.

12 Australia: still a tale of Cinderella?

Chris Aulich

The year 2001 marked the centenaries both of the federation of the six Australian colonies and of the Australian Constitution. This has been a poignant reminder for local government of its formal place in the national polity; constitutional recognition was not accorded in 1901 and later attempts to rectify this were not successful in the referenda of 1988. Hence local government remains a 'creature of the states', its legitimacy and operations depending upon state legislation.

The public sector in Australia has been the subject of two periods of intensive reforms. The first occurred in connection with debates surrounding the development of the constitution, whereas the second has continued since the 1980s. Both periods have been characterized by intensive change, experimentation and attention to system design. The first period was associated with the reconstitution of six colonial systems as six states and the Commonwealth of the Australian Federation in 1901. The second has involved wholesale reform of all public sectors at all three levels of the federal system. Because of the nature of these latter reforms – with the emphasis being on management and the use of markets on the delivery end – local government, as a provider of many services in the Australian federal context, has been one of the main targets of change.

The last decade in particular has seen considerable changes at the local government level, as it has fought to be released from the nineteenth-century stranglehold imposed by state government legislation and regulation. This chapter maps the second period of reforms to the state and territory local government systems in Australia, identifies patterns of change and suggests explanations for these patterns. It concludes that the reforms have focused heavily on managerial change and that issues relating to community governance and the local–state government nexus have remained more immune from significant reform.

Local government in Australia

Six relevant features distinguish local government in Australia:

1   It is part of a complex and diverse federal system comprising three spheres of government – the commonwealth government at the national level, six states and two territories at the intermediate level, and more than 700 units of government at the local level (see Table 12.1).

2   There is enormous diversity within the sphere of local government. This diversity relates to the size and area of population represented (for example Brisbane City, with a population of nearly one million, compared with Murchison, with 145 residents scattered over 43,800 sq km), the range and scale of functions, the councils' fiscal position, the physical, economic, social and cultural environments of local councils, the varying state government legislative frameworks within which councils operate, and the different attitudes and aspirations of local communities (National Office of Local Government 2002: 6).

3   There are 585 councils, or more than 80 per cent of the total number, classified as 'rural' or 'regional'. The urban–rural divide represents one dimension of uneven resource endowments recognized by the provision of national government grants to those councils most in need. This process of 'horizontal equalization' provides additional funding based on 'disadvantage factors' such as the length of roads to be maintained or the capacity to generate income through local taxes and rates. Table 12.2 emphasizes the relative significance of the grants and subsidies for some councils and underlines the range and diversity of councils.

4   Sub-national centralization at the state level, which means a relatively small and weak local government level and a limited inclination to engage in significant redistribution of authority across levels, particularly downwards. While there has been some devolution of functions to the local sphere in the past two decades, the historical reality of administrative subordination of local government continues to be a central feature of central–local relationships (Gerritsen and Whyard 1998).

5   Strict limitations on sub-national capabilities to raise their own revenues. This leads to a major transfer role for the centralized revenue collector to state and local governments and leaves local government with limited revenue-raising capacity beyond the application of taxes ('rates') on the unimproved value of property. Figure 12.1 illustrates the sources of local government revenues.

6   Low formal rates of participation of communities in local government. Voter turnout at local elections, ranges from 12 to 65 per cent with

Table 12.1 *Characteristics of Australian sub-national government*

State/territory	Population	Number of councils	Average population per council	Number of councillors	Average number of councillors per council	Average population per councillor
New South Wales	6,433,572	176	36,554	1,771	10	3,633
Victoria	4,736,717	79	59,958	593	8	7,988
Queensland	3,536,312	157	22,524	1,037	7	3,410
Western Australia	1,871,021	142	13,176	694	5	2,696
South Australia	1,496,207	74	20,219	757	10	1,976
Tasmania	470,749	29	16,233	280	10	1,681
Northern Territory	194,297	69	2,816	762	11	255

Source: National Office of Local Government (2002: 13). Reproduced with the permission of the Commonwealth of Australia.

Table 12.2 *Characteristics of selected Australian councils, 2000–01*

Council	State	Classification	Population	Area (sq km)	Road length (km)	Rate income ($000s)	Rate income ($/capita)	Common-wealth grant ($)	Grant per capita ($)
Monash	Victoria	Metropolitan	162,577	82	651	37.6	231.1	3,322,398	20.4
East Fremantle	Western Australia	Metropolitan	6,649	3	36	4.0	604.5	144,611	21.8
Gosford City	New South Wales	Urban fringe	158,172	1,028	1,034	37.6	553.7	7,368,568	46.6
East Gippsland	Victoria	Regional town	39,352	20,946	3,289	17.2	436.7	6,415,550	163.0
Glenorchy	Tasmania	Regional town	43,860	2,522	290	28.3	645.2	1,436,944	32.8
Surf Coast	Victoria	Rural growth	19,226	1,554	949	10.6	551.1	1,668,831	86.8
Bogan Shire	New South Wales	Rural agricultural	3,252	14,610	1,410	2.4	743.8	1,932,564	594.3
Central Darling Shire	New South Wales	Remote	2,396	51,395	1,602	0.5	209.9	2,426,120	1,012.6
Murchison	Western Australia	Remote	145	43,800	1,721	0.068	468.1	1,092,773	7,536.4

Source: National Office of Local Government (2002: 7). Reproduced with the permission of the Commonwealth of Australia.

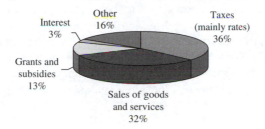

Figure 12.1 *Sources of Australian local government revenue*

Source: National Office of Local Government (2002: 5). Reproduced with permission of the Commonwealth of Australia.

averages in the low 30s. For most rural local governments only a minority (about 30 per cent) of all seats are contested at elections, although this figure is higher in urban elections (about 60 per cent) (Gerritsen and Whyard 1998: 42).

The local sphere of government has been described as the 'Cinderella' of Australia's public administration as it 'simply has not won for itself that place in our polity which a long history has given it in Britain' (Finn 1990: 49). Apart from the lack of constitutional recognition at the national level, local government powers and functions are prescribed through state and territory legislation. These powers and functions have been confined to a relatively narrow range of functions, described as the weakest range of local government functions of any Western country (Gyford 1986). Together with the fragmentation of the system this has worked against high levels of autonomy.

At the same time it is generally acknowledged that local government has satisfactorily met its intended functions of service delivery, adequate representation and participation, and advocacy of constituent needs to higher levels of government (Marshall 1998). Self (1997: 298) argues that the local sector of government 'remains genuinely local and grass roots in a way that is no longer true of most overseas systems'.

While local government accounts for only 7 per cent of the total public-sector outlays, this translates into expenditure of over A$16 billion per year or 2.5 per cent of GDP, the collection of 4 per cent of the total taxation revenue, employment of about 140,000 staff or about 10 per cent of the total government civilian workforce, and responsibility for more than a quarter of the public-sector capital formation, including 30–40 per cent of all construction on electricity distribution, roads and highways, water distribution and sewer systems (National Office of Local Government 2002: 5;

Australian Bureau of Statistics 1997). State and national governments have recognized the importance of this contribution to the national economy and local government reform has been inextricably tied to the national economic reform agenda. While aiming to make local government more efficient and businesslike, the opportunity has also been taken to reconsider the role and responsibilities undertaken by local government in the federal system.

Local government reform

As with most Anglo-Westminster-based systems, local government in Australia plays a significant role in two primary respects. First, it gives voice to local aspirations for decentralized governance, and, second, it provides a mechanism for efficient delivery of services to local communities. The two roles have given rise to two polar approaches to local government reform – one which focuses primarily on local democracy and stresses democratic and locality values over efficiency values; the other primarily concerned with structural efficiency and emphasizing the importance of efficient distribution of services to local communities. The alternatives can be depicted as in Figure 12.2. The local democracy approach values local differences and system diversity, and reforms are designed to enhance local choice and local voice. It accepts that a local authority can and will make choices that differ from those made by others. A premium is placed upon traditional democratic values of responsiveness, representativeness, accountability (especially to the local community) and access (Stewart 1997;

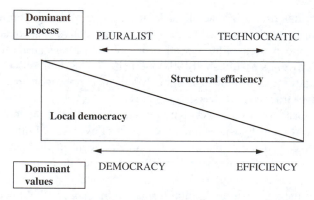

Figure 12.2   *Models of local government reform*
Source: Aulich (1999b: 20). Reproduced with permission from Blackwell Publishing Ltd.

Smith 1985; Sharpe 1981). Collaborative or pluralist processes of reform are more congruent with this focus.

By comparison, where the focus on structural efficiency dominates, local government is perceived more narrowly as a supplier of goods and services, influenced by New Public Management and its instrumental view of public service provision. In this respect, fiscal and economic issues override other social and political concerns: tradition-bound or value-oriented forms of political and social organization are replaced by purely instrumentally rational institutions (Tucker 1997: 3). Such an approach encourages greater state intervention to assert control over the local sphere of government to ensure that mechanisms are in place to advance efficiency and economy. There are inevitably greater pressures for uniformity and conformity and less tolerance of diverse outcomes. In this environment, lower value is placed on collaborative processes, with top-down or technocratic reform processes being more typical.

An earlier renaissance in local government can be identified, dating from the 1960s when 'the combination of grass-roots participation and the dis- covery of the urban problem stimulated wide interest in its potentiality' (Halligan and Wettenhall 1989: 80). Consistent with broader pressures for social change, the reforms focused on democratizing local government and making it more responsive to the communities it served. Targets of reform efforts included moves to widen the franchise beyond 'ratepayers' and embrace universal adult suffrage, to eliminate multiple voting (in some states voting rights were tied to property and multiple owners were entitled to multiple votes), and to redraw boundaries to ensure greater adherence to principles of 'one person, one vote'.

In addition to these attempts to enhance the representative nature of local government, earlier periods saw the refashioning of internal practices to improve strategic planning and financial management systems as well as (generally unsuccessful) efforts to initiate amalgamations of councils. While there was some evidence of reform to local government systems at this time, the impetus appeared to dissipate in the late 1970s under the pressures of fiscal austerity and inflexible management (Halligan and Wettenhall 1989).

System revitalization

The revitalization of local government reform in the late 1980s and early 1990s coincided with the second period in Australian history of intensive administrative change regarding the public sector, and the agendas have by and large been congruent with this change. Reforms were comprehensive at the management, legislative and structural levels of local government and focused on two primary agendas: first, the improved management of resources, and second, the redefinition of roles and responsibilities of local government.

Replacing administration with management

The first agenda involved the rejection of traditional ways – identified with administration – and their replacement by management. There has been a conscious attempt to restrain public-sector expenditure and tighten the accountability of public-sector organizations. Local authorities adopted the language and concepts of New Public Management with support, encouragement and even pressure from state governments. Financial management improvement, devolution, clearer and stronger accountability regimes, performance evaluation and strategic management have been steadily suffused into the management culture of local government during this period (Aulich 1997). In order to deliver services more efficiently, local government has adopted a range of strategies such as resource sharing, competitive tendering and contracting, increasing market influences on pricing of their goods and services, municipal amalgamation and updating technology to facilitate delivery such as one-stop shops, online programmes and quality accreditation.

Redefining roles and responsibilities

More significantly, however, has been the focus on redefining the role and functions of local government during this period. Efforts have been made to clarify the respective roles of state and local government, increase devolution and local capacity (especially to assist in implementing the managerial agenda), mandate consultation and reporting as part of the strategic management process, and enhance provisions for the use of referenda to ensure that councils are more accountable and responsive to the communities they serve. The centrepiece of this activity has been the reformation of state government legislation. State Local Government Acts 'are usually amongst the longest and most complex of the state statutes [and] no state government has tackled the task of reviewing the acts more frequently than once in a generation' (Power *et al.* 1981: 23). Yet, between 1989 and 1996, the Local Government Act in each state and territory was examined and reformed. In the case of New South Wales it represented the first complete reform since 1919.

Despite different traditions of state–local government relations between the states, there was remarkable similarity in the scope and detail of reforms to the Local Government Acts. Common to all changes was the shift away from the prescriptive and limiting powers based on *ultra vires*, which restricted councils to performing only those activities specifically nominated under the legislation. Rather, a form of general competence powers was granted (labelled 'positive' powers in New South Wales) to enable councils to undertake any activities necessary for them to fulfil the functions and powers delegated to them. Typical was the Victorian Local Government Act 1989, which gave councils the power to 'do all things necessary or convenient to be done for or in connection with the performance of its functions and to enable it to achieve its purposes and objectives' (see Aulich 1999b: 14).

Enterprise powers to enable councils to engage in business activities were also granted to New South Wales and Tasmanian local authorities (although with ceilings requiring approval by state ministers), and in Queensland the new legislation enabled local government to become involved in entrepreneurial activities and seek membership of unlisted companies, partnerships and associations. In Western Australia, scope was likewise provided for councils to undertake land development and trading undertakings as commercial activities.

The move towards general competence powers appeared to be a sincere attempt to strengthen local values by enabling councils to engage more in commercial and community activities free of the limitations imposed by the old, prescriptive Local Government Acts. State governments encouraged a conception of councils operating as local businesses, and have often drawn analogies between councils and their representatives and a company's Board of Directors and its shareholders. This shift has also been described as an attempt by state government to reduce their financial responsibilities for local government. Notwithstanding these views, many councils accepted the challenge to become entrepreneurial and operate more commercially. As a result one can find numerous examples of business ventures and commercial activities subsequently developed at the local level (Aulich 1997).

The issue of role clarification has been significant in all state jurisdictions, but this is nowhere better illustrated than in South Australia where state and local governments agreed on developing their partnership. In 1990, a Memorandum of Understanding was signed between representatives of the two spheres of government designed to 'establish new relationships reflecting a co-operative approach to the development of the state' (Bannon and Plumridge 1990). As a consequence of this agreement, the state department with responsibilities for local government was abolished and the role of representing local government devolved to the state Local Government Association. Self-funding for local government was assured by the application of a fuel tax to generate specific local government revenues. Similarly, in Western Australia the 'Better Government Agreement' signed by state and local governments was to signal the beginning of a reform programme designed to enhance local autonomy.

A focus on enhancing local democracy was also high on the reform agendas at this point. Issues such as clarifying intergovernmental roles, improving accountability regimes and management improvement dominated the restructuring of local government. In all states provisions were enacted for councils to develop strategic or management plans (especially to be more responsive to community wishes), to introduce stricter reporting regimes both to the community and to the state government, to introduce community forums, to make key documentation more transparent and to complete electoral reforms begun in the 1960s. These were all designed to strengthen accountability both to the local community and to the state government, improve management capacity and make local government more democratic.

Despite the modernization of the state Local Government Acts, however, there are few examples of significant changes to the state–local power nexus, and few new functions have been added to those already undertaken by local government. Indeed, only in Tasmania was a review of state and local government functions formally included in the reform process. Reserved powers remain with state governments enabling them to overrule local government by-laws (for example, the provision which gives the Queensland government the power to refuse approval to local government by-laws), to overturn existing gazetted by-laws and overturn council resolutions (Aulich 1999b: 14).

The national government played a significant role at this stage, signalling its confidence in local government as an integral part in the national polity, and its contribution to achieving social and community objectives (Marshall 1998). In the 1980s the national government had embarked on a programme to improve Australia's global economic position. This involved both macroeconomic policies (such as reducing and removing import duties and deregulating key industries such as banking and transport) and a programme of microeconomic reform. This programme sought to stimulate competition by removing biases that distorted quick and flexible adjustment to market signals, by minimizing costs and by better deploying resources and eliminating inefficient work practices. Both state and local governments were brought into the ambit of these policies in a consciously collaborative manner.

In the 1980s the national government also introduced Financial Assistance Grants to local government to assist horizontal equalization. In 1988, it assumed a leadership role in attempts to seek constitutional recognition for local government and, although recognition was rejected in the subsequent referendum, the national government invited local government to participate in the Council of Australian Governments (COAG) which consists of the Prime Minister, State Premiers and Territory Chief Ministers, and the President of the Australian Local Government Association. COAG has a charter to 'increase cooperation among governments on reform of the national economy and ongoing structural reform of government', providing a forum for consultation of major overarching government issues.

Pluralist approaches were generally preferred to technocratic ones, perhaps because of the strength of the local government interest groups – such as the state local government associations – and the traditions of involving local government interest groups in political change. Discussion papers, exposure drafts of legislation, inquiries, seminars, community consultations and training programme for newly elected local members became the preferred consultative mechanisms. For example, introduction of the Local Government Act 1989 in Victoria followed three years of consultation and was to be progressively implemented with further community consultation and education over the period up to 1992. In New South Wales the process of review took four years, including the release of a discussion paper and an extensive consultation programme which involved over 3,000 attendees at seminars, 900 written submissions and 450 telephone calls (New South Wales Government 1991: 3). In Tasmania, the 'Modernization' programme was a model of consultation and collaboration, devised to fully engage local government in the reform process.

The collaborative approach generally received active local government support both from individual councils and peak local government bodies (Aulich 1999b; Zwart and Haward 1999). However, there were some complaints from local government associations in several states that their submissions were not sufficiently considered, particularly in relation to the issue of state government reserved powers and its impact on local autonomy. Local government support for reform was often qualified by caveats that indicated a preference for greater local autonomy or that the process of reform should reconsider functional relationships between the local and state governments before the 'form' of local government is determined. Indeed, the Local Government Association of New South Wales (1991: 2) lamented that in the Exposure Draft of the new local government legislation, 'there are some [clauses] which are more prescriptive than existing provisions'. Some argued that reform may well have been designed to reduce state government responsibilities for local government and the financial burden this implied.

Responding to the national competition agenda

The historic agreement reached between states and the commonwealth in 1995 to introduce a national competition policy (NCP) provided an agenda-setting role nationally for both the public and private sectors. The critical feature of the NCP was that it secured agreement between the government of the commonwealth and all states and territories to adopt principles of competition in commercial arrangements involving public organizations. This included competition and commercial pricing for utilities, competitive neutrality when involved in tendering and deregulation of public monopolies where possible.

Divergent responses

The NCP has had a significant effect on local government reform as there has been a divergent response from states in the interpretation of the competition principles and in consequent efforts to promote local government reform from the second half of the 1990s. The governments of New South Wales, Queensland and Western Australia continued to work collaboratively with local government to secure agreed implementation of the principles, but in the states of Victoria, South Australia and Tasmania, state government agendas came to dominate the reform process.

The differences in interpretation were manifested in two critical areas: approaches to service delivery and municipal amalgamation. In New South Wales, Queensland and Western Australia amalgamation has not been a central issue (although voluntary amalgamations have been encouraged and supported), competitive tendering and market testing have been encouraged rather than mandated, and so has the adoption of performance management techniques such as state-wide performance indicators and benchmarking. These state governments continue to accept that reform is necessary, especially in relation to management efficiency and performance, but that it will be internally driven. They have adopted mechanisms to support and encourage, and, perhaps, lead local government efforts. In Queensland, for example, some of the payments to the state from successful implementation of the NCP provisions were specifically earmarked for local government, and in New South Wales financial assistance was provided by the state government to local authorities considering structural reform.

In other states, especially in Victoria, reforms became more technocratic with an increased preference for legislation, regulation, codes of tendering and directives as mechanisms for policy implementation. Early praise by the Victorian Minister for Local Government for the partnership model of South Australia was quickly replaced by processes that permitted little effective consultation and less collaboration with stakeholders. The 210 councils were amalgamated into 78 units and competitive tendering was mandated for all councils within strict timeframes. Rates were capped and local government budgets reduced by 20 per cent across the board. During this process, political and community opposition was blunted by the suspension of elected councillors who were replaced with commissioners appointed for two-year terms by the state government. The state government also managed the appointment of new CEOs for the 78 councils, thereby increasing institutional support for their package of reforms. Contrary to the rhetoric accompanying these changes, 'market-driven managerialism' actually reduced the freedom of managers to form and implement strategy by applying strict controls which generated a pragmatic and compliance-oriented response from councils (Van Gramberg and Teicher 2000; Aulich 1999a).

Although the Victorian government did not come to power with a clear and definite programme of local government reform, and there was no general movement pressing for such reforms, structural reform was nonetheless dramatically and uncompromisingly pursued (Kiss 1997). Local government became conceived primarily as a vehicle for the efficient delivery of services, creating a democratic deficit with the downgrading of traditional local democratic values of representativeness and advocacy of local interests, responsiveness and access, transparency and local accountability (Aulich 1999a). Thus, it was made clear by the state minister responsible for local government that councils were a prime target of the broader state microeconomic reform agenda:

> Municipal reform in Victoria was always seen as part of a wider micro-economic reform agenda. The Government's overarching goal was, and remains, to stimulate investment, wealth creation and employment growth. Increasing the efficiency and reducing the costs of local government is one important means of achieving that goal. (Hallam 1995: 4)

The negative impact of structural reforms on rural local authorities has been cited as one reason for the subsequent demise of the conservative government in Victoria and its replacement by a government more sensitive to traditional local democratic values. The incoming Labour government immediately initiated a variant of the UK's 'best-value' programme to replace compulsory competitive tendering – a programme which explicitly involves greater engagement of communities by local governments.

In South Australia, the 'partnership' between state and local government was similarly reformulated. The establishment of a new state government agency with responsibility for local government services marked a return to the period when state governments assumed overall responsibility for the local government system. The 1995 Ministerial Advisory Group Report (MAG 1995) not only recommended adopting the Victorian approach to, and targets for, compulsory competitive tendering, but also recommended that an extensive programme of amalgamations be initiated. While the government of South Australia did not formally implement the report, the MAG recommendations have clearly influenced subsequent local government policy in that state. This includes the policy of encouraging voluntary amalgamations backed by formal threats to reduce the number of councils if local government is unsuccessful in achieving this through voluntary means. A two-year rates freeze was instituted, performance benchmarks were set for councils and obligations required for reporting to local communities were increased.

In Tasmania, after an exhaustive and collaborative process of modernization, in 1997 the state government unilaterally announced a second round of amalgamations to further reduce the number of local authorities. While this must be seen in the context of broader electoral reforms in the state, it also reflects a shift from a tradition of collaborative reform represented by the earlier modernization process, to one dominated by state government priorities. As Zwart and Haward conclude, 'the failure of the government to effectively engage local government and their communities and convince local government of the need for further amalgamations on either efficiency or community of interest criteria contributed to the collapse of the 1997–98 [reform] process' (1999: 917). It also contributed to the subsequent electoral loss of the government.

The forces for change

The state of the economy has been used as one of the justifications for the more radical local government reform in Victoria, South Australia and Tasmania from the mid-1990s. Collectively labelled as Australia's 'rust belt', the three states had economies that groaned under the transition from primary and secondary-based economies towards ones dominated by service-based industries. The rhetoric that accompanied the reforms in these states was similar and related to the parlous condition of state finances. In Victoria, the Minister for Local Government justified the reforms on the basis that they would generate total savings of A$500 million, lower rates, increase debt retirement, generate employment, streamline planning approval processes and provide greater capacity for strategic decision-making (Hallam 1994). In Tasmania, it was suggested amalgamations would generate cash surpluses to 'improve asset management, reduce the levels of existing debt, improve the range and quality of services to residents ... Real reductions in the levels of rates and charges would also be possible' (Local Government Advisory Board 1997). Significantly, neither mentioned the impact on traditional local democracy and local values.

Differences in traditional state and local government relationships may also have played a part in the divergent responses of local government systems to the national policies of microeconomic reform. Systems that had developed under long periods of conservative governments (Victoria and South Australia) tended to accord lighter responsibilities to local government, but to leave it largely alone in the discharge of those responsibilities. These state governments may have become concerned that the traditions of independence had frustrated system reform in the past (for example, in the municipal amalgamation agenda of the Cain Government in Victoria in the mid-1980s); hence their determination to adopt top-down and regulatory and legislative-based reforms. The tendency of conservative governments to leave local government alone has also been reflected in the level of national government activity with respect to local government matters. Following their election in 1996, the conservative Liberal–National Party coalition downgraded its National Office of Local Government, preferring to leave local government matters more to state governments.

New South Wales and Queensland, by contrast, had their formative periods of development under long periods of Labour government. State and local governments operated more symbiotically, developing tendencies towards joint government activities (Power *et al.* 1981: 21). It has been in New South Wales and Queensland and, lately, in Western Australia where collaborative approaches continue to dominate the reform process. Perhaps the traditions of working more closely with state governments has meant that state government influence has been less overt and less formally utilized or, perhaps, the relatively healthy state economies in those states have not encouraged the attention of state governments to radical reform.

Gauging the level of support for local government reform has been difficult. In states where reform has been more collaborative, senior local officials have been at the forefront of the change process and there have been few public displays of opposition. The peak local government bodies have by and large remained supportive and engaged in the reform process in these states. By contrast, criticism of the state governments employing technocratic approaches has been public and strong from some communities and stakeholders, especially in Victoria and Tasmania (Zwart and Haward 1999; Kiss 1997). Nevertheless, the development of the Victorian government policies was heavily influenced by a cadre of local government managers who played important roles in 'bedding down' the new reforms, especially compulsory competitive tendering (Mowbray 1996; Ernst and Glanville 1995). The backlash in rural communities has been offered as a partial explanation for the electoral losses of the governments in two of these states, and the tensions between some councils and the state government have received considerable media attention.

Conclusions

Discussion of state differences should not obscure similarities that have emerged. After a decade of relentless reform, local government retains much of its traditional focuses of concern yet is demonstrably leaner, more efficient and better-managed (Aulich 1999b; Marshall 1998; Self 1997). The culture and management practices within individual councils are almost unrecognizable from those of a generation ago. Statutory change has included the Westminster distinction between policy and implementation and also mandates community consultation and participation as well as strategic and business planning. But the influence of managerialism has led to an infusion of private-sector techniques that have become enculturated as normal management practice. The workplace has been reshaped with an increasing emphasis on formal qualifications and performance management. For example, senior managers in councils are now appointed solely on the basis of merit and placed on performance-based contracts. Other impacts have variously been reported as providing a more service-orientated culture, a more comprehensive approach to service standards and outputs that reflect community needs, and a focus on service outcomes more than administrative process (Digby 2000; Marshall 1998; Martin 1997).

There are critics who raise 'concerns that economic and managerialist goals have dominated the process and given rise to an instrumental perspective that will change fundamentally the role of councils' (Marshall 1998: 659). While the democratic deficit in particular has been lamented, the reform processes have led to enhancement of democratic practices such as increased accountability, equitable representation, community engagement, access and transparency (Aulich 1999b).

In recent years issues such as the distribution of functions and powers, vertical fiscal imbalance, intergovernmental protocols and concerns for overlap and duplication of functions have been the subject of discussion between representatives of the three spheres of government. However, despite these discussions and the opportunity to radically reform intergovernmental relations, nowhere has the nexus between state and local governments been altered to any marked degree, and nowhere has local autonomy or community governance been pursued with the vigour given to programmes designed to enhance local government efficiency. The fundamental weaknesses of local government are still to be addressed: the range of local government functions is comparatively narrow, principles of subsidiarity have not been embraced, and community governance is only just emerging as an issue.

The reform process can be located within a larger tension which is emerging worldwide, between the centrifugal pressures for decentralization implied in a 'legitimation crisis', and centralizing pressures for increased national control. Centrifugal pressures that threaten the stability of the federal state by demands for increased levels of local and regional autonomy have, in Australia, been weak. The primary manifestation has been an unwillingness in state government to carry the financial 'burden' of local government and the consequent encouragement of local government to engage in entrepreneurial or business activities as a means of reducing state government obligations.

Rather stronger have been centralizing pressures which have led to increasing efforts to secure macroeconomic control. The engagement of state and local governments in the national agenda for microeconomic reform has led to a more cohesive and integrated approach to economic reform. However, this may pose a threat to federalism by concentrating power too heavily in the hands of central governments and allowing national priorities and agendas to subvert state and local policies.

Three emerging influences may challenge the managerialist focus of reform. First, as state government pressure for greater efficiency has yielded fewer, but financially strengthened, local authorities, it may inevitably reduce state government leverage over local government and further enhance claims for increased local autonomy at some future time. Second, the reaction in states that have approached local government reform in a technocratic way serves to remind state governments that local government is perceived by many in the Australian community as more than instruments for the efficient delivery of public services. Third, the emergence of organizations such as the Victorian Local Governance Association, concerned with the promotion of community governance issues, may apply pressure for subsequent reforms designed to address some of the issues of democratic deficit. However, given the long tradition of a constrained local government sector, and the apparent reluctance of Australians to countenance constitutional change, it seems likely that these influences will take some time to mobilize substantial support for reformation of local government as a more significant partner in the Australian federation.

13 The United States: executive-centred politics

Hank V. Savitch and Ronald K. Vogel

War, it is said, is the ultimate litmus test of governments. On 11 September 2001 New York City tragically found itself under such an assault. Two passenger aircraft commandeered by Islamic terrorists crashed into the twin towers of the World Trade Centre. In a few blistering moments the towers became an inferno, sending forth a hail of hot steel, glass and cement onto city streets. Nearly 3,000 people were killed, many more thousands injured and more than 15 million square feet of office space was obliterated. The famed office towers that had loomed into the skyline had collapsed.

For a while part of New York was paralyzed. Tunnels and bridges were closed, water and utilities were shut down, 16 acres of the downtown central business district were turned into a huge pile of rubble and within a week the United States had declared war on an ambiguous enemy, identified as Al-Qaida and its associated network of terrorists and their supporting states. In the meantime New York City faced the dire consequences. The city's economy lost an estimated $83 billion because of the attack. This included $30 billion in capital losses, $14 billion in cleanup and related costs and $39 billion in a loss of economic output (New York City Partnership 2001). Analysts pegged the loss of jobs at 125,000 with a huge number of businesses displaced and resettling in nearby New Jersey. Ever anxious to compete with the city, New Jersey's small municipalities and edge cities welcomed the new business. Even in the face of national disaster the inter-local pirating of business continued. Many of New York's downtown enterprises may never return, and talk abounds about the end of tall buildings. More pessimistic accounts see business moving to less vulnerable suburbs, and emerging through the carnage was a new planning strategy called 'defensive dispersal' (Dudley 2001; New York City Partnership 2002).

Whether these dire forecasts will come to pass remains to be seen. The real issue is how New York will begin its path to recovery. At present there

211

are multiple claimants to the site and even more actors in the process. The site is owned by a bi-state agency called the Port Authority of New York and New Jersey, but has been leased to private developers, who now lay claim to the area. The governors of two states, the mayor of New York, and national, state and local legislators also all have a stake in the outcome. Dozens of municipal agencies, interest groups, realtors, business and unions are involved. Trying to herd all these actors and oversee the process is a public corporation called the Lower Manhattan Redevelopment Corporation (Mollenkopf 2002).

There was also another incident connected to 11 September 2001 that reveals much about the character of local politics in the USA. As a memorial to the fallen, a statue was commissioned of fire-fighters hoisting the American flag over a part of the site. The statue was supposed to be modelled after three identified fire-fighters who, in fact, dramatically lifted the flag amidst all the debris. New York City's fire department is overwhelmingly white and so too were the three fire-fighters. However, in order to portray the diversity of the city, the fire-fighters were depicted as a black, Hispanic and white. The decision caused a commotion in the city and became a national 'cause célèbre'. African American politicians felt the decision fairly portrayed the racial makeup of victims and heroes, while members of the fire department protested that the statue distorted realities of the episode. These feelings were deep enough to cancel the project.

More than anything, 11 September points up the complexities of local government in the USA – its fragmented character, the multitude of interactions among public officials, the numerous ties with interest groups, the intensity of competition between jurisdictions, and the enormity of economic pressure. All this is mixed with racial divisions and political symbolism. These tensions, while most pronounced in places like New York, are present in most medium and large cities in the USA. They have also established a presence in America's suburbs, which heretofore were homogenous, middle-class enclaves where controversy and crises were kept at minimal levels. This allowed for consensual, non-partisan decision-making. Today, older suburbs have become more socially diversified and are experiencing racial and ethnic conflict. Older suburbs have also begun to share economic problems with central cities, including poverty, unemployment and declining central business districts. All this has been compounded by larger forces of globalization, which have created pressures to ensure economic development and made it fashionable for cities to present themselves as international centres for trade and tourism.

A combination of social and economic pressures, in short, has washed onto the steps of local government throughout the country, bringing about shifts in the role of government and in local leadership. In the last decade, major trends in local government management include (1) an emphasis on executive-centred governance, and (2) efforts to fashion public–private partnerships. Before turning to these themes, however, we review the basic organization and features of American local government.

A fragmented and decentralized system

Local government in the United States is noted for its fragmentation. This is because local government is established by the states rather than by the federal government. Each state in its constitution and laws establishes the legal powers, operating procedures, functions, revenue streams and resources available to local government. In reality, therefore, there are 50 systems of local government, not just one. The general grant of authority provided local governments is considered weak in the American context. Judicial interpretations of local powers hold that those powers not specifically authorized by state government are prohibited. Known as *Dillon's rule*, this is much akin to the *ultra vires* doctrine found in the United Kingdom and elsewhere, and leads local governments to be very dependent upon state government for delegating all powers either by general grant or by passage of a *special bill* to allow a particular local government to engage in some activity.

At present there are more than 87,000 local governments in the USA (see Table 13.1), which can be distinguished as *general purpose* or *special purpose* governments. General purpose local governments are set up to provide a full range of public services to residents. These include counties, municipalities, and towns and townships. In addition a variety of special purpose local governments are found. These are set up to provide a single service

Table 13.1   *Number of local governments in the United States by types, 1942–97*

Type of local government	1942	1962	1982	1997
County	3,050	3,043	3,041	3,043
Municipal	16,220	18,000	19,076	19,372
Township and town	18,919	17,142	16,734	16,629
School district	108,597	34,678	14,851	13,726
Special district	8,299	18,323	28,078	34,683
Total	155,067	91,186	81,780	87,453

Source: Data from Statistical Abstract of the United States (2001: 258), table 413.

and include school districts and special districts which manage water and sewer services, pollution controls, parks and other specialized functions.

Counties

Counties are the most basic form of local government in the USA and, with but two exceptions – Connecticut and Rhode Island – are found in all states. The actual number of counties has remained almost unchanged in the last century. In a historically rural nation, the counties were subdivisions of the state government responsible for providing state services to the local population. At present counties provide basic record-keeping, including births and deaths, marriages and divorces, and property records. County government is also usually responsible for supervising elections, maintaining county roads, and local jails. In recent years, county governments have also been under pressure to provide *urban* services to the *unincorporated area*, that is, those areas in the county which are not in a city and which have experienced rapid growth.

There has been a movement to modernize county government and adopt a stronger executive model either by electing a county mayor or appointing a county manager and placing formerly independent county agencies more directly under the administrative control of the executive. Other reforms include a home-rule charter movement seeking to expand the authority granted to counties. In the absence of home-rule, a county (or city) has to make a request to the state legislature to pass a special bill extending county authority to provide new services or functions or to pass regulations or laws.

The most radical local government reorganization proposed to modernize county government, however, is city–county consolidation. This involves merging the political and administrative organization of the core city with county government, with the result being a single mayor and council for the new city. But less than one in five such merger proposals have won approval from voters in referenda, and there have been only four successful consolidations in cities of over 250,000 people since the early 1900s. The number of consolidations nonetheless belies the significance of city–county consolidation; as a solution to the plight of declining central cities (Rusk 1995), this strategy continues to be on the agenda of many cities and counties, both large and small, despite the unlikelihood of success.

Recently *new regionalists*, who see inter-local organization as solutions to sprawl, social disparities and racial segregation, have largely abandoned comprehensive government restructuring (Downs 1994). Instead, new regionalists opt for incremental approaches to inter-local cooperation and stress federative models of governance rather than single embracing structures (Savitch and Vogel 2000). In fact empirical evidence casts doubt upon or refutes merger claims regarding cost savings, better economic performance, and reduced social and economic disparities (Altshuler *et al.* 1999). A more promising strategy, it is argued, can be found in the movement for 'smart growth', which focuses on intergovernmental aid and improved infrastructure in targeted areas in an effort to combat metropolitan sprawl.

Cities

A city or municipality is an *incorporated place* set up as a municipal corporation under state laws. Cities have typically been created to provide services to the more densely populated areas of the states in a rural nation. Municipalities are under direct state authority. Each state decides the specific circumstances under which a municipality can be created and what authority it will have. Under these circumstances the city in most instances receives a municipal charter from the state government that serves as a mini-constitution. Over the years most cities have greatly expanded their municipal services and physical infrastructure (DiGactano 1991: 345).

During the last half century, the US population has experienced a strong trend to suburbanization. The number of cities increased significantly as suburbs grew and subsequently acquired city status. This is because state legislatures made *annexation* – the extension of city boundaries to encompass new growth on the fringe of the city – exceedingly difficult. Often, a *dual majority* election – a majority of residents in the area to be annexed and in the city – would have to approve the boundary adjustment. Thus, a small suburban enclave could block the annexation.

No discussion of US cities would be complete, moreover, without mentioning the variables of race and ethnicity. Most cities are quite segregated, with concentrated populations of black or Hispanic residents. Race in the United States plays much the same role as social class does in Europe: it is the fault-line that divides society, it often defines the country's politics and it determines how sides line up on issues of policy. Those who ally themselves with African Americans are often on the left side of the political spectrum, whereas those who are less interested in these alliances are often on the right side of that spectrum (Kirtzman 2001). In many cities more recent Asian and Hispanic minorities now compete with blacks for economic and political benefits, heightening conflict.

Special purpose districts

Special districts are created by state or local government (if permitted under
state law) to provide specialized functions to a particular geographic area
not otherwise addressed by municipal (city) and county governments.
School districts are a particular kind of special district often found in the
southern and western parts of the country. The special district may operate
with an elected or appointed board and finances its activities by collecting
a property tax, income tax, or a fee from those living within the district
boundaries. Special districts are also set up to provide services that span the
boundaries of existing cities or counties and are thus a mechanism to provide regional services. Special districts may also be created to provide a
higher level of service to an area than it would otherwise have received. For
example, a county government may set up an urban service district in an
unincorporated area of the county to provide garbage collection or other
services to residents and businesses lacking these services. Or a city might
establish a downtown management district to provide more police services,
more frequent garbage collection, street cleaning and so forth.

Special purpose districts are one of the major reasons for the accelerat-
ing fragmentation of local government in the USA. Examining Table 13.1,
we note that the number of special districts has been growing exponentially
in the last several decades even while the number of school districts has
plummeted, especially in the decades after the Second World War. Most of
the decline stems from consolidation of single-school systems (US Census
Bureau 1997: VIII), a move undertaken to save money as administrative
costs of providing education increased. Nonetheless, the overall number of
special districts has grown to provide for specialized functions not otherwise
addressed by municipal and county governments. Another significant factor
underlying the increase in special districts is that a city or county can,
by spinning off a service to a special district, keep the money that otherwise
would have been expended to provide those services, and thus gain
discretionary spending money without having to raise taxes. This is because
the special district tax or fee is not charged against city or county revenue
sources (US Census Bureau 1997: VII–VIII).

The proliferation of special districts has been criticized, however,
because the districts tend to lack direct accountability to voters. These special purpose bodies also lead to concerns about the lack of coordination
among the independent and invisible governments in the metropolis.
Mayors of large cities, for example, complain that schools operate outside
of their authority and yet they are expected to make the schools perform.
Special purpose governments are a legacy of the reform era in the late

nineteenth and early twentieth centuries, which held that politics should be divorced from administration and that political machine influence should not taint professional decision-making. Believing that management should be free of politics, these governments were usually appointed by a mayor and/or governor and officeholders served for specific, renewable terms. The upshot was the rise of politically insulated, functional fiefdoms that today perform critical functions within the cities and metropolises (Harrigan and Vogel 2003: 10–1).

Organization of cities and the federal system

The USA now is predominantly *an urban* and suburban nation. For this reason for the remainder of this chapter we concentrate our attention on city government and city governance.

Models of city government

There are at present four basic models of city government in use in the USA: (1) mayor-council, (2) council-manager, (3) commission and (4) town meeting. Because the commission and town-meeting models are not frequently found in US cities of more than 25,000 inhabitants, the focus of the following discussion is on the two remaining types.

The **mayor-council model** is based upon a separation of powers with checks and balances between the executive (mayor) and the legislature (council). In the *weak-mayor* variant, the mayor lacks a veto and the council dominates the city government decision-making system. In the *strong-mayor* version, by comparison, the balance of power shifts towards the mayor, who has centralized control of city government under his or her authority.

The **council-manager model** is based on the corporate model. Voters (shareholders), elect councillors (board of directors), who in turn appoint a city manager (as the chief executive officer). This city manager has day-to-day responsibility for administering the government. The council is responsible for setting broad policy and providing general direction to the manager, who is responsible for implementing council policies and for managing public services in a professional manner. The model is premised on a policy (politics)-administration dichotomy. Reformers advocating this model had hoped to isolate politics in the council, but the model has been criticized as setting up a false and unworkable dichotomy between politics and administration. The council routinely intervenes in administration, and the manager who waits for policy direction from the council will not succeed.

Adoption of the council-manager reforms was accompanied by electoral and other reforms to ensure the model worked as intended. For example, the council-manager model was tied to *at-large* rather than *single-member (ward)* elections to ensure that councillors took a broad view of the public interest instead of a parochial view in favour of their specific district. Similarly, elections under this model were to be *non-partisan*, councillors were expected to be part-time, and city workers were to be covered by *civil service* protection.

As Table 13.2 reveals, larger cities (that is, those with over 250,000 inhabitants) tend to use the mayor-council form of government, whereas medium-sized cities with 25,000 to 250,000 inhabitants tend to favour the council-manager form of government. The mayor-council model is more frequent in large cities with diverse populations and interests that are often characterized by intense political conflict, whereas the council-manager model is more frequent in the new suburban cities, especially in the south and west where it predominates (Harrigan and Vogel 2003).

The mayor-council and council-manager models represent two distinct views about the purpose of city government. The reform model, prevalent in the suburbs, sees the primary purpose of the government as providing basic public services (for example, roads, police, fire, sewers) in the most efficient manner while keeping taxes low. Politics, especially partisan politics, is viewed as antithetical to good governance. In large urban areas, on the other hand, government is not just important as a provider of basic public

Table 13.2 *Distribution of different forms of city government in the United States by size of government, 2002 (%)*

Form of city government	Population size		
	2,500 to 25,000	*25,000 to 250,000*	*Over 250,000*
Mayor-council	46.2	32.4	56.9
Council manager	45.0	63.7	40.0
Commission	2.1	2.0	3.1
Town meeting	6.7	1.9	0.0
Total	100	100	100
N	*5,613*	*1,228*	*65*

Source: Data from International City/County Management Association, table 2 (2002: xii).

services. Rather, it is also important as a facilitator of group advancement, employment, social justice and even redistribution. Efficiency in this context is but one value. The two major forms of government organization embody these distinct philosophies and political cultures.

Changing intergovernmental relations

While the US Constitution creates a federal system from which both the federal and the state governments derive their authority and powers, the nature of intergovernmental relationships has evolved over the years. The initial view was that of *dual sovereignty* where the states and the federal government were considered to have separate and independent spheres, each sovereign in their own affairs. The federal government was primarily responsible for defence and foreign policy, whereas the states were the primary governments responsible for domestic policy, including local government and politics. This view predominated until the 1930s when an era of *cooperative federalism* was launched under the New Deal. Here the theory of federalism was modified so that the states and federal governments were jointly responsible for the welfare of the American people. At this point a pattern of federal financing through grants-in-aid was established, with the federal government setting national policy goals (Kleinberg 1995). Although the federal government lacked authority under the Constitution to directly regulate or interfere in state and local affairs, the power of appropriation became the vehicle for expansion of national activity in areas previously reserved to the states.

In the 1960s, the Great Society programmes of Lyndon Johnson ushered in a new era of *Creative Federalism* with the US government bypassing states to forge a direct relationship with the cities. Categorical grants, providing aid to local governments but including many requirements, became the main mechanism to implement this new extended version of federalism. Then in the 1970s, Richard Nixon introduced *New Federalism*, suggesting that the federal government had become too big and too intrusive in state and local affairs. The solution was devolution in the form of *fiscal federalism*, with the federal government providing cash assistance for state and local governments through revenue-sharing. Nixon also deemphasized categorical grants in favour of broader block grants with fewer regulations and oversight. A consequence was to deemphasize aid to cities and to shift it over time to suburbs and the Sunbelt. Under Jimmy Carter, however, the federal government returned to the notion of a partnership with larger cities and created several grants to spur economic revitalization and redevelopment.

Ronald Reagan also sought to devolve more authority to state and local governments, but his version of New Federalism was aimed at returning to an era of dual sovereignty, believing as he did that the period since the New Deal was a deviation from the proper workings of federalism. Revenue-sharing was eliminated alongside severe cuts in federal aid to cities (Eisinger 1998).

Although Reagan succeeded in reducing the federal role, the intergovernmental system is still best characterized as cooperative. For the most part entitlement programmes remain in place. In addition, an extensive grant-in-aid system weaves the three levels of government together through policy networks. Although differing in priorities, both Bill Clinton (1993–2000), a neo-liberal, and George W. Bush (2001–) a 'compassionate' conservative, sought to use federal resources to shape local agendas. And state and local governments continue to press the federal government to provide leadership and resources on a range of domestic issues including the environment, education, health, crime, welfare and economic development.

Local autonomy and financing of local government

The relationship between state and local governments is akin to a unitary state, so familiar to Europeans. As noted earlier, Dillon's rule is a major limitation on local authority. Legally, there are few constraints on state power to reorganize local government, but that power is rarely exercised for two reasons. First, American political culture pays high regard to *localism*. Local areas are expected to address their own problems and are resentful of interference from higher levels. Second, governors and state legislators are reluctant to intervene in local affairs. This reticence has less to do with constitutional prescriptions than with the limited political gains to be derived from intervening in local or urban affairs. Urban problems are complex and urban politics is intense. Also, since most of the population resides in suburbs and few state governors, legislators or representatives in Congress or the President owe their election to city voters, where 49 per cent of city residents are now members of minority groups, there is little benefit to entering the urban arena (Waste 1998).

Thus, in spite of Dillon's rule, local governments in the USA have a great deal of legislative and fiscal autonomy in practice. Indeed, given various 'home-rule' powers extended to local government and their revenue-raising capacity, local governments have a great deal of independence. In the period from 1977 to 1997 federal aid to cities declined from 15 to 5 per cent of total city revenues, whereas state aid declined from roughly 23 to 21 per cent in

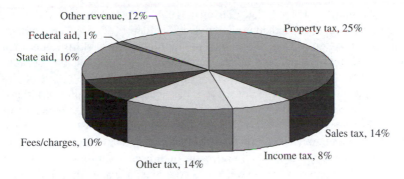

Figure 13.1   *General fund revenue composition for the US municipal sector, 2000*

Source: Pagano (2001: 5). Findings based on a survey of municipalities. Reproduced with permission from the National League of Cities.

the same period (US Census Bureau 1997). This means that local governments have to derive the lion's share of their revenues from other sources. Figure 13.1 provides a general profile of city revenue sources and illustrates the continuing importance of property taxes for city revenues as of 2000. Only a handful of cities have access to city income taxes and cities increasingly rely on user fees.

Recent policy development

The years from 1981 to 1992 under the Reagan and Bush administrations were notable for a belief that urban problems were best treated by unregulated markets and a federal withdrawal from cities. The budget deficits of the 1980s foreclosed any major new initiatives for cities. Bill Clinton's election victory in 1992, however, with strong support from urban areas, brought urban issues back to the forefront. But the deficits and recession at the beginning of his term limited the extent of aid that could be offered to cities. As a result, the Clinton administration sought to fuse the liberal agenda of providing aid to revitalize *places* with concentrated poverty, and particularly inner-city areas in large cities, with the conservative agenda of fostering free markets and providing regulatory relief.

Despite limited federal support for cities and an overall decline in federal aid to local government, the federal government retains a strong presence in local affairs, a fact best illustrated by welfare reform and national crime legislation. Yet a sign of the limited place cities have in the national consciousness is that these general *non-urban* policies overshadow urban policy initiatives. Indeed, Peter Eisinger (1998: 308) has suggested that the 'growing local fiscal and administrative self-reliance [of cities] create pressures on local politicians to focus on public management skills rather than on the pursuit of social and racial agendas that were the focus two decades ago'. Thus, urban politics is now about good governance and not equality of opportunity. A new breed of mayors has accepted the challenge to keep taxes low, bring spending under control, and focus on the maintenance of order in cities (Siegel 2001). The booming economy in the 1990s, alongside the building boom in downtowns in the form of new athletic stadiums and convention centres, gives the imprimatur of success. But mayors now face a greater challenge due to the weakened economy, a change that could raise welfare expenditures or result in increased crime, taxing cities' fiscal capacity. The Cincinnati riots in 2001 are a reminder that most American cities are potential powder kegs given the right catalyst of real or imagined police excesses towards minority members. Even in the face of the new war against terrorism, mayors realize that they will be largely left to fight this war alone with limited federal assistance. This is the new urban reality.

Mayoral-centred cities – pulling it together

Both the form and substance of local politics highlight the importance of US mayors. While it is true that there are more cities with a council-manager system, the largest and most important cities continue to follow the mayor-council model. Moreover, as medium-size cities grow larger, they often incorporate aspects of the strong-mayor model into the council-manager system.

There are many good reasons for this tendency, including the role of history and the desire to personify the city through a mayoral office. Globalization has given an added incentive to this tendency; cities have become anxious to achieve international recognition and have gone through great lengths to achieve global status. Sometimes this was as trivial as designating airports and convention centres with the title of 'international', while at other times it has meant developing centres for international trade and waterfronts for increased tourism. This required that mayors take a leading role and increased their visibility.

Other reasons for the rise of mayoral leadership included the necessity of dealing with the centrifugal nature of local government and providing a mechanism to centralize influence. In order to function in this fragmented system, cities must operate simultaneously at multiple levels. They must work to obtain aid and cooperation from national and state governments;

they must raise revenues by stimulating economic activity and must continuously develop – simply to remain fiscally viable. In addition cities and often counties are responsible in varying degrees for delivering municipal services. This can be a dizzying experience, and the responsibilities may include public housing, police, fire, sanitation, water supply, road maintenance, public transit, education, parks, recreation and healthcare. Amidst these obligations, larger urban areas are often racked by internal, multisided and multilateral conflict. Douglas Yates (1977: 34) refers to this as 'street-fighting pluralism', which he poignantly describes as a 'political free-for-all, a pattern of unstructured, multilateral conflict in which many different combatants fight continuously with one another in a very great number of permutations and combinations'.

The sheer complications, diffuse nature and intensity of a big city require that somebody step into the breach, take charge and ease tensions. Unlike Europe, political parties in the USA lack discipline and are not capable of acting as informal centralizing mechanisms. Indeed, a good many big cities are formally 'non-partisan' and lack an organizational base through which to organize power. As a result, business and interest groups often step into the breach and back a local personality or politician for the mayoralty.

Since the mid-1990s the exigencies and pressures of the system have accentuated these characteristics and produced a number of high-profile, entrepreneurial mayors who have left distinct marks on American urban politics (Walters 1991; Goldsmith *et al.* 1999). At least one of these marks has been a combination of fiscal conservatism and strong measures to combat crime, aspects of what has been termed the 'new political culture' (Clark and Hoffmann-Martinot 1998). Both Rudy Giuliani (New York) and Richard Riordan (Los Angeles) took the lead on these issues and set national standards for what city halls needed to do in order to win popular support. It may be significant that both of these men are white, moderate Republicans who succeeded black, liberal Democrats. They entered office on the heals of fiscal stress, high crime and racial rioting and took steps to reduce the size of the city bureaucracy and began cutting the cost of government.

These mayors are held up as national models of *reinventing government*. The way to revitalize cities was to privatize, employ performance measurements, and clamp down on deviancy. Crime posed the greatest challenge for both mayors. Giuliani, for example, took steps to boost the number of police officers and began a no-tolerance policy towards criminal transgressions. Clearly mayoral leadership during the 1990s had a conservative tone. Black and to some extent Hispanic voters were upset with the agenda and sometimes with their conservative mayors. Giuliani was the most controversial in this respect, and his administration faced a number of highly publicized scandals regarding police brutality.

By the year 2000 many of these 'new' mayors were not reelected, but they did set the pace for the era. Mayors like Giuliani and Riordan magnified the mayoral office, they pointed up the limits of a municipal welfare state, and they struck a popular chord by coming down hard on crime. Beyond this, globalization had increased economic pressures on the city, and mayors sought to leverage their budget by enlisting the support of business. Mayors had always been close to business, but in recent years they have been drawn into even firmer relationships by taking up the business agenda. As mayors saw it, if the resources of government and business could be combined, cities would stand a better chance of strengthening their competitive presence.

Unequal partnerships and the New Public Management

Cities have long endorsed commercial boosterism and used it as a way of promoting development. These partnerships became particularly intense with the advent of massive urban-renewal projects during the 1950s and continued through subsequent decades. The collaboration over urban renewal involved a three-way partnership between the federal government who provided the funds, local government who acquired and cleared vast tracts of land, and private developers who bought the land at highly discounted rates and built mega projects. Many of those projects engulfed downtown neighbourhoods and entailed massive dislocation of small business and blue-collar households. Black neighbourhoods were especially affected by renewal projects and the programme was given the dubious accolade of 'Negro removal' (Anderson 1964).

In recent years power has dispersed from the more centralized elite models found in the 1950s (see Savitch and Thomas 1991); indeed, hyperpluralism has been decried as a problem in many cities. The movement towards strong mayors has led to a new power relation – the *corporate-centred regime* – described by Stone (1989). Relationships of this type are not only found in Atlanta, where Stone conducted his research, but also in a good number of other cities today. Here, the public sector, under the mayor, forges an alliance with the business community to enhance downtown development. In doing so, the mayor gains needed resources for his or her vision for the city while the business community gains support for development goals. Together, the business community and mayor manage conflict and the transition from an industrial to a post-industrial economy. The exact balance between business and government, however, varies by city and the personalities of the public and private business leaders.

Despite the rise of absentee-owned firms and multinational corporations, business has continued to increase its presence in local politics. Downtown organizations that tie together government and business are quite common, with the collaboration falling under the rubric of chambers of commerce or downtown partnerships. Another vehicle used to promote partnerships is the *public benefit corporation* (PBC). New York City has relied on PBCs to develop its airports, bridges and highways; it has used them to build office towers in its central business district and to develop housing. Most other big cities use PBCs, as vehicles for development, building industrial parks, office complexes and tourist attractions.

What makes the PBC so attractive is its ability to insulate itself from legislative accountability, its ability to invoke public power, and its capacity to raise tax-free finances. Their governing boards are not elected but rather appointed by political executives (mayors, governors) for specific terms, the boards usually consisting of leading business figures, banking officials or corporate lawyers. PBCs can commonly rely on laws of eminent domain to purchase and clear land, and often have the power to bypass local legislation and zoning ordinances. They raise money by issuing tax-free bonds and using potential sources of revenue to secure and pay off those bonds. Since bonds are secured in the private market and must be paid off within a specified time, PBCs are tied to profit-making activities. They therefore naturally shy away from deficit-prone services and are apt to invest in projects like toll bridges rather than public transit, or to sponsor rent-producing buildings rather than subsidized housing. Over the last decade or so, PBCs have grown enormously and today they mark the fiscal landscape of most major cities. Furthermore, so long as cities had to raise their own sources of income and PBCs could deliver funds, there was little public outcry.

Cities rely on an array of supply side incentives to create public–private partnerships. More often than not, the public side takes most of the risk by providing guarantees and hard assets. Free land, tax abatements, publicly built infrastructure and employee training are just some of the means through which unequal partnerships are carried out. In Detroit, for example, land was confiscated or bought, cleared and prepared in order to build automobile factories. The public sector also provided hundreds of millions of dollars in tax abatements and facilities.

Finally, the idea of the New Public Management (NPM) has won considerable popularity during the last decade. While NPM is a broad term encompassing a variety of techniques, a typical approach is to distinguish between the provision of public services and their production. NPM advocates argue that localities should not try to generate (produce) all services, but rather make arrangements to furnish (provide) them through other sources. Smaller municipalities, for instance, might contract for police services with larger cities that can deliver them more efficiently. In the same vein garbage can be collected by private firms rather than through a municipal department. And some NPM advocates suggest that vouchers be granted to citizens so they can 'purchase' educational services from independent schools rather than rely on a system of public schools. Some states and localities have also been able to contract with private firms to manage prisons and jails. Still other NPM supporters look for ways in which government can be improved rather than replaced. Accordingly they have turned to ways in which municipal services can be decentralized or ways in which citizen preferences can be measured (surveys, focus groups) and fed back to municipal bureaucracies or ways to make government more flexible (retaining unexpended funds for more effective use in subsequent years).

While many cities pay lip-service to the New Public Management, and it is fashionable for mayors to claim the title of entrepreneur, few have radically changed their approach to governance in practice. Indianapolis' Mayor Stephen Goldsmith is well-known for having introduced market incentives into government operations: he forced municipal unions to compete with private contractors for the city's business and he encouraged religious institutions to deliver social services. Thus far, however, much of the impetus for reinvention has taken place in middle-class, 'sunbelt' cities of the south and southwest. The city of Phoenix, for example, recently won an international award (the Bertelsmann Foundation prize) for being among the world's 'best-run' cities. Among Phoenix's virtues was its attention to neighbourhood improvement through decentralized management, its use of citizen surveys to establish high-quality services, and its reliance on competitive contracting to provide street cleaning and repair.

It is not by chance that 'sunbelt cities' like Phoenix should turn out to be exemplars of the new approach. By contrast, big industrial cities in the northeast and midwest have found it more difficult to incorporate reinvention into their operations. Reinvention, in short, has been a fashion of the 1990s for mayors anxious to promote their cities, but its impact has been limited (Thompson and Riccucci 1998). In fact, one study found that there is a tendency for local governments to report innovation that further investigation revealed did not take place (London 1996). What has changed is the focus of local policy initiatives which are now oriented towards scaling back the local welfare state (Siegel 1997) and fostering urban economic development (Peterson 1981).

Conclusions

There is doubt that US cities have experienced important changes during the last decade. Still, in terms of institutions, modes of operation and patterns of behaviour many current practices reflect the past. Thus, going back to the nineteenth and early twentieth century of 'bosses' and 'machine politics', mayors became powerful figures. By the late twentieth century, the old-fashioned machines were gone, but mayors still loomed as dominant figures. Much of this is due to the highly fragmented nature of local government in the USA, and the consequent need to centralize power. The case of 11 September 2001 dramatically points out some of these complexities. As of late, mayors have come to symbolize and represent big American cities to both an internal audience and an external world. Whether in law or fact, the pressure of economic development, globalization and competitive politics have brought mayors to the fore.

Finally, business has also sought to increase its traditional influence in local government. The withdrawal of the federal government from local affairs, pressures to secure private investment, scarce resources and sheer politics have augmented the political clout of business. PBCs, lavish supply-side incentives, and public–private partnerships are some of the key vehicles used by business to shape the local agenda and preserve an important role in governance.

Does this threaten local democracy? It is difficult to generalize. In some cities, such as New York and Chicago, a vibrant press and lively citizen participation act as a useful counterpoint. City halls in these cities are often cross-pressured and this represents a healthy pluralism. Other cities lack an energetic press and an alert citizenry, and are often steeped in a mundane, lock-step boosterism, whose agenda is dictated by a handful of personalities. There are many variations to these patterns, but this comes as no surprise; American cities are known for their variation (Savitch and Thomas 1991).

14   A New Intergovernmentalism?

Mike Goldsmith

All of the countries reported upon in this volume are themselves unique, with differences of detail that are important for understanding the processes of local politics and government in each country. Intergovernmental processes are no different in this respect, yet all of the countries have had to respond to a common set of challenges over the last 30 years (see Table 1.1 in the introductory chapter). These challenges have to do with

- stronger interdependencies between authorities in metropolitan regions due to increasing urbanization,
- the effect of increased competition as a result of globalization (or, within Europe, changes brought about by the development of the European Union),
- pressures to 'work smarter' – that is, to be both more efficient and economic in the provision of public services through the adoption of some of the ideas of the New Public Management (NPM), and
- the need to respond to apparent democratic weaknesses, as some politicians and other commentators suggest is evidenced by declining electoral turnout at all levels.

All of these challenges have contributed to changes in intergovernmental relations. Of particular interest in this regard is how far they have brought about a change from largely direct patterns of control to more indirect ones through the adoption of regulatory regimes and a shift from local government to local governance. In a recent book Peter John (2001) argues that such a shift has indeed occurred. A good case can be made for this point of view, but stressing governance in characterizing the responses to the set of challenges faced by local governments runs the danger of ignoring the importance of formal rules and constitutions in determining patterns of intergovernmental relations. And the suggestion of a uniform movement towards governance across countries also ignores the importance of differences in national contexts, even though governments at all levels increasingly share experience and practice in the face of similar problems. One such contextual difference, for example, is that pertaining to variations between federal and unitary systems of government (see Table 1.2). Whether a system is federal or unitary is likely to produce different patterns of intergovernmental relations. Within similar types of systems, moreover, cultural differences will also lead to variations in vertical and horizontal intergovernmental relations. Thus, for the EU-countries Table 14.1 illustrates not only the continuing importance of regional and local governments, but also the variability in terms of shares of public expenditure that such governments have within the Union, which reflect contextual differences within the Union.

The systems of local government within the countries included in this volume also differ in another important respect. Page and Goldsmith (1987a) and Page (1991) made a distinction between Northern and Southern European systems of local government, arguing that this distinction is important for understanding the way in which local politics and government operated at that time between countries as diverse as Norway and

Table 14.1 *Public expenditure by EU regional and local governments as a percentage of gross domestic product, 1996*

Country	Public expenditures as percentage of GDP	Regional/local government as percentage of GDP
Austria	57.3	15.3
Belgium	56.5	6.8
Denmark	75.7	30.9
Finland	68.7	18.3
France	50.7	8.4
Germany	53.7	17.7
Greece	53.0	3.9
Ireland	44.8	9.8
Italy	59.4	12.0
Luxembourg	40.7	4.5
Netherlands	60.5	13.5
Portugal	42.4	3.8
Spain	48.5	9.9
Sweden	64.3	23.1
United Kingdom	48.5	10.8

Source: Data from OECD National Accounts 1998. OECD definition of public expenditure does not include investments.

Italy, Sweden and Spain. A major theme raised by John (2001), and important in the context of this book, is how far the widely accepted distinction between the Southern/Napoleonic systems and the Northern systems (both of the Middle European and the Anglo variant) continues to persist in the new millennium. Given the processes of change to which governments at all levels in advanced industrial democracies have been subject over the last 20 years, it would be surprising if such a distinction was as clear-cut today as it was 20 years ago (Goldsmith 2000). This is a question to which we shall return in the concluding part of this chapter. In what follows the changes that have taken place in intergovernmental relations in a broad spectrum of countries in recent years – particularly in those countries reported upon in this book – are reviewed. In doing so, the chapter seeks first to understand these changes, and second to evaluate their importance.

Political systems and local government

In undertaking a more comprehensive review of developments in intergovernmental relations, it is at the outset most useful to make a distinction between countries with federal systems on the one hand and those with more unitary systems on the other, though even here each of the categories contains significant variations. Federalism in Germany or Switzerland, for example, is different in kind to that of Australia or the United States. Similarly, unitary states differ. Compare the formally highly centralized state in France with the rather more formally decentralized state in the Scandinavian countries. Or compare Britain, with its unwritten constitution but which gives local government little formal discretion, with the Netherlands, where local governments formally have rather more discretion but remain heavily dependent on the centre for finance. Here these differences must be borne in mind, even though the aim is to consider experiences within the two broad categories.

Federal systems – the importance of the intermediate tier

In federal systems, the position of the central government is generally quite weak in the intergovernmental relationship, whereas in unitary systems the central government looms large in the affairs of most localities. In countries such as Australia, Canada and the USA, though the federal level has from time to time been involved in the affairs of cities – most notably in the 1960s and 1970s – more recently one has seen the federal level seeking to withdraw from such involvements, as for example under Reagan in the USA. In Australia, by comparison, one saw the state governments reassert their predominant position in the 1970s (Chapman and Wood 1984; Jones 1991), and as Aulich makes clear in Chapter 12, federal government involvement is now much less. In European countries such as Germany and Switzerland, the federal government has always been distanced from local affairs, though issues concerning intergovernmental transfers and welfare provision have been matters which have involved federal or central levels of government – a point to which we shall return. It is thus the intermediate tier – the states, provinces, *Länder* or cantons – which in these countries has key responsibility (both formally and informally) for local government matters. In this they have been joined increasingly by the quasi-federal systems found in countries such as Belgium (Chapter 4) and, debatably, Italy (Chapter 3) where a process of what might be best called 'bottom-up regionalism' has seen the emergence of important intermediate tiers. Hence in Belgium, for example, Flanders and Wallonia have responsibility for most governmental functions. Although not treated in this book, the creation of the autonomous communities in Spain has similarly increasingly led them to becoming the important intermediate tier, first in the nationalist Basque and Catalonia areas, and more lately in the rest of the country.

One result of the growing importance of this meso-tier is that local government systems have become even more diverse, as the country chapters dealing with federal systems demonstrate. Thus Savitch and Vogel in Chapter 13 refer to the USA's 50 systems of local government, some operating with small councils elected on an areawide basis and run by a city manager, others being run by strong mayors, and yet others by weak mayors with strongly partisan councils. By comparison, local government in Australia has, as Aulich points out, been a virtual 'Cinderella'; so much so that the State of Victoria decided virtually to abolish elected local government in the mid-1990s, replacing 210 municipalities with 78 councils, each of which was run by an appointed Chief Executive Officer, though there was later to be a return to elected local government in the State. Despite the different states passing new local government acts designed to produce local government reform, making it more consumer oriented and competitive, Aulich concludes that in effect little has changed.

In the federal systems of Germany and Switzerland, on the other hand, one can see a trend towards some degree of convergence, especially in Germany. In both countries, cooperation between the two tiers is common, despite the differing constitutional arrangements which result in the *Länder* and cantons having differing responsibilities, and the respective municipalities likewise. After reunification in Germany, there has likewise been a trend towards the adoption of similar forms of municipal government across the *Länder*, with the widespread introduction throughout the country of the strong mayor-council system previously most commonly found in northern Germany.

In both of these countries the principle of subsidiarity – namely the idea that governmental functions should be undertaken at the lowest possible level – is engrained, though in Switzerland it seems to have a different meaning to that in Germany. In the former, subsidiarity means that those functions not explicitly assigned to higher levels are left to the local level, whereas the local tier is given more explicit constitutional autonomy in the German system. Thus, Ladner suggests in Chapter 9 that Swiss municipalities enjoy a high degree of autonomy over organizational form, their range of responsibilities and in fiscal matters. He also indicates that they have become increasingly important as 'executive organs and administrative units of the state'. But more recently there have been pressures for reform, with municipalities facing service and fiscal difficulties in a number of areas. The result has been increasing vertical and intergovernmental interdependence. In particular, inter-municipal cooperation in service provision has become more common, and nationally there have been discussions concerning minimal standards and the possible introduction of a new regional layer, but little has happened to date.

Fiscal arrangements between the different tiers in federal systems are often complicated and vary substantially. Gabriel and Eisenmann (Chapter 8) highlight the complicated nature of the German arrangements which help to underpin the cooperative nature of intergovernmental arrangements, as does the party system. In Switzerland, by comparison, there has been some move towards the reform of local finance with the introduction of block grants to replace specific ones, based on the notion of fiscal equivalence – that is, those who decide what should be done also have to provide the necessary resources.

In Belgium the culture is very different between Flanders and Wallonia, as Plees makes evident in Chapter 4. As a consequence their local government systems show some variation, though overall Belgian local government remains relatively unimportant within the political system. Both regions are so dominant within the Belgian political space that it is difficult to see what really remains for the Belgian state to do.

Finally, as Bobbio makes clear in Chapter 3, Italy remains one of the more difficult countries in which to understand the process of change. Bobbio notes that extensive reforms have taken place in the 1990s, yet in some cases (for example proposals for metropolitan reform) these have not been implemented. This is in keeping with the fact that Italy has a history of introducing reforms but not implementing them. The most important reforms of the period, however, have been those which strengthen the intermediate tier, but here Italy has two tiers – both regional and provincial – and as Bobbio indicates it is the provincial tier which has been strengthened and now 'act as fairly strong meso-governments'. Local governments have also been given increased powers, but Bobbio suggests there remains a 'drive towards increased cooperation' between the different tiers in the face of 'the continuing fragmentation of local governments'. In the light of these changes, it is difficult to be certain about the final outcome and to assess the full impact of the changes, especially in the light of the election of the Berlusconi government, which shows tendencies towards a recentralization of powers and is 'intolerant of the tortuous processes of intergovernmental negotiation' despite its commitment to further (regional) decentralization. Furthermore, the question of local fiscal resources has not yet been properly addressed.

Unitary systems – moves towards decentralization

With the possible exception of the Netherlands, where moves towards the establishment of an intermediate tier have been spasmodic, a move towards an increasingly important meso- or intermediate tier is also to be found in virtually all the unitary countries considered in this book. Local government reforms across Northern Europe in the 1960s and 1970s saw a reduction in the numbers of municipalities and the introduction or strengthening of a new county tier, although except for Britain most municipalities remained relatively small in population size. More recently there have been moves towards the creation of new regions in most of the Nordic countries. Denmark has made fewer changes than the others, though a commission to consider the structure and organization of Danish local government issued its report early in 2004 recommending major changes. France introduced regions as part of the Mitterrand decentralization reforms of the 1980s, but commentators suggest that the new regions are still fighting to establish their own political space, with a few notable exceptions such as Nord Pas de Calais and Rhone-Alpes. And in the light of more recent reforms involving state encouraged voluntary cooperation of communes in both rural and metropolitan areas, it seems likely that French regions will continue to struggle to obtain political importance.

Even Britain has acknowledged the importance of the meso-level, with some devolution of power to the nations of Scotland and Wales and to the Province of Northern Ireland in the late 1990s. Such devolution is bringing about disparities between the different parts of the United Kingdom; for example, university students pay no fees in Scotland, unlike the rest of the United Kingdom. More recently the Blair Labour government has introduced legislation which will permit English regions to have elected assemblies with some powers, if such a move is approved by a regional referendum. The north and northwest regions, together with Yorkshire and Humberside, are those most likely to move in this direction, but in some parts of the country (especially London and the southeast) it is difficult to define the regional boundaries in any meaningful way.

Although the Dutch have engaged in a number of reforms (Toonen 1987b, 1991; Bekke 1991), they have not adopted regional structures similar to those found elsewhere (Toonen 1998), despite the fact that the 1980s and 1990s saw a move towards functional decentralization. The centre thus remains strong. Denters and Klok (Chapter 5) also note that the Dutch system reveals 'a highly complex system of shared responsibilities in which hardly any policy sector is the exclusive domain of one tier of government', notwithstanding the constitutional implication that municipalities are 'free to define tasks and create competences so long as these do not conflict with national or provincial statutes'. They also note that almost half of the municipalities' income comes in the form of categorical grants, with over a third coming in the form of a general grant designed to equalize municipal differences in ability-to-pay and service-cost variations. Though Denters and Klok suggest that the categorical grants vary in the amount of discretion they give to municipalities, many either involve obligatory functions or quite detailed regulation. The result is that the amount of local discretion is likely to vary from one grant to another. Hence, according to Groenendijk (1998: 174), the present Dutch system inevitably stifles innovation and change.

The other recent development in Dutch intergovernmental relations noted by Denters and Klok is the increasing use of what they call *covenants* or agreements on the principles and procedures of governing the relationship between different tiers, a process which has been in place since 1987. Similar moves towards what might be called the contractualization of intergovernmental relations can also be found in France and Italy (see Chapters 2 and 3). Denters and Klok admit that the effect of such agreements on intergovernmental relations is difficult to assess, since on the one hand they provide the centre with opportunities under which it can exert greater control over municipalities. On the other hand it allows municipalities an opportunity to win recognized discretion and possibly additional funding in many policy areas, while increasing municipal access to central government decision-making.

A further feature of the Dutch system is voluntary cooperation amongst municipalities as well as the creation of quasi-regional authorities, the latter in effect being indirectly elected bodies covering seven of the Netherlands' major urban areas. Another form of cooperation involves what are known as *intercommunales* or voluntary cooperation agreements, which Denters and Klok suggest are highly subject to veto politics, though apparently working reasonably well as part of the EU sponsored Interreg or cross-border system of cooperation.

In more or less formalized forms, such voluntary cooperation is found in many other countries. France, for example, is a country with a recent history of encouraging municipal cooperation, as Borraz and Le Galès (Chapter 2) make clear. Since Napoleonic times, France has lived with its 36,000 *communes*, an almost sacred number which has hardly varied for two centuries. The formal decentralization moves associated with the Mitterand instance was to strengthen the old departmental levels and the large cities. More recent reforms introduced under the Jospin government between 1997 and 2002 have been to continue the process, especially developing the status of the large cities. Three programmes are worth noting. The first promoted cooperation among what are essentially rural *communes* through the introduction of what are called *communautés des communes*, under which a number of *communes* voluntarily cooperate in the provision of a number of services – mainly those concerned with economic development. The other two programmes emerged as a result of the Chevènement and Voynet laws where emphasis was placed on the major urban areas, both through the development of new *communautés urbaines* and the new *communautés d'agglomérations*. As Baraize and Negrier (2001) note, within the first two years following passage of the Chevènement law an extra two *communautés urbaines* were created and over one hundred *communautés d'agglomération* came into place.

Commentators have differed in their interpretation of what triggered these events. Some believe that financial incentives were important, while others stress the efforts of some prefects in bringing about agreements to join the new bodies. In part the developments reflect the important part which the central French state still plays in the intergovernmental relationship – but one in which it is perhaps more heavily dependent on the willing cooperation of the communal levels than would have been the case some thirty or forty years ago. Borraz and Le Galès suggest that local autonomy is 'a very mixed picture ... an illusion for small communes ... but a great opportunity for powerful municipalities'. They support this view by indicating how municipal functions had been increased under the Mitterand reforms, and by the growing financial autonomy of local governments generally, but also highlight the extent to which the fragmentation in the system undermined this growing autonomy. Borraz and Le Galès stress the importance of *contractualization* between levels of government and between the public and private sectors as 'the central instrument of cooperation between actors'. They also highlight the potential for local governments offered by developments at the EU level, whether it be for example by contesting state decisions at the European Court, lobbying Brussels, networking, or acquiring funding from regional schemes for specific projects, albeit they note the limitations on this autonomy.

Reforms introduced by the Jospin government (Chevènement, Voynet) have produced rapid change. Borraz and Le Galès argue that the speed of change reflects local patterns of leadership and existing cooperative experience rather than the financial incentives offered by central government, though admittedly the latter helped reduce the variety in the form of cooperative arrangements. Given their recent introduction, it is difficult to assess their likely impact. Much will depend, as Borraz and Le Galès emphasize, on how the legitimacy of the new voluntary agglomeration communities develops, and how far they avoid veto politics under which those less willing to cooperate delay or obstruct new developments. What is clear from this process of change is that, as Borraz and Le Galès put it, 'the intercommunal revolution is gradually reorganizing a vast array of 36,000 communes within 4,000 to 6,000 intercommunal governments'. Recent developments also suggest that the regional tier, which has been fighting to establish its political space ever since its creation almost 20 years ago, was further strengthened after the 2002 elections when Prime Minister Raffarin secured reforms leading to increased regional decentralization towards the end of the year.

Turning to the Nordic countries, there have to date been what Rose and Ståhlberg in Chapter 6 describe as major reforms but no revolution in local government. The free commune experiments of the late 1980s and early 1990s provided a stimulus for a decline in the level of administrative oversight provided by central government over local government activities, especially in Norway and Sweden. Though the Nordic municipalities in theory enjoy powers of general competence, they have been subject to a great deal of detailed administrative oversight and legislative dictates which in reality still subject local governments to considerable limitations on their autonomy.

Fiscal crisis and economic downturn in both Sweden and Finland provided further impetus for reform and new developments. As Rose and Ståhlberg note, these developments have been concerned mainly with process rather than structure. There have been some moves towards regionalism, especially in Finland through the creation of joint boards and in Sweden by a strengthening of county tiers, and a general encouragement of inter-municipal cooperation, but little real structural reform. In part this reflects earlier reforms which reduced the number of municipalities and generally increased their size. More important, despite extensive discussion about reforming local government in metropolitan areas, structural reform has up to now been set aside in the face of public opposition. The alternative has been to seek improved arrangements designed to secure voluntary cooperation between the various bodies. As elsewhere, however, such arrangements raise the problems posed by the use of veto politics by those less willing to cooperate. But to one degree or another Oslo, Helsinki and Copenhagen have all moved along this cooperative path. Even so, the issue of structural reform remains alive as the appointment of a new public commission in Denmark in 2002 with a mandate to review existing political-administrative boundaries and responsibilities clearly indicates.

Last, but not least, membership of the EU has had an impact on working relations especially within Sweden and Finland, both of which became extremely active within various EU networks following their admission to membership in the 1990s. Though Norway is not a member of the EU, it too has felt the impact of some of the changes associated with the EU's development. But it is Denmark which appears to have undergone the least change within the recent past, not only in the face of changes brought about within the EU, but also from other pressures. In part this may be a reflection of the relative economic prosperity which Denmark has enjoyed for most of the last twenty years and its commitment to the values implied in the consensus about the Nordic welfare state. Clearly these values have been challenged most heavily in Sweden with its reforms in the 1990s, and they are also under question in Denmark with the recent election of a more rightwing government.

Not all countries are the same

Within the context of the countries reviewed in this volume, there are some interesting 'outliers'. Like other Central and East European countries, Poland can be considered a special case of a political system undergoing extensive change as part of the post-communist reform era. It does appear to share some faith in the process of decentralization generally found elsewhere in Europe, but despite the rapid introduction of elected local government after the collapse of communism, Central and East European countries generally have weak local government systems that are poorly financed and have a meso-tier that is hardly in place (Reed 2002).

Britain and New Zealand, on the other hand, are both unitary states in which the recent history of intergovernmental relations is virtually the opposite of that found elsewhere. Under both right- and leftwing regimes, local government has been undergoing almost constant change in the past two decades, especially in the UK. As Bush makes clear in Chapter 11, by the early 1990s New Zealand had become recognized as a pioneer in many reforms. Here the Labour government at the end of the 1980s had reduced the number of regional authorities, reduced the number of local governments from over 200 to 74, abolished some 500 special-purpose bodies and had introduced extensive privatization of services. The successor rightwing National government adopted a pragmatic approach to its predecessors' reforms, but continued, as Bush puts it, a 'focus on managerial innovations, performance measurement, consultation, strategic development, better financial management and alternative methods of service delivery'. The return of a Labour government after 1999 promised a further period of reform, one encouraging more 'genuine' local government in the sense of considering a general competence power and more community-based decision-making.

In many cases local governments have some general competence power which, without ensuring complete freedom of action for local authorities, offers them greater constitutional discretion than is the case where such a power has not been given. In Australia and the USA, however, local governments remain dependent on state governments for their powers. Furthermore, in the case of Britain and New Zealand, local governments are even more dependent on central government for their existence and powers. In both cases local governments are subject to the doctrine of *ultra vires* – the doctrine that local governments can only do those things on which the national parliament has passed enabling legislation. And in both cases central governments have been very willing to use their powers effectively to pull up the plant and constantly reexamine the roots of local government.

In this context, even if Britain is not an exceptional case, it is certainly an extreme one. For over 20 years it has been undergoing constant change, at one time in the 1980s being considered 'the most centralized (state) outside eastern Europe' (Goldsmith and Newton 1983). Even after further change introduced by New Labour it remains one of the most centralized systems in the world. Under Prime Ministers Thatcher and Major, local government lost status. Funding and expenditure was centrally controlled and many functions and responsibilities given to non-elected agencies, so that elected local governments became only one of many bodies concerned with local service provision. It was, to quote Stoker (1999a: 1), 'a brutal illustration of power politics'. More than anything it reflected the unequal distribution of power and resources between centre and periphery in a system where local government has never been properly defined constitutionally but allowed to emerge piecemeal. And the last 20 years have seen innumerable pieces of British legislation, all having some impact on local government, as the centre has sought to impose one initiative after another on local authorities.

As Wilson notes in this volume, the arrival of the New Labour government in 1997 did not herald a return to the previous glory days of all-powerful, all-providing multi-purpose local governments. Above all control of the purse-strings has remained as tight under New Labour as it had been under the previous regime. Through the 1990s structural change also continued, so that the number of local governments had been reduced from over 1,800 in 1970 to over 500 in 1980 to just 442 by 2000. In population terms, Britain has the largest local governments in the developed world, and one of the highest constituent/elected representative ratios as well. In this context, New Labour has been as much concerned with measures designed to address the so-called democratic deficit at the local level, seeking to improve accountability and transparency of decisions, as it has been to improve service provision in terms of service outputs. But like its predecessor, the Labour government has been only too willing to adopt a plethora of initiatives, often without allowing earlier ones to prove their worth. As Wilson makes clear, government rhetoric which promises British local governments the chance of increased 'earned autonomy' is in practice 'anything but liberating'. Far from speaking with one voice, government at the centre remains fragmented, and what is promised by one part is quickly reversed by another. The New Labour centre continues to distrust elected local government in Britain as much as its Tory predecessors did.

The impact of globalization and Europeanization

One important dimension on which many of the European authors included here touch upon but do not review extensively is the impact of the European Union on intergovernmental relations. Processes of economic globalization and political integration within the EU have also had their impact on intergovernmental relations and on the ability of central governments to control the sub–national level. Economic globalization has forced national governments to adopt new policies and adapt old ones in areas like labour markets, and with respect to welfare services such as education and care for the elderly, in order to remain economically competitive. One result has been that local governments, especially in the larger urban areas, have become much more concerned about promoting the economic competitiveness of their areas than was the case thirty or forty years ago (Le Galès 2002; John 2001).

At the same time, political integration within the EU constrains the ability of national governments to operate independently of fellow member states. This integration takes place in both a formal and informal fashion. Formal political integration within the EU occurs in three ways. First, it follows the adoption of binding treaties from Rome to Nice; second, it follows from decisions of the European Court of Justice, which national courts have accepted as binding on member states; and finally, it occurs through national acceptance of EU Commission-issued directives and regulations.

Informal processes of integration occur mainly through policy-making, which has become increasingly Europeanized in the sense that the policy process has become both more complex and involves a wide variety of actors drawn from across the member states and from different sectors (Fligstein and McNichol 1998). Thus the Commission and its directorates, the European Parliament, member-state governments, sub-national units and a host of national and trans-national interest groups are all involved in policy-making through a process best described as involving an extensive bargaining network or game characterized by interdependence amongst the different actors. The term multi-level governance perhaps best describes EU policy-making, a system in which the different actors and levels operate under a series of varying opportunities and constraints (Hooghe and Marks 2001; Hooghe 1996).

In the present context two areas of EU activity are particularly relevant. The first concerns the process of EU regulatory activity through regulations and directives, which, together with relevant EU Court of Justice decisions, have impacted markedly on sub-national governments. Such policy arenas as health and safety, environmental matters, consumer standards, transport and contracts all provide examples which impact on sub-national levels. In each of these cases, sub-national governments have found themselves obliged to implement directives from Brussels, and thus find themselves subject to direction from another higher and somewhat remote tier of government. However, research also reveals differences in the ways in which different member states comply with such directives, reflecting in part the difficulties the European Commission has in effectively policing its own regulations (Héretier *et al.* 1996). Indeed, the very credibility of the EU regulatory system has been questioned by one of its foremost researchers (Majone 2000).

The other area, now extensively researched, concerns the operation of EU cohesion policy and the use of the structural funds (cf. Hooghe 1996; Heinelt and Smith 1996; Goldsmith and Klaussen 1997; Le Galès and Lequesne 1998). Research shows that eligible sub-national units have derived considerable benefit from access to the structural funds which have allowed them to pursue projects or develop cross-national agreements, albeit always with the support of the relevant central governments, through whom the funds flow. Research also reveals considerable variation in experience within and across countries and over time. In some cases (Belgium and Germany for example) sub-national levels have been able to exercise considerable influence, if not complete independence of action, over the use of the funds, while in others (such as France and the UK) the degree of control exercised by central governments has remained extensive.

But as Balme and Le Galès (1997) suggest, it is also true that not all regions, and even more so not all cities and municipalities are equally able to exploit the benefits of EU funding. There are both bright stars and black holes. Thus, Italian regions and cities have generally speaking, been less able to exploit the structural funds, despite their extensive eligibility. In Britain, cities such as Glasgow, Birmingham, Manchester and more recently Liverpool, by comparison, have been strong players on the European scene. Indeed in the late 1980s, through their exploitation of the EU integrated development programmes, Birmingham and Manchester appeared to be almost bypassing central government, a factor which no doubt influenced the latter in its introduction of the English regional offices as a means of reestablishing control over the British use of regional funds.

In terms of our main theme here two points are relevant. First, the growing importance of Brussels and some of its policy initiatives have changed the nature of intergovernmental relations both within the EU and subsequently within the member states. The result has been changes in the pattern of both vertical and horizontal intergovernmental relations. Central governments remain major players, and while sub-national proposals still go through the centre and must effectively have its support, localities also deal directly with Brussels, reflecting the vertical change. Second, localities are also often obliged or encouraged to work together, including cross-border cooperation, to win Brussels funding – a change in horizontal relations. In part these changes reflect the influence of Brussels and the changing rules of the intergovernmental game. The acceptance of two principles for the operation of the structural funds – subsidiarity and partnership – has meant that national governments sometimes find it more difficult to dominate sub-national units with respect to relevant European matters. Given that the subsidiarity principle is interpreted differently in different countries, in part it is this difference of interpretation which explains how it is that the Belgian regions and the German *Länder* are able to play a different role in the use of regional funds from that of British or French cities.

Partnership, on the other hand, has obliged central governments to work with cities and regions in developing appropriate programmes designed to use the funds. Partnership changes the nature of *vertical* intergovernmental relations, bringing the Commission, national governments, regions and localities together into a partnership network. At the same time the sub-national units are obliged to develop local partnerships with other bodies drawn from the public, private and voluntary sectors. Furthermore, in order to exploit some EU funding opportunities, such partnerships may well be cross-border. In both senses partnership changes the nature of *horizontal* intergovernmental relations. Additionally sub-national units, as with other organized interests, have been quick to exploit the lobbying possibilities offered in Brussels both to put pressure on their own national governments over the ways in which regional funds should be implemented, and also to shape EU policy in this area (John 1994). Although the degree of success such lobbying activity has achieved is variable, this activity is another example of the changing nature of intergovernmental relations to which European local governments, especially in the EU and in the candidate countries, are subject.

However, one must not overexaggerate these changes. Within the EU, and especially since the Amsterdam Treaty, national governments remain the most important actors, whereas regions and localities remain relatively minor actors. Furthermore, given concerns about the Commission's ability to enforce its regulatory regimes and the probable further downgrading of regional policy in EU priorities generally following expansion to the east, Brussels' ability to influence intergovernmental relations is also limited.

Conclusions

This review suggests that changes in the macro-context of local government (like urbanization, globalization and Europeanization) have resulted in changing patterns of intergovernmental relations generally and more specifically in those countries reported in this book. A number of conclusions can be drawn. First, the patterns of change are formally and constitutionally markedly different between federal and unitary systems, in that in the former it is the intermediate tier (state, province or whatever) which frequently has constitutional responsibility for local government, while in the latter that responsibility lies with the central government. But the unitary countries are not uniform in their approach to local government: some grant localities a general competence, whereas in others, notably Britain and New Zealand, the doctrine of *ultra vires* applies. Second, practically everywhere, a move from local government to local governance is clearly discernible, in that local governments increasingly have to work with other agencies and sectors to maintain and/or to improve economic competitiveness and service performance. This holds even in countries like those in the Nordic area which still retain extensive responsibility for service delivery. Third, there are changes in intergovernmental relations in both vertical and horizontal directions. Generally, as a response to the challenges of urbanization, globalization and Europeanization, there are signs of more inter-municipal cooperation in nearly all countries from the United State to France, and from Switzerland to Sweden. Such cooperation may also be encouraged by developments introduced by higher tiers of government – state or national – but is probably most marked in the unitary systems in Europe – for example Italy and France. And such cooperation is likely to be underpinned by an increasing use of some form of contractual arrangement concerning particular activities, be they matters of economic development or service delivery.

Fourth, in terms of the vertical dimension, in both federal and unitary states there are signs of a willingness to grapple with some of the major problems of service delivery, economic development and fiscal stress which most countries face. Increasing healthcare costs, educational demands, aging populations, and economic restructuring pose problems for governments at all levels everywhere. In federal systems it is generally the inter-mediate tier (state, province, *Länder*) which has been willing to consider change: in the United States by encouraging moves towards more voluntary regional cooperation and in Australia by a willingness to do away with elected local government in Victoria, albeit for only a limited period. The changes in unitary countries reforms have been different. In New Zealand and the United Kingdom they have been extensive. In France, Italy, Spain, Central and East Europe they have also been far-ranging if not quite as dramatic. In the case of the Nordic countries and the Netherlands, on the other hand, they have been more gradual.

Last but not least in the European context there has been a clear tendency towards a system of multi-level governance, involving complicated patterns of vertical and horizontal relationships between different municipalities which cross borders and produce new economic and political spaces. Such developments may well be seen as breaking down old cultural differences within Europe. In particular they may well be eroding some of the differences between the Northern and Southern European groups of countries identified by Denters and Rose in the introductory chapter of this volume. Three factors contribute to this process of change. First there is the impact of the EU, through its processes of regulation, the setting of new rules (for example partnership), the provision of finance and the encouragement of good practice. Second, changing practices comes about as a result of the rapid spread of ideas and new methods of working, of which those associated with New Public Management are but one example. But they are also encouraged by the increasingly frequent interaction of local politicians and professional officers across borders and in the rapidly growing number of territorial pressure groups such as Eurocities, and RETI. Third there is increasing cross-border cooperation, not only amongst existing EU members but with the accession countries as well. All of these developments encourage regions and cities to do things in a different fashion. The process of change, however, is slow and should not be overestimated. As Wollman (2000) has demonstrated, old practices and customs die hard, while national values persist. Thus path-dependent influences remain strong, and help maintain the cultural differences identified by writers such as Hesse and Sharpe (1991) as well as Page and Goldsmith (1987a) more than a decade ago.

A similar process of change in intergovernmental relations might well occur within North America, with the liberalized market and growing economic cooperation between the United States, Canada and Mexico, but it is perhaps still too early to see that impact at the local level. These latter changes reflect processes of economic globalization as nations, regions and cities seek to maintain their economic competitiveness.

One other feature of intergovernmental relations is also apparent. In the 1960s and to a lesser extent the 1970s, national governments were much more directly involved in municipal affairs, largely as a result of growing welfare-service responsibilities. Governments everywhere appeared willing to 'tear up the map' of local government, reducing the numbers of municipalities, introducing metropolitan-level institutions, and giving municipalities more responsibilities. In the 1980s and 1990s, in many countries but especially the federal ones, there was a move away from such direct involvement in the map and powers of localities by national governments. Under Ronald Reagan, for example, the US federal government withdrew from extensive involvement with local governments, especially in the cities, as did its Australian counterpart. In federal systems such disengagement has placed more responsibility on the intermediate tier, which has reacted with greater or lesser enthusiasm as the case may be. Elsewhere, led by the New Zealand and British examples, and supported by US examples, governments encouraged municipalities to move away from direct service provision – albeit with less enthusiasm in some parts of Europe (the Nordic area generally) than in others. But in other parts, notably Southern Europe, different models of service provision applied, and the introduction of New Public Management techniques was also less marked.

At the turn of the century, in short, change in intergovernmental relations is very much afoot, but in a different form. It is perhaps best described as a move towards more indirect forms of control and influence based on regulation and contractualization rather than on direct intervention, and which depends more on the willing cooperation of sub-national levels than before. France, the Netherlands and to a lesser extent Italy and the UK, provide examples of this new pattern, which it seems likely that others will follow.

15 Towards Local Governance?

Bas Denters and Lawrence E. Rose

In the last few decades the world of democratic local government has changed considerably. In the introductory chapter to this book five major trends were identified, all of which have had an impact in this regard. These trends are as follows:

- Urbanization.
- Globalization.
- Europeanization.
- The rise of new substantive demands.
- The rise of new participatory demands.

The previous chapter by Goldsmith offers a cross-national analysis of the repercussions of such changes for the relations *between* various governments, both vertically (between various layers of government) and horizontally (between different local governments). This chapter offers a similar cross-national analysis of patterns of change in the relations between the various public and private agents that are engaged in efforts to deal effectively with the challenges arising *within* local communities.

The challenges are of a dual character. On the one hand substantive demands require improved local problem-solving capacity and more effective forms of community leadership. On the other hand there are calls for democratic reforms that will assure greater openness, access, transparency and accountability within local government. Meeting these challenges is no small task, not the least because the macro-trends of urbanization, globalization and, for many countries considered here, Europeanization have contributed to the emergence of an increasingly complex multi-level polity. It has become harder to draw clear boundary lines with respect to tasks, responsibilities and actors, and as a consequence of this, it has become not only harder to meet substantive demands, but also harder to realize and protect fundamental values of democratic policy-making.

In the following sections, changes in the responsibilities of local governments and the implications of these changes in terms of a shift from government to governance are discussed, after which the implications of these changes for managerial and leadership reforms and the consequences in terms of democratic reforms are highlighted. The chapter ends with a short conclusion.

Changing responsibilities – beyond the provision of services

It is evident that at the beginning of the new millennium local governments in most of the countries reviewed here either alone or in collaboration with other authorities are responsible for a broad range of tasks and functions (see column 1 in Exhibit 15.1). In Switzerland, the United States, Germany and the Nordic countries there has long been a tradition of strong (*de facto*) local autonomy and local governments operating with a wide range of functional responsibilities. In France, Italy, Poland and the Netherlands, on the other hand, more recent decentralization programmes have resulted in significant extensions in the range of functional responsibilities attended to by local government. In Belgium, by comparison, where local government traditionally engaged in a wide range of activities, no such decentralization operation has taken place.

Despite differences in specific local government responsibilities across the countries mentioned, all but one grant their local governments a power of general competence that endows municipalities with the right to undertake policy initiatives in all areas that are not explicitly precluded or defined as the exclusive responsibility of another layer of government. The exception is the USA, where Dillon's rule does not grant such a general competence to city governments. But in the USA powers of home rule and considerable fiscal autonomy found in many states provide local government with a great deal of independence from state governments. For all of these countries it is therefore fair to say that local governments now have significant *de facto* powers to initiate efforts to address community problems in an integrated fashion, working with other partners as may be deemed best under conditions that pertain. Potentially this enables local authorities to move beyond the role of merely being a provider and producer of a more or less broad range of centrally defined public services.

It is in this context that local governments increasingly engage in new activities. In both France and the Netherlands, for instance, municipalities are now explicitly taking on responsibility for the integration of national social and urban policies and their adaptation to local needs. In several

Exhibit 15.1 Trends in local government responsibilities and structures

Country	Range of responsibilities	New Public Management	Partnerships	Strong executive/mayor
France	Decentralization in the 1980s and a new role for municipalities in territorial integration of policies in the 1990s	Privatization of many services, rise of large private-service companies	New alliances with private partners, often with the use of contracts	French mayor's role strong within municipality; external role affected by rise of intercommunales
Italy	Post-1997: decentralization and tensions between regions and local governments; increasing saliency of developmental policies to boost the attractiveness of cities	More room for public managers to manage; privatization and performance-based management introduced by central government	Territorial pacts for public–private cooperation aimed at economic development	Introduction of strong directly elected mayor
Belgium	No major reallocation of tasks from other levels to the local level	New organizational models as alternatives for in-house-production of services	Autonomous municipal companies, non-profit associations and advisory councils may be used to engage with partners from outside local government	Indirectly elected mayor; debate on introduction of direct election of mayor; attempts to professionalize and strengthen mayoral powers
Netherlands	Decentralization with increasing local responsibilities for housing, urban renewal, social policies and economic policy	Privatization, involvement of third sector, contract-based management of bureaucracy; performance-based management (partly instigated by central government); citizen surveys and charters	Development of local community partnerships aimed at local economic development and urban policy plans	Appointed mayor; debate on direct election; position of executive has been strengthened recently (division of powers)

Norden	Traditionally strong role of local government; increased saliency of developmental policies	Desire to clarify boundaries between politics and administration (MBO); municipal companies; privatization; benchmarks, etc., partly under influence of central governments	Public–private partnerships to pursue economic development policies and other objectives	Indirectly elected mayors; experiments with directly elected mayors in Norway
Poland	Transfer of a wide range of responsibilities to municipalities in the post-communist era	Introduction of new forms of service delivery: municipal companies, privatization etc. and cooperation with NGOs	Change from direct economic activity to strategic economic planning aimed at local development	Recently direct election of mayor (often checked by alternative majority in council); attempts to strengthen position of mayor *vis-à-vis* council
Germany	Local government is traditionally a partner in a complicated system of joint policy-making with other layers of government; no fundamental decentralization	Privatization and contracting-out of delivery and production of services; increased customer orientation; reinforcement of separation between politics and administration; institutionalization of benchmarks	Public–private partnerships in urban planning, utilities and social cultural services	Nationwide adoption of strong mayor model after unification
Switzerland	No further decentralization in already highly decentralized system	Adoption of elements of NPM, though not necessarily the most essential elements for performance-based management; national minimum standards for services	Public–private partnerships in service provision and delivery; widespread involvement of third sector in social and community services	Directly elected mayors, checked by direct democratic controls. Attempts to strengthen executive by reducing its size and expanding its responsibilities; slight trend to professionalize mayor

Exhibit 15.1 Continued

Country	Range of responsibilities	New Public Management	Partnerships	Strong executive/mayor
UK	Increased importance of non-elected local agencies in providing services; hollowing out of local government and fragmentation	Strong national impulses to contract-out or privatize service provision and production; devolution of powers to service departments and other NPM measures	Hollowing out and fragmentation create need for partnerships to tackle cross-cutting issues	Various options for local authorities to strengthen the executive – among others direct or indirect election of mayors
New Zealand	Rather limited set of functions; introduction of a power of general competence to promote well-being of community first in 2002	National policies to adopt NPM practices, alternatives for in-house production; separation of politics and administration; adoption of policy and financial planning		No attempts to strengthen political executive; no strong elected mayor
Australia	Strong focus on service delivery; introduction of power of general competence, but issue of community governance is only just emerging	State encouragement or directives for more efficient service delivery based on NPM recipes; competitive tendering; strategic management; accountability regimes; performance evaluation etc.		
USA	Considerable *de facto* autonomy, but a power of general competence is not common	Adoption of NPM practices in some but not all cities; many cities only pay lip-service to the NPM rhetoric	Corporate-centred regimes; public–private partnerships aimed at economic development	Rise of mayoral leadership to counteract fragmentation: also elected mayors in many council-manager (C-M) cities; strong initiating role in cities with mayor-council model; in C-M cities, facilitative leadership role of mayor

countries, moreover, local governments have sought to find new ways to further local economic development. In part this is in reaction to the declining scope for effective macro-economic and monetary policies at the national level (due, for example, to Europeanization and globalization). Yet it is also motivated by an increased sense of responsibility for the general well-being of the community. This is not only the case in the USA, where there is a long tradition of local government engagement in economic development, but also in other countries. The chapters on Switzerland, Poland and the Netherlands provide some clear illustrations of this. Although these developments may not be entirely new, the extent of local government involvement in economic policies in these countries is unprecedented.

By contrast, local government autonomy in the United Kingdom, New Zealand and Australia has been much more limited, based as it is on a long-standing tradition of *ultra vires* whereby municipal competences are restricted to those that are explicitly attributed to them by central government. In these countries the functions of local government have typically been concentrated in the realm of service-provision and production. Interestingly, however, authorities in all three of these countries have recently decided either to introduce a power of general competence for local governments (New Zealand and Australia) and/or to remove 'consent regimes' that imply the requirement of central approval of local policy initiatives. In doing so, the responsibility of local authorities to promote and develop social, environmental and economic well-being of the community has been explicitly acknowledged. This is especially true in the UK.

Opportunities and uncertainties

In short, whereas the conclusion reached by Hesse and Sharpe (1990/91: 608) over a decade ago – that is, that local governments throughout the Western industrialized world play a 'major role in the delivery of fundamental collective public and quasi-public goods' – is still valid, the nature of local government's role in the delivery of such goods and services has changed considerably, as is evident from material presented in the chapters of this volume and the contents of Exhibit 15.1. As Stoker (1999a: 4–5) has argued, these changes have created opportunities for local government to play 'a leadership role in some of the broader challenges of community governance'. Whether local governments will be able to play such a role effectively, however, is uncertain. David Wilson, for example, notes in

Chapter 10 that without an adequate financial base it remains to be seen whether British local authorities will be able to make community leadership real. Rather similar concerns have been raised for some of the other countries considered (see, for instance, the chapters on Germany and the Netherlands).

Beyond the uncertainties relating to the formal powers and fiscal capacities of local government, tendencies towards *fragmentation* of activity and responsibility also constitute a source of potential uncertainty. In large measure fragmentation is tied to the wave of New Public Management which to a substantial degree has swept over local governments in all countries (see column 2 in Exhibit 15.1). This development has taken a variety of forms, including everything from hiving off services and contracting out production to introducing contract-management and establishing municipal agencies or companies at arm's length from the local political executive. The nature of the reforms and the extent to which such reforms have been implemented, of course, depend very much on national and local factors. Thus, in traditional consociational democracies like the Netherlands and Switzerland, for example, services have not as frequently been contracted out to private firms, but have instead been transferred to publicly subsidized or financed third-sector organizations. Important cross-national variations are also induced by the different role that state and national governments play. In Germany, Switzerland and the USA, for instance, these reforms have been largely based on local initiatives, whereas in the UK and New Zealand and some of the Australian states these reforms have been more or less dictated by central or state government.

The demise of in-house production has given birth to a whole range of what may be called *quasi-private organizations (QUAPRI)*, that is to say more or less autonomous organizations that operate under either public or private law, that are managed in a business-like manner, and that are engaged in the production and delivery of public services. Whereas in the more traditional system of local government the political executive could resort to its hierarchical powers to control and supervise the (service) bureaucracy, it is now necessary to rely more on new steering instruments and institutional arrangements.

In addition to these developments in the domain of the delivery of goods and services, new responsibilities have forced local governments to develop collaborative relationships with a variety of organizations of a local and regional character – public, private and quasi-private alike (see column 3 in Exhibit 15.1). Terms like 'community partnerships', 'organizing capacity', and 'public–private partnerships' have become increasingly popular. This partnership approach is particularly important in the area of economic development, especially where EU funds are involved. As noted in previous chapters, municipalities in many countries have engaged in assorted efforts to stimulate the local economy – for example, by creating favourable conditions for business and furthering tourism. Typically these efforts involve more or less close cooperation between the local business community and local government. Not all of these efforts may be characterized as attempts at building US-type urban growth regimes (cf. Stone 1989): differences between the nature of the local political arenas in the USA and British or continental Europe are too big to warrant such a generalization (Stoker 1995; Denters 2002). Even so it is clear that these new initiatives imply that local governments have become increasingly dependent upon other organizations in the local and regional community for service delivery and policy-making in many areas.

From local government to local governance – a demand for managerial and leadership reform

When taken together, increased fragmentation and dependency of local governments on external actors in taking on new responsibilities which have been evident over the past decade or so seem to justify concluding that there has been a shift from more traditional systems of local government to new forms of local governance. As Leach and Percy-Smith (2001: 1) argue in relation to the British case, the traditional notion in which 'local government is "what the council does" ' has to be replaced by a conception in which it is conceded that public decision-making concerning local issues 'increasingly involves multi-agency working, partnerships and policy networks which cut across organisational boundaries' – in essence governance. Cross-national evidence presented in this book suggests that this shift has taken place not only in the UK, but in other countries as well. Yet it should be acknowledged, as is evident from the exhibits in this chapter, that the exact manifestation of this development is dependent upon the national context in which such changes take place.

Rather than implying a loss of functions and responsibility, this shift involves a new role for local governments. In the words of Le Galès (2002: 13): 'changes in the state, the economy, and society ... are causing upheaval in the model of the nation-state and altering the constraints and opportunities for sub-national territories'. These changes constitute 'the pressures that are pushing these territories either towards social and political fragmentation or towards attempts to create internal coherence and develop strategies to help them evolve towards being actors of European governance' (*ibid.*). The success of such integrative strategies is by no means self-evident. Especially cross-cutting issues such as environmental sustainability, crime and social inclusion require concerted action by a wide array of actors across virtually all sectors of the local community – public organizations, private associations, third-sector organizations, the business community and neighbourhood and residential groups alike (Sullivan and Skelcher 2002: 56–79). Fragmentation, departmentalization and increased external dependencies all imply important obstacles for effective action with respect to such issues and serve to underline the need for reforms of local management practices and local executive leadership.

In order to enhance their capacity for effective and decisive action, municipalities in many of the countries considered here have pursued two main remedies. First, in an attempt to streamline their internal operations and to structure relations with organizations engaged in producing public services, they have adopted various forms of *contract- and performance-based management*. In theory this approach to public management is based on a combination of politically formulated measurable goals, a system of performance measurement to assess the achievement of these goals, and a 'contract' between the in-house department or QUAPRI-agent and its political principal. This agreement typically implies a grant of managerial discretion to the agent by the principal, combined with the agent's promise to strive for the realization of the agreed-upon goals and to provide empirical evidence on the actual achievement of these goals. Such arrangements appear attractive at first sight, but there is growing evidence that such mechanisms are not without problems (see, for example, Sanderson 1998: 8–16; Leeuw 2000; Denters 2001), and it is reasonable to anticipate that they will be subject to greater scrutiny in the years ahead.

A second and related remedy pursued in many countries discussed in this book has been an attempt to strengthen the local political executive. The introduction of a directly elected mayor, especially when endued with strong executive powers, is the most conspicuous expression of this tendency, but strengthened executive leadership has also taken other forms. Although the arguments for such executive reforms vary from one country to another, in broad terms there are three types of motivations. First, strengthening the executive – especially the position of the mayor – is considered as a remedy to the traditional bureaucratic evil of departmentalization. Second, the strong mayor and other forms of strong executive leadership are thought to be favourable for decisive and effective community leadership and for building successful urban regimes. Third, the advocates of such reforms, especially when they imply the direct election of the mayor, believe they will also have important democratic benefits – in particular more public interest and higher turnout for local elections, as well as gains in the democratic accountability of the executive.

Not only do the arguments used differ; the institutional forms employed to strengthen the executive also vary. In the UK, for example, the Labour government has offered local authorities a forced choice between a number of alternative models, all of which share a separation of legislative and executive functions and the introduction of a more or less strengthened executive function. Only one of the options offered, and the least popular among the local authorities, involved a directly elected mayor; most municipalities in the UK opted instead for one of the other models. The recent integral reform of the Dutch model of municipal government (2002) similarly seeks to strengthen executive leadership without introducing a directly elected mayor. The reform combines the retention of a nationally appointed mayor with a stronger, more independent executive board comprised of a mayor and two or more aldermen.

Many other local government systems, however, are characterized by a form of strong mayoral leadership. In France, southern Germany and many large US cities there has been a long tradition of strong monocentric executive leadership by a directly elected mayor. But in recent years the strong mayor system has also been introduced outside these traditional strongholds. Many US cities, even those previously operating with a council-manager model, have introduced directly elected mayors and extended their executive powers. In Switzerland there have likewise been attempts, albeit quiet modest, to strengthen the position of the executive and the elected mayor, whereas in Germany all state governments have now adopted variants of the strong, directly elected mayor model of southern Germany. Italy and Poland have also introduced a relatively strong directly elected mayor. Even countries with a strong tradition of collective executive leadership, either in the form of the council committee system (for example in Norway) or an executive board (for example the Netherlands and Belgium), have made more or less cautious moves towards the introduction of a directly elected mayor in recent years.

Towards a new form of local democracy?

The shift from government to governance has clear implications for the nature of local democracy. Traditionally efforts to understand local democracy have almost exclusively focused on the role of the directly elected municipal council; the council was conceived of as the crucial link in what

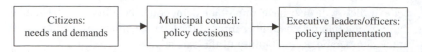

Figure 15.1   *The electoral chain of command model of local democracy*

Dearlove (1973: 25–46) once called the 'electoral chain of command' model of democracy (see Figure 15.1). In this simple and transparent model the council occupies a pivotal position in local democracy and the councillors – as popular representatives – are primarily responsible for translating local inputs (needs and demands) into authoritative decisions that in theory guide the actions and activities of municipal officers.

This model is based on a *general* rather than *issue-specific* primacy of a directly elected representative assembly. Although the empirical validity of this model has been challenged before (for example Newton 1976), it may be argued that recent changes have served to hollow out the traditional model even more substantially (see for instance Stoker 2003). For one thing, relations between citizens and (local) government have changed, a change that is evident on at least two fronts. On the one hand scholars have observed a decline in the absolute as well as the relative importance of traditional forms of electoral and party-oriented forms of political participation in many settings. Many of the country chapters in this volume illustrate that local government in these countries have not escaped these tendencies. Turnout in local elections has been traditionally rather low (typically well below 50 per cent) in the USA, the UK and Switzerland. But in several other countries – for example France, the Netherlands and Norway – there appears to be a clear downward trend in rates of electoral turnout for council elections as well (see column 1 in Exhibit 15.2). On the other hand there also appears to be a tendency whereby citizens increasingly seek alternative opportunities to voice their opinions and demands directly *outside the electoral channel*. Hence, even if turnout rates do not show a clear downward trend, the *relative importance* of electoral participation *vis-à-vis* other channels in the people's repertoire for political participation may have declined. Moreover, tendencies of strengthening the executive, sometimes even the direct election of a chief-executive (see column 1 of Exhibit 15.2), have (further) reduced the influence of the elected council in determining policies and exercising control of its implementation.

Secondly, the fragmentation of emerging systems of local governance puts pressure on the principle of local authorities as general-purpose governments. This fragmentation of authority not only poses functional problems (for example in providing for a coordinated approach to cross-cutting issues), it also raises the issue of securing transparency and democratic accountability. Who is to hold the QUAPRIs and the strengthened executive accountable?

The need to secure transparency and democratic accountability, however, is but one factor behind a host of recent initiatives to renew local democracy. Citizen calls for the introduction of new participatory channels have provided another reason for such reforms. Many reforms have sought to engage citizens in a relatively early stage of the decision-making process, either through consultations or through a process of co-decision or co-production (see column 2 in Exhibit 15.2). Another reform found in countries as different as Germany, France and Australia has been the introduction of various forms of plebiscitary democracy, either as a local initiative or as a dictate of national or state government (see column 3 in Exhibit 15.2). But the scope for citizen influence implied in all these new channels differs greatly. In some cases (for example Germany) the outcomes of these new modes of decision-making are decisive, and one might characterize the reforms as the introduction of elements of direct democracy *à la* Switzerland. In other cases, such as with referenda in Italy and Belgium, the reforms are less radical and the status of citizen inputs are advisory rather than decisive. In a slightly different vein, many countries have sought to secure accountability in local service delivery by the use of satisfaction surveys and focus groups (for example in Belgium) or the use of citizen juries (the UK), through the creation of user boards (for example in the Nordic countries) and the adoption of Citizen Charters (such as are best known from the UK).

In addition to such reforms, may countries have also undertaken a review of the role of the elected council in local government. France, where no major institutional reforms pertaining to the position of the council took place, is the exception rather than the rule. But once again we see that the changes diverge in various directions. In Belgium an attempt is being made to reinvigorate the council's traditional primacy. In Italy, by contrast, reforms were implemented to marginalize the powers of the councils in favour of the directly elected mayor. In yet other countries there has been a *de facto* decline in the influence of councils because of the introduction of an elected mayor (for example in Poland and Germany). In still other countries attempts have been made to redefine the roles of the council and the executive branch. This latter strategy has been adopted in countries like the Netherlands and in the UK. Whereas these two countries had rather different models of local government before the introduction of recent reforms, they have now both adopted a model in which councillors are supposed to play a double role, being popular representatives in the one hand, while

Exhibit 15.2   Trends in local democratic governance

Country	Representative democracy and turnout	New models of citizen involvement	Plebiscitary democracy
France	Role of councils remains rather weak; decline in electoral turnout; weaker position for parties	Introduction of citizen consultations, deliberation, etc., partly initiated by central government	Referenda and initiatives introduced partly by central government
Italy	Role of councils weakened by directly elected mayor; decline in turnout from 1990s onwards	Some developments in urban renewal, Agenda 21 and infrastructure policies	Advisory local referendums (in practice often binding)
Belgium	Attempts to strengthen position of council *vis-à-vis* mayor; compulsory voting and hence no change in turnout	Attempts to increase citizen involvement through citizen surveys, advisory councils and *ad hoc* initiatives	Advisory referendums (consultations) since mid-1990s
Netherlands	Attempts to strengthen the representative, control and scrutiny roles of councillors; decline in turnout, crisis of local parties	Neighbourhood decentralization and procedures for consultation or co-decision in policy process	Local experiments with advisory referenda and initiatives
Norden	Attempts to streamline committee system and experiments with parliamentary model; decline of turnout in Norway	User boards, especially in Denmark and Sweden; modest attempts to use e-democracy to enhance citizen involvement	No initiatives
Poland	Powers *vis-à-vis* mayor reduced; turnout low, but not a clear downward trend; increasing role for parties	Statutory obligation to consult citizens in e.g. planning decisions; new modes of communication with citizens	Recall of elected mayor by popular referenda; referendum to call for new council elections
Germany	Decline of power of council (by more powerful position of mayor and rise of plebiscitary democracy); traditionally high turnout declines in most municipalities	New participatory and consultative initiatives and experiments with e-participation	Right to recall elected representatives; referenda and initiatives

Switzerland	Local executive traditionally dominant over council; but executive power also checked by direct democratic means; traditionally low turnout	Efforts to improve information of citizens and involve them in planning process in order to reduce risk of negative referendum outcomes	In many places popular assemblies; in addition a wide range of referenda, initiatives and rights to recall officials
UK	Reform of committee system and redefinition of role of non-executive councillors (representation, control and scrutiny); traditionally low levels of turnout	Under Conservatives empowerment of citizens as consumers; under Labour broader conception with new methods of citizen consultation	No initiatives
New Zealand	Formal primacy of council; no change in role of council *vis-à-vis* political executive; introduction of council-elected CEO in charge of administrative matters	Adoption of community boards to bridge gap between TLAs and citizens; statutory obligation to consult citizens on strategic planning at local level	No initiatives
Australia	Council in role of 'board of directors': decide on CEO leadership role in shaping policies and implementation; low electoral turnout	Mandated consultations and reporting in the strategic planning process	Local referenda to ensure accountability and responsiveness
USA	Role of council differs between council-manager (C-M) and mayor-council (M-C) model; in C-M cities governance role orientation emphasized by councillors; in M-C cities representational role of councillors more pronounced; traditionally low levels of turnout	Cities across the nation have adopted participatory reforms ranging from administrative decentralization to community control	Initiatives for referenda fairly universal; initiatives and recall procedures more widespread in the West than in the East

controlling and scrutinizing the local executive on the other. Finally, efforts to reinvoke a traditional division of labour between the council's role and the role of the executive branch based on the distinction between policy and politics are also to be observed. The most pronounced example is to be found in New Zealand, but similar efforts can be found elsewhere (for example in Australia, the Nordic countries, Italy, Germany and in Switzerland).

All these changes suggest that local democracy is in the midst of a major transformation. At the same time as new mechanisms of accountability are superimposed on the traditional institutions of local democracy, the development of new relations between the council and the executive branch within local government is evident. These reforms raise complex issues. One may ask, for example, about the compatibility of traditional electoral accountability on the one hand and the new participatory accountability mechanisms on the other. Loughlin (1999: 340) for one has argued that '[m]uch thought needs to go into the kind of institutionalization necessary to make it work and to avoid conflict between the two kinds of representation'. On the other hand, new participatory channels share an element of functional specificity. Whereas the traditional model of local democracy in most Western countries has been based on a *general, undifferentiated relation* between the community of local citizens and an elected council that represented this community, new relations between citizens and their local government are characterized by a higher degree of functional differentiation inasmuch as they allow for citizen participation directed at *particular (sets of) decisions*. Many of these new participatory channels, moreover, target particular groups (either territorially defined as in the case of neighbourhood councils, or in functional terms as in the case of Danish school boards) within the community, based on assumptions about who will be affected by a particular decision.

In sum, whereas the electoral chain of command model of local democracy 'mapped out fairly simple serial flows of power between the represented and their representatives', the emerging system is characterized by a differentiation of the 'represented' and the complexity of their relations with the institutions of local governance (Judge 1999: 121). This, too, raises complex issues. From a democratic perspective one can ask to what extent a common definition of local democracy applies. Thus, in a classic study of democratic authority, Robert Dahl (1970: 59) asked 'Rule by the people: What people?' Who, in short, is to have a right to participate in making particular decisions? Who, for example, should have the right to participate in school boards: Employers? Employees? Parents? Members of the general public with an interest in education? Others? From a functional perspective it may also be asked what this differentiation means for efforts to interconnect and control complex processes of governance.

Conclusion

Answers to these questions are not within the realm of this book. This book has rather focused upon *major changes and continuities in various systems of local government in selected Western countries*. The underlying question has been whether the observation by several British scholars (for example, Rhodes 1997; Stoker 1999 and 2000) that a shift from government to governance has occurred recently, could be generalized to other parts of the Western world. Already in 2001 Peter John claimed that the UK does not stand alone, and on the basis of the contributions in this volume we are able to confirm this conclusion. In many respects the shift from local government to local governance is very much an international phenomenon. If contemporary local political arenas are contrasted with the prevalent model of local government in the Western world of the early 1980s, three major changes are to be observed:

- a widespread adoption of NPM and public–private partnerships;
- involvement of organized local associations, interest groups and private actors in policy partnerships; and
- introduction of new forms of citizen involvement.

Analyses contained in this volume also corroborate another of John's conclusions – namely that there are 'different paths of development away from traditional local government' (John 2001: 175). This conclusion is subject to some refinement however. On the one hand, tendencies relating to the introduction of NPM and public–private partnerships are rather uniform; more or less similar trends are found in most of the countries considered in this book. Yet two provisos should be mentioned in this connection: first, the same label may be used for widely different practices; and, second, new features are at times more symbolic than genuine in character.

On the other hand, there seems to be greater variety in the strategies pursued in terms of involvement of organized local associations, citizens and private actors in policy partnerships, new forms of citizen involvement, and changes in the traditional system of representative democracy. The differences here are so large as to defy any easy generalization. Patterns of change do not reflect simple categorizations based on the distinction between federal and unitary systems or between Northern, Southern and Anglo local government systems.

From a normative point of view the evidence presented in this volume raises important issues regarding the future of local democracy. In terms of *functional effectiveness and efficiency*, it remains to be seen how the emergent systems of local governance will fare in tackling the problems of local communities. In terms of *democratic quality*, a proliferation of accountability mechanisms and participatory channels is to be observed, yet it is unclear whether various parts of this new democratic infrastructure will be compatible. If this is not the case, it will be crucial for the future of democracy to find a well-balanced mix of democratic institutions. The domain of local governance will therefore undoubtedly remain the focus of considerable debate – both academic and political – for many years to come.

Bibliography

Aarts, C.W.A.M. (2000) 'Opkomst', in J. Thomassen, K. Aarts, and H. van der Kolk (eds), *Politieke veranderingen in Nederland 1971–1998: kiezers en de smalle marges van de politiek* (Den Haag: Staatsuitgeverij), pp. 57–75.

Aarts, K. (1995) 'Intermediate Organizations and Interest Representation', in H.-D. Klingemann and D. Fuchs (eds), *Citizens and the State* (Oxford: Oxford University Press), pp. 227–57.

Ackaert, J. (1997) 'De rol van de burgemeester', *Res Publica* 39, pp. 27–44.

Albæk, E., Rose, L., Strømberg, L. and Ståhlberg, K. (1996) *Nordic Local Government: Trends and Reform Activities in the Postwar Period* (Helsinki: The Association of Finnish Local Authorities), Acta 71.

Altshuler, A., Morrill, W., Wolman, H. and Mitchell, F. (eds) (1999) *Governance and Opportunity in Metropolitan America* (Washington, DC: National Academy Press).

Andersen, V.N. (1997) *Brugerbestyrelsen som et demokratisk organ* (Bergen: LOS-senteret), LOS-senter notat 9731.

Anderson, B. (1993) 'Do We Have Better Government?' *Chartered Accountants' Journal* 72(9), pp. 65–6.

Anderson, B.T.W. and Norgrove, K.J. (1997) 'Local Government Reform in New Zealand 1987–1996', in *Comparative Study on Local Government Reform in Japan, Australia and New Zealand* (Sydney: Japan Local Government Centre), pp. 113–82.

Anderson, M. (1964) *The Federal Bulldozer* (Cambridge, MA: MIT Press).

Anheier, H.K., Priller, E. and Zimmer, A. (2000) 'Zur zivilgesellschaftlichen Dimension des Dritten Sektors', in H.-D. Klingemann and F. Neidhardt (eds), *Zur Zukunft der Demokratie. Herausforderungen im Zeitalter der Globalisierung* (Berlin: Edition Sigma), pp. 71–98.

Audit Commission (2001) *Changing Gear: Best Value Annual Statement 2001* (London: Audit Commission).

Aulich, C. (1997) 'Competition in Local Government', in N. Marshall and B. Dollery (eds), *Australian Local Government: Reform and Renewal* (South Melbourne: Palgrave Macmillan), pp. 189–208.

Aulich, C. (1999a) 'Bureaucratic Limits to Markets: The Case of Local Government in Victoria, Australia', *Public Money and Management* 19, pp. 37–43.

Aulich, C. (1999b) 'From Convergence to Divergence: Reforming Australian Local Government', *Australian Journal of Public Administration* 58, pp. 12–23.

Australian Bureau of Statistics (ABS) (1997) *Wage and Salary Earners Australia* (Catalogue 6248.0) (Canberra: Commonwealth of Australia).

Axelrod, R. (1990) *The Evolution of Cooperation* (Harmondsworth: Penguin).

Aziewicz, T. (1994) *Prywatyzacja usług komunalnych w Polsce* (Gdańsk: The Gdansk Institute for Market Economics).

263

Aziewicz, T. (1998) *Gospodarka rynkowa w uslugach komunalnych* (Gdańsk: The Gdansk Institute for Market Economics).
Bache, I. (1998) *The Politics of European Union Regional Policy* (Sheffield: Sheffield Academic Press).
Bäck, H., Gjelstrup, G., Helgesen, M., Johansson, F. and Klausen, J.E. (2004) *Urban Political Decentralisation: Six Scandinavian Cities* (Leverkusen: Verlag Leske + Budrich).
Baldersheim, H. (1992) 'Aldermen into Ministers': 'Oslo's Experiment with a City Cabinet', *Local Government Studies* 18, pp. 18–30.
Baldersheim, H., Illner M., Offeredal, A., Rose, L. and Swianiewicz, P. (eds) (1996) *Local Democracy and the Process of Transformation in East-Central Europe* (Boulder: Westview Press).
Baldersheim, H., Sandberg, S., Ståhlberg, K. and Øgård, M. (2001) 'Norden in Europe of the Regions: A Summary of Perspectives and Results', in K. Ståhlberg (ed.), *The Nordic Countries and Europe II: Social Sciences* (København: Nordisk Ministerråd). Nord 2001: 23, pp. 75–110.
Baldersheim, H. and Ståhlberg, K. (eds) (1994) *Towards the Self-Regulating Municipality: Free Communes and Administrative Modernization in Scandinavia* (Aldershot: Ashgate).
Baldersheim, H. and Ståhlberg, K. (1999a) 'The Internationalisation of Finnish and Norwegian Local Government', in H. Baldersheim and K. Ståhlberg (eds), *Nordic Region-Building in a European Perspective* (Aldershot: Ashgate), pp. 121–49.
Baldersheim, H. and Ståhlberg, K. (1999b) *Making Local Democracy Work: An Evaluation of the Hämeenlinna Model* (Åbo: Åbo Akademi). Meddelanden från Ekonomisk-statsvetenskapliga fakulteten. Ser. A: 505.
Baldersheim, H. and Ståhlberg, K. (eds) (1999c) *Nordic Region-Building in a European Perspective* (Aldershot: Ashgate).
Baldersheim, H. and Ståhlberg, K. (2002) 'From Guided Democracy to Multi-Level Governance: Trends in Central–Local Relations in the Nordic Countries', *Local Government Studies* 28, pp. 74–90.
Baldersheim, H. and Stava, P. (1993) 'Reforming Local Government Policy-making and Management through Organizational Learning and Experimentation', *Policy Studies Journal* 21, pp. 104–14.
Baldersheim, H. and Swianiewicz, P. (2002) 'Mayors Learning Across Borders: The International Networks of Municipalities in East-Central Europe. Do Mayors Matter?', *Regional and Federal Studies* 12, pp. 126–38.
Baldersheim, H. and Øgård, M. (1998) 'The Norwegian CEO: Institutional Position, Professional Status, and Work Environment', in K.K. Klausen and A. Magnier (eds), *The Anonymous Leader: Appointed CEO's in Western Local Government* (Odense: Odense University Press), pp. 128–39.
Baldini, G. and Legnante, G. (2000) *Città al voto. I sindaci e le elezioni comunali* (Bologna: Il Mulino).
Balducci, A. (2001) 'La partecipazione nel contesto delle nuove politiche urbane', in D. Bianchi and E. Zanchini (eds), *Ambiente Italia 2001* (Milano: Edizioni Ambiente), pp. 59–71.
Balme, R., Faure, A. and Mabileau, A. (eds) (1999) *Les nouvelles politiques locales* (Paris: Presses de Sciences Po).
Balme, R. and Le Galès, P. (1997) 'Bright Stars and Black Holes: French Regions and Cities in the European Galaxy', in M. Goldsmith and K. Klaussen (eds),

European Integration and Local Government (Cheltenham: Edward Elgar), pp. 146–71.

Banner, G. (1989) 'Kommunalverfassungen und Selbstverwaltungsleistung', in D. Schimanke (ed.), *Stadtdirektor oder Bürgermeister. Beiträge zu einer aktuellen Kontroverse* (Basel: Birkhäuser), pp. 37–61.

Bannon, J. and Plumridge, L. (1990) *Memorandum of Understanding* (Adelaide: State Government of South Australia and the Local Government Association of South Australia).

Baraize, F. and Négrier, E. (eds) (2001) *L'invention politique de l'agglomération* (Paris: L'Harmattan).

Barbera, F. (2001) 'Le politiche della fiducia. Incentivi e risorse sociali nei patti territoriali', *Stato e mercato* 63, pp. 413–50.

Barthelemy, M. (2000) *Associations: un nouvel âge de la participation* (Paris: Presses de Sciences Po).

Beetham, D. (1996) 'Theorising Democracy and Local Government', in D. King and G. Stoker (eds), *Rethinking Local Democracy* (Basingstoke: Palgrave Macmillan), pp. 28–49.

Bekke, H. (1991) 'Experiences and Experiments in Dutch Local Government', in R. Batley and G. Stoker (eds), *Local Government in Europe* (Basingstoke: Palgrave Macmillan), pp. 123–33.

Bekkers, V.J.J.M. and Hendriks, F. (1998) 'Gemeenten in Europees perspectief', in A.F.A. Korsten and P.W. Tops (eds), *Lokaal bestuur in Nederland: inleiding in de gemeentekunde* (Alphen aan den Rijn: Samsom), pp. 170–80.

Berger, R. and Partner GmbH (1998) *Entwicklung und Einführung einer Kosten- und Leistungsrechnung in der Stadtverwaltung Frankfurt am Main (Abschlussdokumentation); Frankfurt a. M.* (Munich: Berger, Roland & Partner GmbH).

Berger, R. and Partner GmbH (1999) *Aufgabenteilung und Schnittstellenverantwortung in der Konzernorganisation 'Stadt Essen' – Zentrale und dezentrale Steuerungsverantwortung für Beteiligungsunternehmen und Ämter; Essen* (Munich: Berger, Roland & Partner GmbH).

Berger, R. and Partner GmbH (2000) *Entwicklung und Einführung eines Gesamtsteuerungssystems in der Landeshauptstadt Stuttgart; Stuttgart* (Munich: Berger, Roland & Partner GmbH).

Berghuis, J.M.J., Herweijer, M. and Pol, W.J.M. (1995) *Effecten van herindeling* (Groningen: Kluwer).

Berkhout, D.M. (1996) 'Overheid en middenveld in een ontzuilde samenleving', in Chr.L. Baljé, Th.G. Drupsteen, M.P.H. van Haeften and Th.A.J. Toonen (eds), *De ontzuiling voorbij: openbaar bestuur en individualistisch burgerschap* ('s-Gravenhage: Sdu Uitgeverij/Raad voor het binnenlands bestuur), pp. 81–102.

Bettin, G. and Magnier, A. (1995) 'I nuovi sindaci: come cambia una carriera politica', *Rivista italiana di scienza politica* 1, pp. 91–118.

Beyme, K. von (1996) 'Ansätze zur Reform des politischen Systems. Die Institutionen auf dem Prüfstand', in W. Weidenfeld (ed.), *Demokratie am Wendepunkt. Die demokratische Frage als Projekt des 21. Jahrhunderts* (Berlin: Siedler Verlag), pp. 158–76.

Blair, T. (1998) *Leading the Way: A New Vision for Local Government* (London: Institute for Public Policy Research).

Bobbio, L. (2000) 'Produzione di politiche a mezzo di contratti nella pubblica amministrazione italiana', *Stato e mercato* 58, pp. 111–41.

Bobbio, L. (2002) *I governi locali nelle democrazie contemporanee* (Roma-Bari: Laterza).

Bobbio, L. and Zeppetella, A. (eds) (1999) *Perché proprio qui? Grandi opere e opposizioni locali* (Milano: F. Angeli).

Bogumil, J. (2001) *Modernisierung lokaler Politik: kommunale Entscheidungsprozesse im Spannungsfeld zwischen Parteienwettbewerb, Verhandlungszwängen und Ökonomisierung* (Baden-Baden: Nomos).

Borraz, O. (1998) *Gouverner une ville. Besançon 1959–1989* (Rennes: Presses Universitaires de Rennes).

Borraz, O. (2000) 'Le gouvernement municipal en France. Un modèle d'intégration en recomposition' *Pôle Sud* 13, pp. 11–26.

Boston, J., Martin, J., Pallot, J. and Walsh, P. (1996a) 'The Centre and the Periphery: The Continuing Game', in J. Boston, J. Martin, J. Pallot and P. Walsh (eds), *Public Management: The New Zealand Model* (Auckland: Oxford University Press), pp. 162–82.

Boston, J., Martin, J., Pallot, J. and Walsh, P. (1996b) 'Management in Local Government', in J. Boston, J. Martin, J. Pallot and P. Walsh (eds), *Public Management: The New Zealand Model* (Auckland: Oxford University Press), pp. 183–202.

Bouckaert, G., Kampen, J.K., Maddens, B. and Walle, S. Van de (2001) *Klantentevredenheidsmetingen bij de overheid. Eerste rapport 'burgergericht besturen: kwaliteit en vertrouwen in de overheid'* (Leuven: Instituut voor de Overheid).

Bovenschulte, A. and Buss, A. (1996) *Plebiszitäre Bürgermeisterverfassungen. Der Umbruch im Kommunalverfassungsrecht* (Baden-Baden: Nomos).

Brosio, G., Maggi, M. and Piperno, S. (2001) *Governare fuori dal centro* (Ivrea: Fondazione Adriano Olivetti).

Bulpitt, J. (1989) 'Walking Back to Happiness'? in C. Crouch and D. Marquand (eds), *The New Centralism* (Oxford: Blackwell), pp. 56–73.

Burger, A. (2001) 'Verzuiling in de verzorgingsstaat: De non-profit-sector in historisch-theoretisch perspectief', in A. Burger and P. Dekker (eds), *Noch markt, noch staat: De Nederlandse non-profitsector in vergelijkend perspectief* (Den Haag: Sociaal en Cultureel Planbureau), pp. 87–104.

Bush, G.W.A. (1992) 'Local Government: Politics and Pragmatism', in H. Gold (ed.), *New Zealand Politics in Perspective* (Auckland: Longman, Paul), pp. 102–22.

Bush, G.W.A. (1995) *Local Government and Politics in New Zealand* (Auckland: Auckland University Press).

Bush, G.W.A. (2001) 'Local Government', in R. Miller (ed.), *New Zealand Government and Politics* (Auckland: Oxford University Press), pp. 159–68.

Cabinet Office (1999) *Modernising Government* Cm 4310 (London: HMSO).

Cabinet Office (2002) 'Your Region – Your Choice': Revitalising the English Regions (London: Stationery Office).

Caillosse, J., Le Galès, P. and Loncle, P. (1997) 'Les sociétés d'économie mixte locales en France, Outils de quelle action publique urbaine?', in F. Godard (ed.), *L'action publique urbaine et les contrats* (Paris: Descartes), pp. 23–96.

Cassese, S. (2002) *La crisi dello stato* (Roma-Bari: Laterza).

Cassese, S. and Wright, V. (eds) (1995) *La recomposition de l'Etat en Europe* (Paris: La Découverte).

Castells, M. (2002) 'Local and Global: Cities in the Network Society' *Tijdschrift voor economische en sociale geografie Journal of Economic and Social Geography* 93(5), pp. 548–58.

Cazzola, F. (1991) *Periferici integrati. Chi, dove, quando nelle amministrazioni comunali* (Bologna: Il Mulino).

Centre for Public Opinion Surveys (CBOS) (1994) 'Przed wyborami samorządowymi', Bulletin CBOS No. 1189, May 1994.

Centre for Public Opinion Surveys (CBOS) (1995) 'Uczciwoścw polityce', Bulletin CBOS No. 1464, December 1995.

Centre for Public Opinion Surveys (CBOS) (1999) 'Korupcja w życiu publicznym', Bulletin CBOS No. 2220, November 1999.

Centre for Public Opinion Surveys (CBOS) (2000), 'Korupcja i łapownictwo w życiu publicznym', Bulletin CBOS No. 2370, July 2000.

Centraal Bureua voor de Statistiek (CBS) (2001) *Statistisch Jaarboek 2001* (Voorburg/Heerlen: Centraal Bureau voor de Statistiek).

Centraal Bureua voor de Statistiek (CBS) (n.d.) *STATLINE: Statistics Netherlands* (http://www.cbs.nl/en)

Cersosimo, D. and Wolleb, G. (2001) 'Politiche pubbliche e contesti istituzionali. Una ricerca sui patti territoriali', *Stato e mercato* 63, pp. 369–412.

Champion, T. (2001) 'Urbanization, Suburbanization, Counterurbanization and Reurbanization', in R. Paddison (ed.), *Handbook of Urban Studies* (London: Sage), pp. 143–61.

Chapman, R. and Wood, M. (1984) *Australian Local Government – The Federal Dimension* (Sydney: Allen & Unwin).

Cheyne, C. (2002) 'Public Involvement in Local Government in New Zealand: A Historical Account', in J. Drage (ed.), *Empowering Communities? Representation and Participation in New Zealand's Local Government* (Wellington: Victoria University Press), pp. 116–55.

Cheyne, C. and Comrie, M. (2002) 'Involving Citizens in Local Government: Expanding the Use of Deliberative Processes', in J. Drage (ed.), *Empowering Communities? Representation and Participation in New Zealand's Local Government* (Wellington: Victoria University Press), pp. 156–86.

Chiche, J., Haegel, F. and Tiberj, V. (2002) 'La fragmentation partisane', in G. Grunberg, N. Mayer and P. Sniderman (eds), *La démocratie à l'épreuve. Une nouvelle approche de l'opinion des Français* (Paris: Presses de Sciences Po), pp. 203–37.

Christensen, D.A. and Aars, J. (2002) *Teknologi og demokrati: Med norske kommuner på nett!* (Bergen: Rokkansenteret). Notat 29–2002.

Clark, T.N. and Hoffmann-Martinot, V. (eds) (1998). *The New Political Culture* (Boulder: Westview Press).

Clarke, J. and Newman, J. (1997) *The Managerial State* (London: Sage).

Codding, G.A. (1961) *The Federal Government of Switzerland* (Boston: Houghton Mifflin).

Cole, A. and John, P. (2001) *Local Governance in England and France* (London: Routledge).

Conseil de l'Europe (1995) *La taille des communes, l'efficacité et la participations des citoyens* (Strasbourg: Council of Europe). Communes et régions d'Europe, no. 56.

Controller and Auditor-General (1998) *Public Consultation and Decision-Making in Local Government* (Wellington: The Audit Office).

Controller and Auditor-General (2002a) *Local Government – Looking Back and Looking Forward* (Wellington: The Audit Office).

Controller and Auditor-General (2002b) *Managing the Relationship Between a Local Authority's Elected Members and its Chief Executive* (Wellington: The Audit Office).

Dafflon, B. (1998) 'Suisse: Les fusions de communes dans le canton de Fribourg. Analyse socio-économique', in *Annuaire des collectivités locales* (Paris: Crédit local de France et direction générale des collectivités locales).

Dahl, R.A. (1970) *After the Revolution: Authority in a Good Society* (New Haven: Yale University Press).

Dam, M. van (1992) 'Regio zonder regie: verschillen in en effectiviteit van gemeentelijk arbeidsmarktbeleid', Doctoral dissertation (Amsterdam: Thesis Publishers).

Davis, H., Downe, J. and Martin, S. (2001) *External Inspection of Local Government: Driving Improvement or Drowning in Detail?* (York: Joseph Rowntree Foundation).

Dearlove, J. (1973) *The Politics of Policy in Local Government: The Making and Maintenance of Public Policy in the Royal Borough of Kensington and Chelsea* (Cambridge: Cambridge University Press).

Decoster, G. (2000) 'Het pact met de gemeenten en OCMW's: een eerste positieve balans' *Binnenband* (http://aba.ewbl.vlaanderen.be/binnenband/Archief/oud/minister.htm).

Dente, B. and Kjellberg, F. (eds) (1988) *The Dynamics of Institutional Change: Local Government Reorganization in Western Democracies* (London: Sage).

Denters, B., Klok, P.J. and Visser, M. (2002) 'Rebuilding Roombeek: Patterns of public participation and interactive governance', Paper presented at ECPR Joint Sessions of Workshops, Turin, Italy.

Denters, S.A.H. (1987) 'Gemeentelijke samenwerking: de lappendeken in de lappenmand? Een politicologische benadering', in T.P.W.M. van der Krogt, P.B. Boorsma, J.W. van Deth and D.W.P. Ruiter (eds), *Big is beautiful? Schaalveranderingen in overheid en samenleving* ('s-Gravenhage: Vuga), pp. 127–48.

Denters, S.A.H. (2000) 'Urban Democracies in the Netherlands: Social and Political Change, Institutional Continuities?', in O. Gabriel, V. Hoffmann-Martinot and H. Savitch (eds), *Urban Democracies* (Opladen: Leske & Budrich), pp. 73–126.

Denters, S.A.H. (2001) 'Prestatiesturing: pronkstuk of probleem? Prestatiemeting in de theorie en praktijk van het Nederlandse grotestedenbeleid', *Beleidswetenschap* 15, pp. 356–71.

Denters, S.A.H. (2002) *Grootstedelijk bestuur: over stedelingen en stadsbestuurders* (Enschede: Universiteit Twente), Inaugural address.

Denters, S.A.H. and Geurts, P.A.Th.M. (eds) (1998) *Lokale democratie in Nederland: burgers en hun gemeentebestuur* (Bussum: Coutinho).

Denters, S.A.H., Heffen, O. van and Jong, H.M. de (1999) 'An American Perestroika in Dutch Cities? Urban Policy in the Netherlands at the End of a Millennium', *Public Administration* 77, pp. 837–53.

Denters, S.A.H., Jong, H.M. de and Thomassen, J.J.A. (1990) *Kwaliteit van gemeenten: een onderzoek naar de relatie tussen de omvang van gemeenten en de kwaliteit van het lokaal bestuur* ('s-Gravenhage: VUGA).

Denters, S.A.H. and Veldheer, V. (1998) 'Gemeentelijke taken: historie en actualiteit', in A.F.A. Korsten and P.W. Tops (eds), *Lokaal bestuur in Nederland: inleiding in de gemeentekunde* (Alphen aan den Rijn: Samsom), pp. 66–76.

Department of the Environment, Transport and the Regions (1998a) *Modern Local Government: In Touch with the People* (Cm 4014) (London: DETR).

Department of the Environment, Transport and the Regions (1998b) *Modernising Local Government: Local Democracy and Community Leadership* (London: DETR).

Department of Internal Affairs (1996). *Community Boards: 1995 Survey of Functions* (Wellington: Department of Internal Affairs).

Department of Statistics (1990) *New Zealand Official 1990 Yearbook* (Wellington: Department of Statistics).

Department for Transport, Local Government and the Regions (2001) *Strong Local Leadership – Quality Public Services* (Cmnd 5237) (London: DTLR).

Derksen, W. (1998) *Lokaal bestuur* ('s-Gravenhage: VUGA).

Derksen, W., Drift, J.A. van der, Giebels, R. and Terbrack, C. (1987) *De bestuurskracht van kleine gemeenten: een beleidsrapport* (Leiden/Amsterdam: Onderzoekscentrum Sturing van de Samenleving/Stichting voor Economisch Onderzoek).

Derlien, H. U., Gürtler, C., Holler, W. and Schreiner, H.J. (1976) *Kommunalverfassung und politisches Entscheidungs system. Eine vergleichende Untersuchung in vier Gemeinden* (Meisenheim am Glan: Hain).

Deth, J.W., van en Vis, J.C.P.M. (1995) *Regeren in Nederland: het politieke en bestuurlijke bestel in vergelijkend perspectief* (Assen: Van Gorcum).

DiGaetano, A. (1991) 'The Origins of Urban Political Machines in the United States: A Comparative Perspective', *Urban Affairs Quarterly* 26, pp. 324–53.

Digby, P. (2000) 'Victorian Experience of Local Government Reform', Paper to the Local Government and Shires Association of NSW Conference, Sydney, February.

Direction Générale des Collectivités Locales (2002) *Les collectivités locales en chiffres 2002–2003* (Paris: Ministère de l'Intérieur).

Dölle, A.H.M. and Elzinga, D.J. (1993) *Handboek van het gemeenterecht I: organen en bevoegdheden* (Groningen: Wolters-Noordhoff).

Downs, A. (1994) *New Visions for Metropolitan America* (Washington, DC: The Brookings Institution; and Cambridge, MA: Lincoln Institute of Land Policy).

Dudley, M.Q. (2001) 'Sprawl as Strategy: City Planners Face the Bomb', *Journal of Planning Education and Research* 21, pp. 52–63.

Dujardin, J. (1997) 'Verzelfstandiging van gemeentediensten als instrument voor een modern management', in J.E. Krings (ed.), *Liber Amicorum Prof. dr. G. Baeteman* (Deurne: E. Story-Scientia), pp. 479–515.

Duran, P. (1998) *Penser l'action publique* (Paris: LGDJ).

Duran, P. and Thœnig, J.-C. (1996) 'L'Etat et la gestion publique territoriale', *Revue Française de Science Politique* 4, pp. 580–622.

Eikås, M. and Selle, P. (2001) 'New Public Management and the Breakthrough of a Contract Culture at the Local Level in Norway', in A.L. Fimreite, H.O. Larsen and J. Aars (eds), *Lekmannstyre under press* (Oslo: Kommuneforlaget), pp. 103–32.

Eisinger, P. (1998) 'City Politics in an Era of Federal Devolution' *Urban Affairs Review* 33, pp. 308–25.

Ejersbo, N., Hansen, M.B. and Mouritzen, P.E. (1998) 'The Danish Local Government CEO: From Town Clerk to City Manager', in K.K. Klausen and A. Magnier (eds), *The Anonymous Leader: Appointed CEO's in Western Local Government* (Odense: Odense University Press), pp. 97–112.

Elwood, B. (1995) *Local Government Reform* (Wellington: New Zealand Local Government Association).

Ercole, E. (1997) ' "Yes in Theory and Perhaps in the Future": European Integration and Local Government in Italy', in M. Goldsmith and K. Klausen (eds), *European Integration and Local Government* (Cheltenham: Edward Elgar), pp. 189–204.

Ernst, J. and Glanville, L. (1995) *Coming to Terms! The Initial Implementation of CCT Policy* (Melbourne: Outer Urban Research and Policy Unit, Victoria University of Technology).

Faure, A. (1994) 'Les élus locaux à l'épreuve de la décentralisation. De nouveaux chantiers pour la médiation politique locale', *Revue Française de Science Politique* 3, pp. 462–79.

Federal Finance Administration (FFA) (2000). *General Government Operations.* (Internet. http://www.efv.admin.ch/oehfina/e/soehrech.htm).

Ferrera, M. and Gualmini, E. (1999) *Salvati dall'Europa?* (Bologna: Il Mulino).

Finn, P. (1990) 'Myths of Australian Public Administration', in J. Power (ed.), *Public Administration in Australia: A Watershed* (Sydney: Hale & Iremonger), pp. 41–56.

Fiorina, M.P. (1999) 'Extreme Voices: A Dark Side of Civic Engagement', in Th. Skocpol and M.P. Fiorina (eds), *Civic Engagement in American Democracy* (Washington: Brookings Institution Press and Russell Sage Foundation), pp. 395–425.

Fligstein, N. and McNichol, J. (1998) 'The Institutional Terrain of the European Union', in W. Sandhotlz and A. Stone Sweet (eds), *European Integration and Supranational Governance* (Oxford: Oxford University Press), pp. 59–91.

Floris, T. S. and Bidsted, C. (1996) *Brugerbestyrelser på tværs – erfaringer fra kommuner og amter* (København: AKF forlaget).

Forgie, V., Cheyne, C. and McDermott, P. (1999) *Democracy in New Zealand Local Government: Purpose and Practice* (Palmerston North: School of Resource and Environmental Planning, Massey University).

Fuchs, D. and Klingemann, H.-D. (1995a) 'Citizens and the State: A Changing Relationship?', in H.-D. Klingemann and D. Fuchs (eds), *Citizens and the State* (Oxford: Oxford University Press), pp. 1–23.

Fuchs, D. and Klingemann, H.-D. (1995b) 'Citizens and the State: A Relationship Transformed?', in H.-D. Klingemann and D. Fuchs (eds), *Citizens and the State* (Oxford: Oxford University Press), pp. 420–43.

Gabriel, O.W. (2002) 'Bürgerbeteiligung in den Kommunen', in Enquete-Kommission 'Zukunft des Bürgerschaftlichen Engagements' Deutscher Bundestag (ed.), *Bürgerschaftliches Engagement und Zivilgesellschaft* (Opladen: Leske & Budrich), pp. 121–60.

Gaudin, J.-P. (1999) *Gouverner par contrat. L'action publique en question* (Paris: Presses de Sciences Po).

Gaxie, D. (ed) (1997) *L'intercommunalité, Bilan et perspectives* (Paris: Presses universitaires de France).

Gekiere, J. (2001) 'De verkozen burgemeester', in R. Maes and M. Boes (eds), *Proeve van Vlaams Gemeentedecreet* (Brussel: Ministerie van de Vlaamse Gemeenschap), pp. 136–40.

Gerritsen, R. and Whyard, M. (1998) 'The Challenge of Constant Change: The Australian Local Government CEO', in K.K. Klausen and A. Magnier (eds), *The Anonymous Leader* (Odense: Odense University Press), pp. 31–48.

Geser, H., Höpflinger, F., Ladner, A., Meuli, U. and Schaller, R. (1996) *Die Schweizer Gemeinden im Kräftefeld des gesellschaftlichen und politisch-administrativen Wandel* (Zürich: Soziologisches Institut der Universität Zürich). Schlussbericht NF-Projekt N. 12-32586-92.

Gidlund, J. and Jerneck, M. (eds) (2000) *Local and Regional Governance in Europe: Evidence from Nordic Regions* (Cheltenham: Edward Elgar).

Gilbert, G. (1999) 'L'autonomie financière des collectivités locales est-elle en question?', in Caisse des Dépôts et Consignations (eds), *Quel avenir pour l'autonomie des collectivités locales?* (Paris: Editions de l'Aube), pp. 159–90.

Gilbert, G. and Thoenig, J.-C. (1999) 'Les cofinancements publics – des pratiques aux rationalités', *Revue d'Economie Financière* 1, pp. 7–40.

Goldsmith, M. (1995) 'Autonomy and City Limits', in D. Judge, G. Stoker and H. Wolman (eds), *Theories of Urban Politics* (London: Sage), pp. 228–52.

Goldsmith, M. (2000) 'Local Politics in Europe', in R. Balme, A. Faure and A. Mabileau (eds), *Les Nouvelles Politiques Locales* (Paris: Presses de Sciences Po), pp. 149–68.

Goldsmith, M. and Klausen, K. (eds) (1997) *European Integration and Local Government* (Cheltenham: Edward Elgar).

Goldsmith, M. and Newton, K. (1983) 'Central–Local Government Relations: The Irresistible Rise of Centralised Power', *West European Politics* 6, pp. 216–33.

Goldsmith, S. Giuliani, R. and Daley, R.M. (1999) *The Entrepreneurial City: A How-To Handbook For Urban Innovators* (New York: Manhattan Institute).

Grauhan, R.-R. (1969) 'Modelle politischer Verwaltungsführung' *Politische Vierteljahresschrift* 10, pp. 269–84.

Groenendijk, J.G. (1998) 'Local Policy Making under Fiscal Centralism in the Netherlands: Consequences for Local Environmental Policy', *Government and Policy* 16, pp. 173–89.

Gunlicks, A.B. (1986) *Local Government in the German Federal System* (Durham: Duke University Press).

Gyford, J. (1986) 'Diversity, Sectionalism and Local Democracy', in Department of the Environment, *The Conduct of Local Authority Business*, Research Vol. 4 (London: HMSO), pp. 106–31.

Haglund, R. (1998) 'Turbulence as a Way of Life: The Swedish Municipal CEO', in K.K. Klausen and A. Magnier (eds), *The Anonymous Leader: Appointed CEO's in Western Local Government* (Odense: Odense University Press), pp. 140–58.

Haldemann, T. and Schedler, K. (1995) 'New Public Management-Reformen in der Schweiz – Aktuelle Projektübersicht und erster Vergleich', in P. Hablützel, T. Haldemann, K. Schedler and K. Schwaar (eds), *Umbruch in Politik und Verwaltung* (Berne, Stuttgart, Vienna: Haupt), pp. 99–127.

Hall, W. and Weir, S. (eds) (1996) *The Untouchables* (London: The Scarman Trust for Democratic Audit).

Hallam, R. (1994) *It's Coming Together* Minister's Review Local Government in 1994 (Melbourne: Minister for Local Government, Victoria).

Hallam, R. (1995) *First Fruits of Reform* Minister's Review Local Government in 1995 (Melbourne: Minister for Local Government, Victoria).

Halligan, J. and Wettenhall, R. (1989) 'The Evolution of Local Governments', in *The Australian Local Government Handbook* (Canberra: Australian Government Publishing Service), pp. 77–87.

Harrigan, J.J. and Vogel, R.K. (2003) *Political Change in the Metropolis*, 7th edn (New York: Addison-Wesley, Longman Press).

Haugsjerd, E. and Kleven, T. (2002) 'Ånden som går? Om utbredelse og utforming av kommunal målstyring i Sverige, Danmark og Norge', *Norsk statsvitenskapelig tidsskrift* 18, pp. 195–224.

Heinelt, H. and Smith, R. (1996) *Policy Making and European Structural Funds* (Aldershot: Avebury).

Heinz, W. (1999), 'Public Private Partnership', in H. Wollmann and R. Roth (eds), *Kommunalpolitik: Politisches Handeln in den Gemeinden* (Opladen: Leske & Budrich), pp. 552–70.

Hellevik. O. (1996) *Nordmenn og det gode liv: Norsk Monitor 1985–1995* (Oslo: Universitetsforlaget).

Hendriks, F. (1997) 'Regional Reform in the Netherlands: Reorganizing the Viscous State', in M. Keating and J. Loughlin (eds), *The Political Economy of Regionalism* (London: Frank Cass), pp. 370–87.

Hennekens, H.Ph.J.A.M. (2000) 'De gemeente verbouwd, niet versterkt', *Bestuurskunde* 9, pp. 62–6.

Héretier, A., Knill, C. and Minders, S. (1996) *Ringing the Changes in Europe: Regulatory Competition and the Redefinition of the State: Britain, France, Germany* (Berlin: de Gruyter).

Hesse, J.J. (ed.) (1990/91) *Local Government and Urban Affairs in International Perspective: Analyses of Twenty Western Industrialised Countries* (Baden-Baden: Nomos).

Hesse, J.J. and Sharpe, L.J. (1990/91) 'Local Government in International Perspective: Some Comparative Observations', in J.J. Hesse (ed.), *Local Government and Urban Affairs in International Perspective: Analyses of Twenty Western Industrialised Countries* (Baden-Baden: Nomos), pp. 603–21.

Hoffmann-Martinot, V. (1999) 'Les grandes villes françaises: une démocratie en souffrance', in O.W. Gabriel and V. Hoffmann-Martinot (eds), *Démocraties urbaines. L'état de la démocratie dans les grandes villes de 12 pays industrialisés* (Paris: L'Harmattan), pp. 77–121.

Hooghe, L. (ed.) (1996) *Cohesion Policy and European Integration: Building Multi-Level Governance* (Oxford: Oxford University Press).

Hooghe, L. and Marks, G. (2001) *Multi-Level Governance and European Integration* (Lanham, MD.: Rowman & Littlefield).

Hooydonk, E. van (1997) 'De Gemeentebedrijvenwet van 28 maart 1995 en het juridisch statut van de autonome gemeentebedrijven', *Tijdschrift voor gemeenterecht* 10, pp. 4–57.

Hovedstadskommissionen (1995) *Betænkning fra hovedstadskommissionen om hovedstadsområdets fremtidige struktur* (Copenhagen: Indenrigsministeriet). Betänkning no. 1307.

Hughes, C. (1975) *Switzerland* (New York: Praeger).

Indenrigsministeriet (2000) *Den kommunale sektor: Størreseseffekter i den kommunale sektor* (Copenhagen: Indenrigsministeriet).

International City/County Management Association (2002), 'Inside the Year Book', in *The Municipal Year Book 2002* (Washington, DC: International City/County Management Association).

Jenssen, A.T., Pesonen, P. and Gilljam, M. (eds) (1998) *To Join or Not to Join: Three Nordic Referendums on Membership in the European Union* (Oslo: Scandinavian University Press).

Jessop, B. (2000) 'The Crisis of the National Spatio-temporal Fix and the Tendential Ecological Dominance of Globalizing Capitalism', *International Journal of Urban and Regional Research* 2, pp. 321–60.

Joana, J. (2001) 'La Commune contre le municipalisme. Débat public et politiques municipales à Avignon sous la IIIe République (1884–1903)', *Genèses* 43, pp. 89–111.

John, P. (1994) 'UK Subnational Offices in Brussels: Regionalisation or Diversification', *Regional Studies* 26:739–746.

John, P. (2001) *Local Governance in Western Europe* (London: Sage).

Jones, G. and Stewart, J. (1992) 'Selected not Elected', *Local Government Chronicle*, 13 November, p.15.

Jones, G. and Stewart, J. (1993) 'When the Numbers Don't Add Up to Democracy', *Local Government Chronicle*, 8 January, p. 15.

Jones, M. (1991) 'Australian Local Government: Waiting for a Challenge', in J.J. Hesse (ed.), *Local Government and Urban Affairs in International Perspective: Analyses of Twenty Western Industrialised Countries* (Baden-Baden: Nomos), pp. 13–44.

Jouve, B. and Lefèvre, C. (eds) (1999) *Villes, Métropoles. Les nouveaux territoires du politique* (Paris: Economica).

Judge, D. (1999) *Representation: Theory and Practice in Britain* (London: Routledge).

Kaase, M. (1990) 'Mass Participation', in M.K. Jennings and J.W van Deth, *Continuities in Political Action: A Longitudinal Study of Political Orientations in Three Western Democracies* (Berlin/New York: de Gruyter), pp. 23–64.

Kahila, P. (1999) 'The Changing Pattern of Local Economic Development Policy in Finnish Municipalities', *Finnish Local Government Studies* 3/99, pp. 365–72.

Karrenberg, H. and Münstermann, E. (1999) 'Kommunale Finanzen', in H. Wollmann and R. Roth (eds), *Kommunalpolitik: Politisches Handeln in den Gemeinden* (Opladen: Leske & Budrich), pp. 437–60.

Kautto, M., Fritzell, J., Hvinden, B., Kvist, J. and Uusitalo, H. (eds) (2001) *Nordic Welfare States in the European Context* (London: Routledge).

Kautto, M., Heikkilä, M., Hvinden, B., Marklund, S. and Ploug, N. (eds) (1999) *Nordic Social Policy: Changing Welfare States* (London: Routledge).

Keith-Lucas, B. and Richards, P. (1978) *A History of Local Government in the Twentieth Century* (London: Allen & Unwin).

Kirtzman, A. (2001) *Rudy Giuliani: Emperor of the City* (New York: Perennial).

Kiss, R. (1997) 'Governing Local Communities – Top Down or Bottom Up? The Case of Victoria', in R. Chapman, M. Howard and B. Ryan (eds), *Local Government Restructuring in Australasia* (Hobart: Centre for Public Management and Policy, University of Tasmania).

Klausen, J.E., Helgesen, M. and Aardal, B. (2002) *Et valg av betydning?*
Videreføring av evaluering av forsøk med direkte valg til fire bydeler i Oslo kom-
mune (Oslo: Norsk institutt for by- og regionforskning). NIBR-rapport 2002: 1.

Klausen, K.K. and Magnier, A. (eds) (1998) *The Anonymous Leader: Appointed*
CEOs in Western Local Government (Odense: Odense University Press).

Klausen, K.K. and Ståhlberg, K. (eds) (1998) *New Public Management i Norden:*
Nye organisations- og ledelsesformer i den decentrale velfærdsstat (Odense:
Odense Universitetetsforlag).

Kleinberg, B. (1995) *Urban America in Transformation: Perspectives on Urban*
Policy and Development (Thousand Oaks: Sage).

Klok, P.J., Denters, S.A.H. and Visser, M.A. (2002a) 'Veranderingen in de
Bestuurscultuur', in S.A.H. Denters and I.M.A.M. Pröpper (eds), *Naar een poli-*
tiek profiel voor de gemeenteraad; Eindrapportage Project duale gemeenten
(Den Haag: VNG Uitgeverij), pp. 53–71.

Klok, P.J., Denters, S.A.H. and Visser, M.A. (2002b) 'Veranderingen in de
Bestuurspraktijk', in S.A.H. Denters and I.M.A.M. Pröpper (eds), *Naar een poli-*
tiek profiel voor de gemeenteraad; Eindrapportage Project duale gemeenten
(Den Haag: VNG Uitgeverij), pp. 73–82.

Knemeyer, F.-L. (1999) 'Gemeindeverfassungen', in H. Wollmann and R. Roth
(eds), *Kommunalpolitik: Politisches Handeln in den Gemeinden* (Opladen: Leske &
Budrich), pp. 104–22.

Kowalczyk, A. (2000) 'Local Government in Poland', in T. Horvath (ed.),
Decentralisation: Experiments and Reforms (Budapest: Open Society Institute),
pp. 217–55.

Kristensen, N.N. (1998) *Skolebestyrelser og demokratisk deltagelse – Støvets*
fortælling (København: Jurist- og økonomforbundets forlag).

Ladner, A. (1991a) *Politische Gemeinden, kommunale Parteien und lokale Politik.*
Eine empirische Untersuchung in den Gemeinden der Schweiz (Zürich: Seismo).

Ladner, A. (1991b) 'Direkte Demokratie auf kommunaler Ebene – Die Beteiligung
an Gemeindeversammlungen', in H. Kriesi (ed.), *Schweizerisches Jahrbuch für*
Politische Wissenschaft 31/1991 (Bern: Paul Haupt), pp. 63–86.

Ladner, A., Arn, D., Friederich, U., Steiner, R. and Wichtermann, J. (2000)
Gemeindereformen zwischen Handlungsfähigkeit und Legitimation (Bern:
Institut für Politikkwissenschaft und Institut für Organisation und Personal,
Universität Bern).

Ladner, A. and Steiner, R. (1998) *Gemeindereformen in den Schweizer Kantonen.*
Konzeptuelle Grundlagen und empirische Ergebnisse einer Kantonsbefragung
(Bern: Institut für Organisation und Personal, Universität Bern). Arbeitsbericht
Nr. 28.

Lafitte, P. (1987) *Les institutions de démocratie directe en suisse au niveau local*
(Chavannes-près-Renens: Cahiers de l'Idheap).

Lako, C.J. and Daaleman, C. (1999) 'Lokale monitoring', *Bestuurswetenschappen*
53, pp. 445–61.

Lane, J.-E. (1997) 'Introduction: Public Sector Reform: Only Deregulation,
Privatization and Marketization?', in J.-E. Lane (ed.), *Public Sector Reform:*
Rationale, Trends and Problems (London: Sage), pp. 1–18.

Laux, E. (1999) 'Erfahrungen und Perspektiven der kommunalen Gebiets- und
Funktionalreformen', in H. Wollmann and R. Roth (eds), *Kommunalpolitik:*
Politisches Handeln in den Gemeinden (Opladen: Leske & Budrich), pp. 168–85.

Le Galès, P. (1999) 'Le desserrement du verrou de l'Etat', *Revue Internationale de Politique Comparée* 3:627–52.

Le Galès, P. (2001), 'Etudier les politiques. Les politiques locales et la recomposition de l'action publique', in D. Renard, J. Caillosse and D. de Béchillon (eds), *L'analyse des politiques publiques aux prises avec le droit* (Paris: LGDJ), pp. 285–303.

Le Galès, P. (2002) *European Cities: Social Conflicts and Governance* (Oxford: Oxford University Press).

Le Galès, P. and Lequesne, C. (1998) *Regions in Europe: The Paradox of Power.* (London: Routledge).

Le Galès, P. and Mawson, J. (1995), 'Contract versus Competitive Bidding: Rationalising Urban Policy in Britain and France', *Journal of European Public Policy* 2, pp. 205–41.

Le Saout, R. (2000a) 'L'intercommunalité, un pouvoir inachevé?' *Revue Française de Science Politique* 3, pp. 439–61.

Le Saout, R. (2000b) *Le pouvoir intercommunal* (Orléans: Presses Universitaires d'Orléans).

Leach, R. and Percy-Smith, J. (2001) *Local Governance in Britain* (Basingstoke: Palgrave).

Leemans K. de (2001) 'De bestuurskracht van landelijke gemeenten', *Tijdschrift voor de Vlaamse Gemeentesecretaris* 3, pp. 4–11.

Leeuw, F.L. (2000) 'Onbedoelde neveneffecten van outputsturing, controle en toezicht?', in Raad voor Maatschappelijke Ontwikkeling (ed.), *Aansprekend burgerschap: de relatie tussen organisatie van het publieke domein en de verantwoordelijkheid van burgers* (Den Haag: SDU), pp. 149–71.

Leonardis, O. de (1998) *In un diverso welfare. Sogni e incubi* (Milano: Feltrinelli).

Lidström, A. (2003) *Kommunsystem i Europa*, 2nd edn (Stockholm: Norstedts Juridik AB).

Lijphart, A. (1977) *Democracy in Plural Societies: A Comparative Exploration* (New Haven and London: Yale University Press).

Linder, W. (1991) 'Local Government: The Case of Switzerland', in J.J. Hesse (ed.), *Local Government and Urban Affaires in International Perspective* (Baden-Baden: Nomos Verlagsgesellschaft), pp. 409–28.

Linder, W. (1998) *Swiss Democracy: Possible Solutions to Conflict in Multicultural Societies*, 2nd edn (Basingstoke: Macmillan).

Linder, W. and Nabholz, R. (1999) 'Switzerland', in B.M. Jacob, W. Linder, R. Nabholz and C. Heierli (eds), *Democracy and Local Governance: Nine Empirical Studies* (Bern: Institute of Political Science, University of Bern), pp. 125–155.

Lippi, A. (2001) *Valutazione e controlli di gestione nei governi locali italiani. Una teoria, molte pratiche* (Torino: Giappichelli).

Local Government Advisory Board (1997) *1997 Tasmanian Local Government Review*, Exposure Draft (Hobart: Local Government Advisory Board).

Local Government Association of NSW and Shires Association of NSW (1991) *Submission to the Department of Local Government and Co-operatives in Response to Local Government Reform: Proposals for Legislation* (Sydney: Local Government Association of NSW and Shires Association of NSW).

Loncle, P. (2000) 'Partenariat et exclusion sociale en France: expériences et ambiguïtés', *Pôle sud* 12, pp. 47–62.

London, R. (1996) 'Checking Perceptions and Reality in Small-town Innovation Research', *American Behavioral Scientist* 39, pp. 616–29.

Lorrain, D. (1991) 'De l'administration républicaine ou gouvernement urbain', *Sociologie du Travail* 4, pp. 461–83.

Lorrain, D. (1993) 'Après la décentralisation. L'action publique flexible', *Sociologie du Travail* 3, pp. 285–307.

Lorrain, D. (1996) 'Introduction', in D. Lorrain and G. Stoker (eds), *The Privatization of Urban Services in Europe* (London: Frances Pinter), pp. 9–30.

Lorrain, D. and Stoker, G. (eds) (1996) *The Privatization of Urban Services* (London: Frances Pinter).

Loughlin, J. (1999) *Regional and Local Democracy in the European Union.* (Luxembourg: Office for Official Publications of the European Communities).

Lowndes, V. (2002) 'Between Rhetoric and Reality: Does the 2001 White Paper Reverse the Centralising Trend in Britain?' *Local Government Studies* 28, pp. 135–47.

Lundqvist, L.J. (1998) 'Local-to-Local Partnerships among Swedish Municipalities: Why and How Neighbors Join to Alleviate Resource Constraints', in J. Pierre (ed.), *Partnerships in Urban Governance: European and American Experience* (London: Macmillan), pp. 93–111.

Lynch, J. (2002) 'Working in Partnership', in J. Drage (ed.), *Empowering Communities? Representation and Participation in New Zealand's Local Government* (Wellington: Victoria University Press), pp. 258–76.

Mabileau, A. (1995) 'De la monarchie municipale à la française', *Pouvoirs* 73, pp. 7–17.

Maes R. (ed.) (1997) 'De burger in de politieke, bestuurlijke en sociale vernieuwingen', in R. Maes (ed.), Democratie, legitimiteit, nieuwe politieke cultuur (Leuven: ACCO), pp. 91–105.

Majone, E. (2000) 'The Credibility Crisis of Community Regulation', *Journal of Common Market Studies* 38, pp. 273–302.

Marcou, G., Rangeon, F. and Thiébault, J.-L. (eds) (1997) *La coopération contractuelle et le gouvernement des villes* (Paris: L'Harmattan).

Marsh, D., Richards, D. and Smith, M.J. (2001) *Changing Patterns of Governance in the United Kingdom: Reinventing Whitehall* (Basingstoke: Palgrave Macmillan).

Marshall, N. (1998) 'Reforming Australian Local Government: Efficiency, Consolidation – and the Question of Governance', *International Review of Administrative Sciences* 64, pp. 643–62.

Martin, J. (1997) 'Workplace Reform: HRM and Enterprise Bargaining', in N. Marshall and B. Dollery (eds), *Australian Local Government: Reform and Renewal* (South Melbourne: Macmillan), pp. 209–26.

Martins, M.R. (1995) 'Size of Municipalities, Efficiency, and Citizen Participation: A Cross-European Perspective', *Environment and Planning C: Government and Polity* 13, pp. 441–58.

Mayer, M. (2000) 'Post-Fordist City Politics', in R.T. LeGates and F. Stout (eds), *The City Reader*, 2nd edn (London: Routledge), pp. 230–9.

McRae, K.D. (1983) *Conflict and Compromise in Multilingual Societies*, vol. 1, *Switzerland* (Waterloo, Ontario: Wilfred Laurier University Press).

Mény, Y. (1992) 'La République des fiefs', *Pouvoirs* 60, pp. 17–24.

Ministerial Advisory Group on Local Government Reform (MAG) (1995) *Reform of Local Government in South Australia: Councils of the Future.* Report to the Minister for Housing, Urban Development and Local Government Relations (Adelaide: SA Government Printer).

Ministerie van Binnenlandse Zaken en Koninkrijksrelaties (2000) *Kerngegevens Overheidspersoneel, Stand ultimo 1997, 1998 en 1999* (Den Haag: Ministerie van Binnenlandse Zaken en Koninkrijksrelaties).

Ministerie van Financiën (2001) *Financiële verhoudingen Rijk – decentrale overheden* (Den Haag: Ministerie van Financiën).

Mollenkopf, J. (2002) 'Who Decides, and How? Government Decision-Making after 9/11' (unpublished manuscript).

Mønnesland, J. (2001) *Kommunale inntektssystemer i Norden* (Oslo: Norsk institutt for by- og regionforskning). NIBRs PLUSS-serie 2–2001.

Montin, S. and Elander, I. (1995) 'Citizenship, Consumerism and Local Government in Sweden', *Scandinavian Political Studies* 18, pp. 25–51.

Mowbray, M. (1996) 'Local Government in Victoria: Hijacked or Returned to its Roots?' *Just Policy* 8, pp. 28–35.

Muijen, M.L. van (2001) 'Bestuursakkoorden: Een praktijk met méér dan goede bedoelingen', *Bestuurswetenschappen* vol 55, pp. 175–88.

Mulgan, R. (1994) *Politics in New Zealand* (Auckland: Auckland University Press).

Muller, P. (1992) 'Entre le local et l'Europe, La crise du modèle français de politiques publiques', *Revue Française de Science politique* 2:275–97.

Naschold, F. (1995) *The Modernisation of the Public Sector in Europe: A Comparative Perspective on the Scandinavian Experience* (Helsinki: Ministry of Labour).

Naschold, F. (1997) 'Umstrukturierung der Gemeindeverwaltung: eine international vergleichende Zwischenbilanz', in F. Naschold, M. Oppen and A. Wegener (eds) (1997), *Innovative Kommunen: Internationale Trends und deutsche Erfahrungen* (Stuttgart: Kohlhammer), pp. 15–48.

National Office of Local Government (2002) *2000–2001 Local Government National Report* (Canberra: National Office of Local Government).

New South Wales Government (1991) *Reform of Local Government in New South Wales: Exposure Draft Local Government Bill 1992* (Sydney: Department of Local Government and Co-operatives).

New York City Partnership and Chamber of Commerce (2001) 'Working Together to Accelerate New York's Recovery Economic Impact Analysis of the September 11th Attack on New York' [http://www.nycp.org/impactstudy/EconImpactStudy.pdf].

New York City Partnership and Chamber of Commerce (2002) 'Working Together To Accelerate New York's Recovery: Update of The NYC Partnership's Economic Impact Analysis of the September 11th Attack on New York City' [http://www.nycp.org/impactstudy/Update_02_11_02.pdf].

Newton, K. (1976) *Second City Politics: Democratic Processes and Decision-Making in Birmingham* (Oxford: Clarendon Press).

NOU (1992) *Kommune- og fylkesinndelingen i et Norge i forandring* (Oslo: Kommunal-departementet). Norges offentlige utredninger 1992: 15.

NOU (1997) *Grenser til besvar:* Lokaldemokrati og forvaltning i hovedstadsområdet (Oslo: Kommunaldepartementet). Norges offentlige utredninger 1997: 12.

Øgård, M. (2002) *Forvaltningsinnovasjon i de nordiske regionene/komunene: I felles takt mot new public management?* (Oslo: Institutt for statsvitenskap, Universitetet i Oslo). Doctoral dissertation.

Osborne, D. and Gaebler, T. (1992) *Reinventing Government: How the Entrepreneurial Spirit is Transforming the Public Sector* (New York: Plume).

Ostrom, E. (1972) 'Metropolitan Reform: Propositions Derived from Two Traditions'. *Social Science Quarterly* 53, pp. 474–93.

Oulasvirta, L. (1991) *Statsbidragspolitik i Norden: En jämförande undersökning om Finlands, Sveriges, Norges och Danmarks statsbidragssystem och stat-kommun relationer* (Stockholm: Företagsekonomiska institutionen, Stockholms Universitet). Institut för kommunal ekonomi IKE 1991:24.

Overheyden H. van and M. Verhulst (2000) 'Naar een grotere betrokkenheid van de Vlaamse gemeenten bij de intercommunale besluitvorming?' *Binnenband* (http://aba.ewbl.vlaanderen.be/binnenband/betrok.htm).

Pagano, M.A. (2001) 'City Fiscal Conditions in 2001' (Washington, DC: National League of Cities). [http://www.ncl.org/nlc_org/site/files/reports(fiscal01.pdf)].

Page, E.C. (1991) *Localism and Centralism in Europe: The Political and Legal Bases of Local Self-Government* (Oxford: Oxford University Press).

Page, E.C. and Goldsmith, M.J. (eds) (1987a) *Central and Local Government Relations: A Comparative Analysis of West European Unitary States* (London: Sage).

Page, E.C. and Goldsmith, M. (1987b) 'Centre and Locality: Explaining Cross-national Variation', in E.C. Page and M. Goldsmith (eds), *Central and Local Government Relations: A Comparative Analysis of West European Unitary States* (London: Sage), pp. 156–68.

Parry, G., Moyser, G. and Day N. (1992) *Political Participation and Democracy in Britain* (Cambridge: Cambridge University Press).

Pelczynska-Nalecz M. (1998) 'Opinia publiczna wobec samorzadu terytorialnego w Polsce w latach 1989–1997' (Warszawa: Foundation in Support for Local Democracy). Unpublished manuscript.

Peppel, R.A. van de and Prummel, M.T. (2000) 'De selectiviteit van interactief beleid', *Bestuurskunde* 9, pp. 15–24.

Peterson, P.E. (1981) *City Limits* (Chicago: University of Chicago Press).

Phoenix Rising: A Study of New Zealand Local Government Following Reorganisation, (1993). (London: Audit Commission for Local Authorities in England and Wales). Occasional paper no. 19.

Pierre, J. (1998) 'Local Industrial Partnerships: Exploring the Logics of Public-Private Partnerships', in J. Pierre (ed.), *Partnerships in Urban Governance: European and American Experience* (London: Macmillan), pp. 112–39.

Pinson, G. (2002) 'Les projets urbains et la recomposition de l'action publique à Venise, Turin, Nantes et Marseille', PhD dissertation (Rennes: University of Rennes).

Plees Y. and Laurent, T. (1998) 'The Belgian Municipal Secretary: A Manager for the Municipalities?', in K. Klausen and A. Magnier (eds), *The Anonymous Leader: Appointed CEOs in Western Local Government* (Odense: Odense University Press), pp. 173–87.

Pollitt, C. (2000) 'Is the Emperor in his Underwear? An Analysis of the Impacts of Public Management Reforms', *Public Management: An International Journal of Research and Theory* 2, pp. 181–99.

Pollitt, C., Birchall, J. and Putnam, K. (1999) 'Letting Managers Manage: Decentralisation and Opting Out', in G. Stoker (ed.), *The New Management of British Local Governance* (Basingstoke: Macmillan), pp. 40–61.

Pollitt, Ch. and Bouckaert, G. (2000) *Public Management Reform: A Comparative Analysis* (Oxford: Oxford University Press).

Power, J., Wettenhall, R. and Halligan, J. (eds) (1981) *Local Government Systems of Australia* (Canberra: Australian Government Publishing Service). Advisory Council for Intergovernment Relations Information Paper No. 7.

Pratchett, L. (2002) 'Local Democracy and Local Government at the End of Labour's First Term', *Parliamentary Affairs* 55, pp. 331–46.

Putnam, R. (1993) *Making Democracy Work: Civic Traditions in Modern Italy* (Princeton: Princeton University Press).

Putnam, R. (2000) *Bowling Alone: The Collapse and Revival of American Community* (New York: Simon & Schuster).

Raad voor het Openbaar Bestuur (1998) *Wijken of herijken: Nationaal bestuur en recht onder Europese invloed* (Den Haag: Raad voor het Openbaar Bestuur, Den Haag).

Reed, M. (2002) 'Cities at Risk: Challenge and Opportunity', in R. Hambleton, H. Savitch and J. Stewart (eds), *Globalism and Local Democracy* (Basingstoke: Palgrave), pp. 95–124.

Regulski, J. (1999) 'Building Local Democracy in Poland', (Budapest: Open Society Institute). Discussion Paper No. 9, Local Government and Public Service Reform Initiative.

Regulski, J. (2000) *Samorzad III Rzeczypospolitej: koncepcje i realizacje* (Warszawa: PWN).

Reid, M. (2002) 'Exploring the Rhetoric of Partnership', in J. Drage (ed.), *Empowering Communities? Representation and Participation in New Zealand's Local Government* (Wellington: Victoria University Press), pp. 304–42.

Reignier, H. (2001) *Les DDE et le politique* (Paris: L'Harmattan).

Rhodes, R.A.W. (1997) *Understanding Governance: Policy Networks, Governance, Reflexivity and Accountability* (Buckingham: Open University Press).

Rihoux B. (2001) 'Iedereen naar het centrum en voorstander van de nieuwe politieke cultuur?' *Tijdschrift van Dexia bank* 55, pp. 7–18.

Rose, L.E. (1990) 'Nordic Free Commune Experiments: Increased Local Autonomy or Continued Central Control?', in D.E. King and J. Pierre (eds), *Challenges to Local Government* (London: Sage Publications), pp. 212–41.

Rose, L.E. (1996) 'Kommunenes stilling i Norden', in L.E. Rose (ed.), *Kommuner og kommunala ledare i Norden*(Åbo: Åbo Akademi). Meddelanden från Ekonomisk-statsvetenskapliga fakulteten. Ser. A: 469, pp. 1–16.

Rose, L.E. (1999) 'Citizen (Re)orientations to the Welfare State: From Public to Private Citizens?', in J. Bussemaker (ed.), *Citizenship and Welfare State Reform in Europe* (London: Routledge), pp. 131–48.

Rotelli, E. (1999) 'Le aree metropolitane in Italia: una questione istituzionale insoluta', in G. Martinotti (ed.), *La dimensione metropolitana. Sviluppo e governo della nuova città* (Bologna: Il Mulino), pp. 299–327.

Ruegg, J., Découtère, S. and Méttan, N. (eds) (1994) *Le partenariat pulic-privé* (Lausanne: Presses polytechniques et universitaires romandes).

Rusk, D. (1995) *Cities Without Suburbs*, 2nd edn (Washington, DC: Woodrow Wilson Center Press).

Sandberg, S. (1998) 'The Strong CEOs of Finland', in K.K. Klausen and A. Magnier (eds), *The Anonymous Leader: Appointed CEOs in Western Local Government* (Odense: Odense University Press), pp. 113–27.

Sandberg, S. (2000) 'Folkligt samarbete under förändrade villkor. Vänortssamarbetet i Norden vid ingången till 2000-talet', in *Mångkulturalitet och folkligt samarbete* (København: Nordisk Ministerråd). Nord 2000: 29, pp. 35–49.

Sandberg, S. (2001) 'Region- och kommunpolitikernes kontaktnätverk', in H. Baldersheim, S. Sandberg, K. Ståhlberg and M. Øgård (eds), *Norden i regionernas Europa* (København: Nordisk Ministerråd). Nord 2001: 18, pp. 159–78.

Sandberg, S. and Ståhlberg, K. (2000) *Nordisk regionalförvaltning i förändring* (Åbo: Åbo Akademi). Meddelanden från Ekonomisk-statsvetenskapliga fakulteten. Ser. A: 513.

Sandberg, S. and Ståhlberg, K. (2001) 'Utvecklingspolitiska inställningar hos nordiska region- och lokalpolitiker', in H. Baldersheim, S. Sandberg, K. Ståhlberg and M. Øgård (eds), *Norden i regionernas Europa* (København: Nordisk Ministerråd). Nord 2001: 18, pp. 89–113.

Sanderson, I. (1998) 'Beyond Performance Measurement? Assessing "Value" in Local Government', *Local Government Studies* 24, pp. 1–25.

Savitch, H.V. and Thomas, J.C. (eds) (1991) *Big City Politics in Transition* (Newbury Park, CA: Sage).

Savitch, H.V. and Vogel R.K. (2000) 'Paths to the New Regionalism', *State and Local Government Review* 32, pp. 158–68.

Sawicki, F. (1997) *Les réseaux du Parti socialiste. Sociologie d'un milieu partisan* (Paris: Belin).

Scharpf, F.W. (1976) 'Theorie der Politikverflechtung', in F.W. Scharpf, B. Reissert and F. Schnabel (eds), *Politikverflechtung: Theorie und Empirie des kooperativen Föderalismus in der Bundesrepublik* (Kronberg: Scriptor), pp. 13–70.

Scharpf, F.W. (1996) 'Negative and Positive Integration in the Political Economy of European Welfare States', in G. Marks, F.W. Scharpf, P.C. Schmitter and W. Streeck (eds), *Governance in the European Union* (London: Sage), pp. 15–39.

Scharpf, F.W., Reissert, B. and Schnabel, F. (1976) *Politikverflechtung I. Theorie und Empirie des kooperativen Föderalismus in der Bundesrepublik* (Kronberg: Athenäum).

Schedler, K. and Proeller, I. (2000) *New Public Management* (Bern: Haupt. UTB).

Schmidt, M.G. (1999) 'Die Europäisierung der Öffentlichen Aufgaben', in T. Ellwein, and E. Holtmann (eds), *50 Jahre Bundesrepublik Deutschland* (Opladen: Westdeutscher Verlag), pp. 385–94.

Sclavi, M. (2002) *Avventure urbane. Fare urbanistica partecipata* (Milano: Eleuthera).

Self, P. (1997) 'The Future of Australian Local Government', in N. Marshall and B. Dollery (eds), *Australian Local Government: Reform and Renewal* (South Melbourne: Macmillan), pp. 297–310.

Swiss Federal Statistical Office (SFSO) (2000a) *Amtliches Gemeindeverzeichnis der Schweiz* (Neuchâtel: Bundesamt für Statistik – SFSO).

Swiss Federal Statistical Office (SFSO) (2000b) *Permanent Resident Population by Municipality in 1998* (Neuchâtel: Bundesamt für Statistik – SFSO).

Sharpe, L.J. (1981) 'Theories of Local Government', in L. Feldman (ed.), *Politics and Government of Urban Canada* (Toronto: Methuen), pp. 28–39.

Sharpe, L.J. (ed.) (1993) *The Rise of Meso Government in Europe* (London: Sage).

Siegel, F. (1997) *The Future Once Happened Here: New York, D.C., L.A., and the Fate of America's Big Cities* (New York: The Free Press).

Siegel, F. (2001) 'The Rebirth of America's Cities', in F. Siegel and J. Rosenberg (eds), *Urban Society*, 10th edn (Guilford, CT: McGraw-Hill/Dushkin), pp. 222–4.

SKTF (2002) *Hur står det till med e-demokratin?* Om elektronisk demokrati i samtliga Sveriges kommuner och i Stockholms och Göteborgs stadsdelar (Stockholm: SKTF). Rapport.

Smith, A. (1995) *L'Europe au miroir du local, La réforme des fonds structurels* (Paris: L'Harmattan).

Smith, B.C. (1985) *Decentralisation: The Territorial Dimension of the State* (London: Allen & Unwin).

Sørensen, E. (1998) 'New Forms of Democratic Empowerment: Introducing User Influence in the Primary School System in Denmark', *Statsvetenskaplig Tidskrift* 101, pp. 129–43.

SOU (1993) *Kvalitetsmätning i kommunal verksamhet. Rapport till Lokaldemokratikommitten* (Stockholm: Fritzes kundtjänst). Statens offentliga utredningar 1993: 74.

Speybroeck, J. van, Hecke, R. van and Claeys, D. (2000) 'Meer inspraak met een volksraadpleging of met een algemene bevolkingsenquête?' *De Gemeente* 75, pp. 37–41.

Ståhlberg, K. (1996) 'Finland', in E. Albæk, L. Rose, L. Strømberg and K. Ståhlberg (eds), *Nordic Local Government: Trends and Reform Activities in the Postwar Period* (Helsinki: The Association of Finnish Local Authorities). Acta 71, pp. 87–157.

Ståhlberg, K. (1998) 'Regionala reformer i Norden', in H. Baldersheim and K. Ståhlberg (eds), *Perspektiv på regioner i Norden* (Åbo: Åbo Akademi). Meddelanden från Ekonomisk-statsvetenskapliga fakulteten. Ser. A: 487, pp. 29–103.

Statistical Yearbook of Poland (2001) (Warszawa: Główny Urząd Statystyczny).

Statystyka wyborow do rad gmin (1990) (Warszawa: Główny Urząd Statystyczny).

Steinberg, J. (1996) *Why Switzerland?*, 2nd edn (Cambridge: Cambridge University Press).

Steiner, R. (2000a) 'Benchmarking in den Gemeinden der Schweiz', in R. Schauer (ed.), *Interkommunale Leistungsvergleiche – wie stark sind unsere Gemeinden?* (Linz: Tauber), pp. 45–77.

Steiner, R. (2000b) 'New Public Management in the Swiss Municipalities', *International Public Management Journal* 3, pp. 169–89.

Stewart, J. (1997) 'The Government of Difference', in M. Chisholm, R. Hale and D. Thomas (eds), *A Fresh Start for Local Government* (London: Public Finance Foundation), pp. 65–78.

Stewart, J. and Stoker, G. (eds) (1989) *The Future of Local Government* (London: Macmillan).

Stoker, G. (1990) 'Regulation Theory, Local Government and the Transition from Fordism', in D.E. King and J. Pierre (eds), *Challenges to Local Government* (London: Sage), pp. 242–64.

Stoker, G. (1995) 'Regime Theory and Urban Politics', in D. Judge, G. Stoker and H. Wolman (eds), *Theories of Urban Politics* (London: Sage), pp. 54–71.

Stoker, G. (1996) 'Introduction: Normative Theories of Local Government and Democracy', in D. King and G. Stoker (eds), *Rethinking Local Democracy* (London: Macmillan), pp. 1–27.

Stoker, G. (1999a) 'Introduction: The Unintended Costs and Benefits of New Management Reform for British Local Government', in G. Stoker (ed.),

The New Management of British Local Governance (Basingstoke: Macmillan), pp. 1–21.

Stoker, G. (ed.) (1999b) *The New Management of British Local Governance* (Basingstoke: Macmillan).

Stoker, G. (ed.) (2000) *The New Politics of British Local Governance* (Basingstoke: Macmillan).

Stoker, G. (2003) *Transforming Local Governance: From Thatcherism to New Labour* (Basingstoke: Palgrave Macmillan).

Stone, C.N. (1989) *Regime Politics: Governing Atlanta, 1964–1988* (Lawrence: University Press of Kansas).

Stone, C.N. (1993) 'Urban Regimes and the Capacity to Govern: A Political Economy Approach', *Journal of Urban Affairs* 15, pp. 1–28.

Stucke, N. and Schöneich, M. (1999) 'Organisation der Stadtverwaltung und deren Reform/Modernisierung', in H. Wollmann and R. Roth (eds), *Kommunalpolitik: Politisches Handeln in den Gemeinden* (Opladen: Leske & Budrich), pp. 411–29.

Sullivan, H. and Skelcher, C. (2002) *Working Across Boundaries: Collaboration in Public Services* (Basingstoke: Palgrave Macmillan).

Sutcliffe, J. (2000) 'The 1999 Reform of the Structural Fund Regulations: Multi-Level Governance or Renationalisation?', *Journal of European Public Policy* 7, pp. 290–309.

Swianiewicz, P. (1992) 'The Polish Experience of Local Democracy: Is Progress Being Made?', *Policy and Politics* 20, pp. 87–99.

Swianiewicz, P. (1997) 'Local Services in Poland in the Wake of Public Provision', in D. Lorrain and G. Stoker (eds), *The Privatisation of Urban Services in Europe* (London: Pinter), pp.168–188.

Swianiewicz, P. (2000) 'Institutional Performance of Local Government Administration in Poland', in J. Jabes (ed.), *Ten Years of Transition: Prospects and Challenges for the Future of Public Administration*, proceedings from the 10th NISPAcee Annual Conference, Budapest 13–15 April 2000, pp. 162–87.

Swianiewicz, P. (2001) 'Sympathetic Disengagement: Public Perception of Local Governments in Poland', in P. Swianiewicz (ed.), *Public Perception of Local Governments in East-Central Europe* (Budapest: Open Society Institute), pp. 169–223.

Swianiewicz, P. and Bukowski, J. (1992) 'Krytyczna analiza dzialalnosci wladz lokalnych', *Wspolnota*, no. 13.

Swianiewicz, P. and Dziemianowicz, W. (1999) *Atrakcyjność inmwestycyjna miast 1998/99* (Gdańsk-Warszawa: The Gdansk Institute for Market Economics).

Swianiewicz, P. and Klimska, U. (2003) 'Czy wielkie miasta są sterowalne? Wpływ sytuacji politycznej na warunki zarządzania największymi miastami Polski', *Samorząd Terytorialny*, 3, pp. 12–28.

Thiel, S. van (2002) 'Lokale verzelfstandiging: trends, motieven en resultaten van verzelfstandiging door gemeenten', *Beleidswetenschap* vol 16, pp. 3–31.

Thiel, S. van and Buuren, A. van (2001) 'Ontwikkeling van het aantal zelfstandige bestuursorganen tussen 1993 en 2000: zijn zbo's uit de mode?' *Bestuurswetenschappen* 55, pp. 386–404.

Thompson, F.J. and Riccucci, N.M. (1998) 'Reinventing Government', in N.W. Polsby (ed.), *Annual Review of Political Science,* vol. 1 (Palo Alto, CA: Annual Reviews), pp. 231–57.

Toonen, Th.A.J. (1987a) *Denken over binnenlands bestuur: theorieën van de gede-centraliseerde eenheidsstaat bestuurskundig beschouwd*, Doctoral dissertation ('s-Gravenhage: VUGA).

Toonen, Th.A.J. (1987b) 'The Netherlands: A Decentralized State in a Welfare Society', in R.A.W. Rhodes and V. Wright (eds), *Territorial Politics in Western Europe* (London: Allen and Unwin), pp.108–29.

Toonen, Th.A.J. (1991) 'Change in Continuity: Local Government and Urban Affairs in the Netherlands', in J.J. Hesse (ed.), *Local Government and Urban Affairs in International Perspective: Analyses of Twenty Western Industrialised Countries* (Baden-Baden: Nomos), pp. 291–331.

Toonen, Th.A.J. (1993) 'Dutch Provinces and the Struggle for the Meso', in L.J. Sharpe (ed.), *The Rise of Meso Government in Europe* (London: Sage), pp. 117–53.

Toonen, Th.A.J. (1998) 'Provinces versus Urban Centres in the Netherlands', in P. Le Galès and C. Lequesne (eds), *Regions in Europe: the Paradox of Power*, (London: Routledge), pp. 131–48.

Toonen, Th.A.J. and Hesse, J.J. (1991) 'De Nederlandse eenheidsstaat in Europees vergelijkend perspectief; internationalisering en het binnenlands bestuur', in N.F. Roest, K.J.M. Mortelmans, A.P. Oele and J.H. Boone (eds), *Europa binnen het bestuur* ('s-Gravenhage: Raad voor het Binnenlands Bestuur), pp. 73–122.

Toonen, Th.A.J., van Dam, M.J.E.M., Glim, M.C.S. and Wallagh, G.J. (1998) *Gemeenten in ontwikkeling: herindeling en kwaliteit* (Assen: Van Gorcum).

Topf, R. (1995a) 'Electoral Participation', in H.-D. Klingemann and D. Fuchs (eds), *Citizens and the State* (Oxford: Oxford University Press), pp. 27–51.

Topf, R. (1995b) 'Beyond Electoral Participation', in H.-D. Klingemann and D. Fuchs (eds), *Citizens and the State* (Oxford: Oxford University Press), pp. 52–91.

Traag, J.M.E. (1993) *'Intergemeentelijke samenwerking: democratie of verlengd lokaal bestuur?'*, Doctoral dissertation (Enschede: Faculteit Bestuurskunde Universiteit Twente).

Travers, T. (2003) *Governing London: Power and Politics in a Global City* (Basingstoke: Palgrave Macmillan).

Tschäni, H. (1990) *Das neue Profil der Schweiz. Konstanz und Wandel in einer alten Demokratie* (Zürich: Werd Verlag).

Tucker, D. (1997) 'From Administration to Management', in N. Marshall and B. Dollery (eds), *Australian Local Government. Reform and Renewal* (South Melbourne: Macmillan), pp. 69–88.

US Census Bureau (1997) *Census of Governments, V. 1 Government Organization* (Washington, DC: electronic version) [http://www.census.gov/prod/gc97/gc971-1.pdf].

Van Gramberg, B. and Teicher, J. (2000) 'Exploring Managerialism in Victorian Local Government' (Melbourne: Faculty of Business and Economics, Monash University). Working Paper 19/00.

Vandelli, L. (1990) *Poteri locali. Le origini nella Francia rivoluzionaria. Le prospettive nell'Europa delle regioni* (Bologna: Il Mulino).

Veldheer, V. (1996) 'Van planmatig naar onderhandelend bestuur: veranderingen in het welzijnsbeleid tussen 1976 en 1996', in P. Hulsen and R. Reussing (eds), *Keuzen maken: Nederland tussen 1976 en 1996* (Enschede: Twente University Press), pp. 109–26.

Vion, A. (2002) 'Le gouvernement urbain saisi par l'internationalisation', in J. Fontaine and P. Hassenteufel (eds), *To change or not to change*. *L'analyse des politiques publiques à l'épreuve du terrain* (Rennes: Presses Universitaires de Rennes), pp. 95–113.

Walter-Rogg, M. (2002) *Politische Macht und Responsivität in der Großstadt. Eine Studie zur Einstellungskongruenz kommunalpolitischer Akteure am Beispiel der Stadt Stuttgart* (Stuttgart: Department of Political Systems and Political Sociology, University of Stuttgart). Dissertation: http://elib.uni-stuttgart.de/opus/volltexte/2002/1026.

Walters, J. (1991) 'Urban Crisis: Cities on Their Own,' *Governing Magazine* [http://www.governing.com/archive/1991/apr/urban.txt].

Waste, R. (1998) *Independent Cities: Rethinking U.S. Urban Policy* (New York: Oxford University Press).

Weir, S. and Beetham, D. (1999) *Political Power and Democratic Control in Britain* (London: Routledge).

Weiss, Karin (2002) *Das Neue Steuerungsmodell – Chance für die Kommunalpolitik?* (Opladen: Leske + Budrich)

Wiktorowska, A. (2000) *Komunikacja i wspolpraca sektorow w gminie* (Warszawa: Municipium).

Wille, A. (2001) 'Politieke participatie en representativiteit in het interactieve beleidsproces', in J. Edelenbos and R. Monnikhof (eds), *Lokale interactieve beleidsvorming: Een vergelijkend onderzoek naar de consequenties van interactieve beleidsvorming* (Utrecht: Lemma), pp. 87–115.

Wilson, D. (2002) 'Unravelling Control Freakery: Redefining Central-local Government Relations'. Paper presented to ESRC seminar on local government and local governance, University of Birmingham, February 2002.

Wilson, D. and Game, C. (2002) *Local Government in the United Kingdom*, 3rd edn (Basingstoke: Palgrave Macmillan).

Wojciechowski, E. (1997) *Samorzad terytorialny w warunkach gospodarki rynkowej* (Warszawa: Wydawnictwo Naukowe PWN).

Wollmann, H. (1998) 'Entwicklungslinien lokaler Demokratie und kommunaler Selbstverwaltung im internationalen Vergleich', in R. Roth and H. Wollmann (eds), *Kommunalpolitik*. (Opladen: Leske & Budrich), pp. 186–206.

Wollmann, H. (1999) 'Kommunalpolitik – zu neuen (direkt-) demokratischen Ufern?', in H. Wollmann and R. Roth (eds), *Kommunalpolitik: Politisches Handeln in den Gemeinden* (Opladen: Leske & Budrich), pp. 37–49.

Wollmann H. (2000) 'Local Government Systems: From Historic Divergence towards Convergence? Great Britain, France and Germany as Comparative Cases in Point', *Government and Policy* 18, pp. 33–55.

Yates, D. (1977) *The Ungovernable City: The Politics of Urban Problems and Policy Making* (Cambridge, MA: MIT Press).

Zintl, R. (1999) 'Politikverflechtung und Machtverteilung in Deutschland', in T. Ellwein and E. Holtmann (eds), *50 Jahre Bundesrepublik Deutschland. Rahmenbedingungen, Entwicklungen, Perspektiven* (Opladen/Wiesbaden: Westdeutscher Verlag), pp. 471–81.

Zwart, I. and Haward, M. (1999) 'Local Government Restructuring in Tasmania 1990–1999: Modernisation to Partnerships' (Sydney: Australian Political Studies Association), Conference Proceedings, pp. 909–22.

Index